Eric Hansen's
MOTORING WITH MOHAMMED

Leaving Mahall al-Dabri, we walked north as dense clouds closed in around us. We increased our pace to keep warm, but within a mile of the village we became disoriented. Lost in a sea of mountain mist, we followed narrow, rock-piled switchbacks that seemed to lead us in circles. Large patches of prickly pear appeared in the mist, and *Aloe vera* drooped listlessly from fissures in the cliff faces. During one ascent we broke through the cloud cover; in the sunlight the air was warm, and mountain peaks were visible in all directions. The distant views made me feel as if I had regained my sight. When we plunged back into the clouds, our vision became limited, and sounds provided the few clues to our surroundings. Young voices drifted to us, conjuring scenes of children taking their sheep to the mountain pastures. The distinctive thud of an axe bit into wood. Later we could hear the sounds of a *mizmar,* a double-reed pipe, and much later the distant voice of a woman singing.

BOOKS BY ERIC HANSEN

STRANGER IN THE FOREST:
On Foot Across Borneo

MOTORING WITH MOHAMMED:
Journeys to Yemen and the Red Sea

MOTORING WITH MOHAMMED

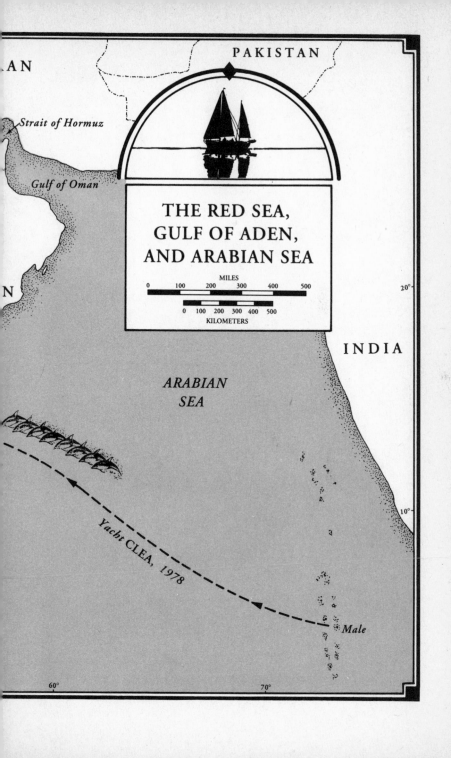

PAKISTAN

Strait of Hormuz

Gulf of Oman

THE RED SEA,
GULF OF ADEN,
AND ARABIAN SEA

MILES

0   100   200   300   400   500

0   100   200   300   400   500
KILOMETERS

INDIA

20°

*ARABIAN
SEA*

Yacht CLEA, *1978*

Male

10°

60°   70°

Motoring with Mohammed

Journeys to Yemen and the Red Sea

Eric Hansen

VINTAGE DEPARTURES

VINTAGE BOOKS • A DIVISION OF RANDOM HOUSE, INC. • NEW YORK

FIRST VINTAGE DEPARTURES EDITION, FEBRUARY 1992

Copyright © 1991 by Eric Hansen

All rights reserved under International and Pan-American Copyright
Conventions. Published in the United States by Vintage Books, a division of
Random House, Inc., New York, and distributed in Canada by Random
House of Canada Limited, Toronto. Originally published in hardcover by
Houghton Mifflin Company, Boston, in 1991. Reprinted by special
arrangement with Houghton Mifflin Company.

AUTHOR'S NOTE: The names of certain people in Yemen have been changed in
order to protect those who helped me. They put their careers at risk, and I
regret not being able to thank them here, because without their assistance this
book could not have been written. In order to protect the privacy of several
mountain villages, I have taken the precaution of moving their locations and
altering their names as well. I have also changed the names of my shipmates in
1978. Finally, because the events in this book span nearly twelve years, I have
either condensed or deleted many situations for the sake of brevity.

Library of Congress Cataloging-in-Publication Data
Hansen, Eric.
Motoring with Mohammed : journeys to Yemen and the Red Sea /
Eric Hansen.
p.   cm. — (Vintage departures)
ISBN 0-679-73855-X (pbk.)
1. Yemen—Description and travel—1981-   2. Hansen, Eric—Journeys—
Yemen.   I. Title
[DS247.Y42H34 1992]
915.33204—dc20   91-58001
CIP

Maps by George Ward
Author photograph copyright © Jim Williams

Manufactured in the United States of America
10 9 8 7 6 5 4 3

TO MY PARENTS

and in memory of
my grandmother

EDNA MOORE, 1906–1988

Contents

Invitation to a Voyage

The room where I work in Manhattan overlooks Central Park. I grow tomatoes and basil on the windowsill to remind me of the ground far below. There is a sea gull that comes to my window most mornings, and I have trained it to dive for pieces of bread. The bird can fold its wings and drop fifteen floors to grab the morsels. He seldom misses. The sea gull then rides the air currents to regain altitude, sometimes circling as far as the green-and-gold rooftop of the Carlyle Hotel before once again soaring past my window, ready for the next piece. He is perched on the sill now, pecking at the glass, but I think I will let him wait awhile.

I haven't always worked in this room with its view of both the Hudson and the East River. Between 1971 and 1978 I traveled through North Africa, the Middle East, Asia, the South Pacific, and Australia. It was a different life. I worked in places like Mother Teresa's Home for the Destitute Dying in Calcutta, as well as in a bakery at the edge of the Sinai Desert where on Friday nights I stood at a table until dawn braiding thousands of loaves of challah for Shabbat, the holy day. I supported myself by smuggling Chinese erasers from Tibet to North India and

Revlon lipstick and false eyelashes to Rangoon (far more exciting and profitable than it sounds). One night at a waterfront bar
in Tahiti I saw an Italian seaman stabbed to death with a broken
beer bottle. A year later I was drinking hot rakshi for breakfast
with Tibetan Buddhist monks who lived in a remote monastery
surrounded by rhododendron forest and three glaciers. The place
is called Kyimolung, the Valley of Happiness. It is a two-week
walk from the nearest road and accessible only by a rickety log
footbridge that spans a gorge seventy-five feet wide and nine
hundred feet deep. There was a summer night in the south of
India when I sat on the balcony of my hotel room and smelled
the delicious fragrance of a flowering shrub called raat kee rani,
the Night Queen. Pony carts, with their bells ringing, moved
through the darkened laneways, and bats wheeled overhead
against the night sky. I once lived with the sultan's drummer in
the Maldive islands where a pretty village girl taught me the local
language by day — and returned after dark.

For seven years I wrote about these people and places in my
travel diaries. In addition to observations on everyday life, the
notebooks contain a collection of short stories, hand-drawn
maps to remote Afghan villages near the Russian border, pencil
sketches, and recipes for things like the sticky rice flavored with
coconut cream and steamed in sections of green bamboo that I
ate while floating down the Mekong River past soldiers of the
Khmer Rouge. Another recipe explains the procedure for making
yak blood sausages by stuffing garlic, salt, and cornmeal into the
small intestine. The recipe begins with the Tibetan technique for
killing a yak (thrust hand and forearm through small incision in
chest and give aorta a good tug) and ends with how much butter
to donate to the local monastery to compensate for the death of
the animal. The tail, which is also donated to the monastery, is
later sold to make Santa Claus whiskers in Europe and North
America.

In the notebooks there are addresses from all over the world,
old love letters, and a large collection of paper labels and pressed
flowers. The language sections include lists of words and phrases
in Greek, Turkish, Urdu, Hindi, Nepalese, Thai, Malay, and

Divehi (the language of the Maldives). There are directions to a riverside flower market in Bangkok and to a nightclub where a female entertainer puffs the customers' cigarettes in a most unconventional manner. Simple instructions explain how to test the purity of gold and, on a more practical note, how to subdue a camel by sitting on its head. I noted the daily rental rates for elephants in Bangladesh, as well as the address of a shop in Madurai that sells the best cassette tapes of Kari Kuri Arinatchulam, the celebrated South Indian *nageswaram* (clarinet) player.

Thumbing through the journals this morning, I found myself walking in the mountains of the Malay Peninsula searching for the giant scarab beetle *Oryctes rhinoceros*. In a different section I am on board a cruise ship in the middle of the Pacific Ocean trying to persuade a young woman to come down from the handrail where she is standing at 2 A.M. with a drink in her hand, telling me there is nothing to worry about because she was once a gymnast.

The spine of the notebook where I found these last two stories is broken, and the cover is coming to pieces. The pages are brittle and the writing faded. But this is not surprising, considering that the book, and several more like it, was buried for more than ten years. I have only just retrieved them. I now keep the journals on a bookshelf, wrapped in a faded purple Dacron bag. The bag has its own story. It came from a yacht that disappeared while sailing in the Red Sea. On the night of February 2, 1978, the sailboat was shipwrecked on a desert island twenty miles off the coast of North Yemen. In the darkness five people were washed ashore. I was one of them.

Just before our rescue two weeks later, I buried some of my belongings in the sand flats near our camp, thinking that I would return within a few days to dig them up. Among the buried items were my travel journals from years of wandering.

Until fairly recently I used to look out of my window in New York City and try to remember some of the stories I had lost. Listening to the muted sounds of jackhammers and sirens echoing up from the grid of concrete canyons, I would think about my old journals. I started thinking about the journals so often that one day I decided to go in search of them. The chances of success seemed remote, and friends clearly thought me a fool to make such an absurd journey. But in the end the lure of those lost pages and the dimly remembered experiences they chronicled drew me back to Yemen. Part of my desire to return was purely sentimental, but I also felt that the journals held significant moments to be relived — scenes from a past life. I wanted to find out who I was as a young man and to remember how my journey of seven years finally came to an end. At least, that was the original plan.

Sorting through old memories for facts is a very hazardous thing indeed. Many of the events from that time still confuse me, and so before describing my return journeys to Yemen, I think it best to explain the shipwreck and how I came to lose the journals in the first place.

The sea gull is still tapping at the window. It is time for his breakfast, and I suppose I shouldn't keep him waiting any longer. He leaps clear of the ledge and I throw the stale crust. As it falls, the bread turns over and over in the air, buffeted by the updrafts. The bird hovers for a moment, then dives. Forty-one floors above the street, he plummets through space without hesitation. Watching him, I once again remember what it was like to let go completely, to abandon all caution and feel the freedom of floating in the world.

ERIC HANSEN
New York City, 1990

MOTORING WITH MOHAMMED

The Joys of Yachting

I HAD NEVER CONSIDERED visiting North Yemen. I arrived quite by accident while sailing with four others from the Maldives to Athens by way of the Red Sea. The little I had heard about Yemen convinced me that it was a place I didn't want to visit, although the rumors were tempting enough. There were stories that the entire male population was hopelessly addicted to a narcotic leaf called qat, that the men wore skirts, and that during public circumcisions the foreskin was thrown into the crowd, where people rolled on it as a sign of joy. If this was how friends and family members fared, I wondered, what would happen to people the Yemenis didn't like? Intertribal warfare had been going on for 1500 years, and child brides were sold for twenty times the average yearly income. Alcohol was prohibited, and before having intercourse husbands were known to mutter *"Bismillah"* (In the name of God). It didn't sound like my kind of place.

Ellen, the American woman who owned the yacht, didn't know how to sail, but that hadn't kept her from acting on the middle-class fantasy of buying a sailboat and embarking on an ocean cruise. I admired her courage. Many dream of making such a journey, but few act. *Clea* was the name of her beautiful sailboat. With a cutter rig, an eight-foot bowsprit, teak decks, oak ribs, and a varnished cedar interior, she was a classic example of the ideal small cruising yacht of the 1930s and 1940s. The yacht measured forty-two feet overall, thirty-one feet at the waterline, and with a ten-foot beam and a six-foot draft she was slow, sturdy, and comfortable. She had an easy, gentle motion under sail, and a speed that rarely exceeded five knots.

Accompanying Ellen was her penniless twenty-seven-year-old lover, Robert, who liked to be called Captain Riley. The yacht's crew consisted of Georgik and Suzanne, a young French couple from the neighborhood of Montmartre. Georgik was an unemployed leatherworker, and Suzanne at twenty-one had only just left her family house to come on the big adventure. Neither of them knew how to sail. Before joining the crew I had spent six months smuggling dried bonito, a common ingredient in Asian cooking, from the Maldives to Sri Lanka. Years earlier I had worked as a cook and deckhand on a prawn trawler off the north coast of Australia. Considering our backgrounds, there seemed little chance of having the sort of sailing idyll one reads about in yachting magazines. Even before we raised anchor, extraordinary events seemed inevitable.

We left Furana lagoon in the Maldives shortly after eight on the morning of December 29, 1977. Several events stand out from the nineteen days it took to cross the Indian Ocean. On the tenth night, as we sailed south of the Persian Gulf, yellow-green patches of eerie, glowing sea light became visible. Ten to twenty feet in diameter, these patches looked like giant amoebas. They pulsated, stretched, and contracted in slow, irregular motions. At first we assumed they were dense clusters of plankton, but up close there were no telltale dots of light. Our curiosity was aroused, and when we sighted a large patch ahead, we decided to alter course to sail through the thing. The yacht moved into the big green blob, and as the hull passed through its center I wondered if the substance would stick to the sides of the boat. It didn't, but as I looked astern I noticed that the blob had been neatly cut in two. A large black gap, the exact width of the hull, divided the two halves. Yet within moments two thin tendrils of watery light reached out, joined each other, and rapidly increased in thickness. In amoeba-like fashion, the thing pulled itself back together in a fluid motion that left the green pool of light intact, with no sign that it had been disturbed. I was relieved that it didn't start following us. We continued to see the patches of light in the sea for several nights, but we never again attempted to sail through them.

Two days later we encountered the disappearing wave. I was in the habit of climbing the mast to the second set of spreaders, where I could sit quietly and enjoy near-perfect solitude. From that vantage point the ocean seemed circular, as well as much larger. I felt detached from the boat as I watched it moving through the pristine blue water. The hull churned a wake, but the frothy trail soon settled, and not a mark was left on the gentle ocean swells.

One day while I was sitting on the spreaders, thirty feet above the water, I noticed an unusual wave approaching the boat. Although it was difficult to judge from a distance, the wave appeared to be a hundred yards wide but no more than four to five feet high. The strangest thing about it was its habit of rising up out of the sea and then vanishing for several seconds before reappearing. It didn't have the motion of a normal wave. I could not understand what I was looking at, so I yelled down to those on deck and pointed in the direction of the wave. We all fell silent, but as it drew closer, flying fish began to appear in great numbers. They filled the air and in their panic flew haphazardly in all directions, pursued by thousands of sleek, midnight blue, bullet-shaped bonito, which leapt two feet out of the water and caught them in midair. The surface of the sea exploded with fish, and as the frenzy of flight and feeding increased, I looked up to check on the mysterious wave. To my astonishment, it had become transformed into a line of dolphins leaping in unison. I found this spectacle even more mesmerizing than the frantic fish surrounding the boat. I estimated that there were more than 150 dolphins, but it wasn't the numbers that impressed me. I was enchanted by the sight of these wild creatures leaping out of the water with such precision. The dolphins, the entire one hundred yards of them, rose out of the water, leapt to exactly the same height, and re-entered the water simultaneously. After a few moments they again broke through the surface of the ocean and repeated their maneuver in perfect synchronization. The behavior of the bonito and the dolphins seemed to be linked, and I assumed I was witnessing an oceanic joint venture for food.

During the commotion, someone on deck had the presence of mind to throw a baited hook overboard, and less than twenty feet from the boat the fish took the bait. I climbed down from the mast as it was brought aboard.

"Grab him by the eyes — it will immobilize him!" yelled Captain Riley, the vegetarian.

It was a dorado, a shimmering, electric, yellow-green water jewel. With the hook through the side of its mouth, it thumped across the wet teak deck. Its sides were so outrageously opalescent and liquid that I thought the color might come off on my fingers. Stepping forward to demonstrate a quick and compassionate death, Captain Riley immobilized the two-and-one-half-foot-long fish with his bare foot and, in one easy motion, stuck a knife into the dorado's right eye.

Ouch! I said to myself, wincing.

"Just like pithing a frog's brain," the captain explained. The fish continued to flap on deck. "It'll stop soon — those are just the reflexes," he added. But the beautiful fish refused to die.

Flap . . . flap, flap.

Wrong eye? I wondered. During twelve months at sea as a professional fisherman I had never seen this trick, and so I watched with interest as the captain, with mounting impatience, shoved the knife in and out of the dorado's left eye socket, probing for the brain. The fishing lesson had somehow become muddled in this display of male pride and lost skills.

"That's got him!" the captain finally exclaimed, folding the blade into its handle.

. . . flap . . . flap, flap . . .

The fish was placed head first into a bucket, where I found it a short while later, blinded, mutilated, but, incredibly, still alive.

When no one was watching, I grabbed it by the tail and quickly smacked its head against the hull of the sailboat. No finesse, certainly, but an effective end to the poor creature's struggle. I put the dead fish back into the bucket and went below deck, where I climbed into my bunk in the main cabin to read Thesiger's *Arabian Sands* and reflect on compassionate vegetarian killers.

That night I again climbed the mast. The sails were barely visible, and I was exhilarated by the rocking, lurching, swaying motion, which was exaggerated up in the rigging. Standing on the spreaders with one hand on the mast and the other on the shrouds, I was enclosed by the big ghostly sails. The hull gurgled through the water, and a series of vibrations traveled up the mast to mingle with the deep humming bass notes from the rigging under tension. These vibrations passed through my body and created the illusion that I had climbed into a large stringed instrument that was being played by the wind and waves. It was a sensation that I rarely experienced on deck. Galaxies in the night sky . . . galaxies in the ocean. Shooting stars burned their brief paths across the heavens, and sparkling phosphorescence blinked and bubbled in our wake far below. Up in the rigging, I felt as if I were free from gravity, and ready to be carried on the wind.

By the morning of February 1, 1978, a steady five-knot wind from the east was carrying us toward Bab al-Mandab, the Strait of Lamentations. We passed Perim Island and sailed north into the Red Sea. The wind freshened, and by late afternoon we were sailing under a triple-reefed main and storm staysail. We ate a hurried meal of rice and fresh fish before preparing the boat for rough weather. I noticed an uneasiness to the flight of the birds. The seas became more unsettled, the sun disappeared, and we sailed into the darkness.

The wind increased, and by midnight we were having difficulties. Suzanne and Ellen were extremely seasick, and Georgik was incapacitated by saltwater boils on his bottom. We were afraid Suzanne might fall overboard while vomiting, so we put her into one of the twin bunks in the main cabin with a plastic bucket alongside. The scene below deck was one of utter chaos. Because of the movement of the boat, dozens of bananas had parted company with their stalk, which dangled from a coat hook. The below-deck activity of stowing wet sails and fastening the hatches had spread the bananas from one end of the boat to the other. Blackened skins and mashed pulp were plastered to the countertops, floors, heater grate, and engine cover. With the hatches closed there was insufficient ventilation, and the stench of vomit, mildewing towels, bilge water, and overripe bananas was difficult to stomach in such rough weather.

When we finally finished readying the ship for the storm, I climbed into my bunk opposite Suzanne's, but the maddening commotion of unseen tin cans, tools, teacups, cooking utensils, and other, unidentified objects kept me awake and irritated. Metal pots clattered in the sink, and a stack of enameled dinner plates thudded against the inside of a cabinet. I finally fell asleep to the sound of Suzanne sobbing in her bunk. Georgik, covered by wet sails, groaned to himself in the forepeak.

At around one-thirty in the morning I was awakened by a terrific jolt, then heard a powerful whooshing sound, followed by the splintering of wood. A blast of wind filled the cabin, and suddenly I was submerged beneath a torrent that pinned me to my bunk. I was sure we had capsized. Instead, a wave had slammed the boat and washed across the deck. Its force had wrenched open the main cabin skylight and emptied what felt like the equivalent of five bathtubs full of cold sea water on top of me. When the powerful cascade subsided, I sat up in the dark, coughing and terrified. Miraculously, Suzanne had not been touched by the water, but her bucket was gone and its contents were everywhere. The floorboards were floating, and I was up to my ankles in water. In darkness, I stood on my bunk to secure the skylight before going to get help.

Georgik and Ellen came on deck to take the helm as Robert made his way below deck to help get the engine and pump working. The boat lurched and rolled violently in the confused seas. As we hand-cranked the engine to life, the empty banana stalk beat crazily against the walls of the cabin. Robert went to check the intake hose to the pump in the aft cabin while I knelt down in the sloshing bilge water to manipulate the pump. The engine had been installed as an afterthought, and to keep the pump engaged you had to crouch near the running engine with one hand on a control lever. In near darkness, I remained in this position as the flywheel of the engine began to throw a warm, steady spray of sump oil, diesel fuel, vomit, banana pulp, sea water, and dead cockroaches into my face. I couldn't leave the pump handle unattended or avoid the spray, and hoped only that I wouldn't get wound up in the generator belt or pass out from the nauseating smell. Heat and fumes from the engine added to the discomfort. The boat lurched unexpectedly, and I was thrown against the cabin wall. When the boat completed the roll, I flew back against the engine and cracked my head solidly on the valve cover.

"Fuck you!" I screamed at the engine. Suzanne retched in her bunk, and I could see Captain Riley, illuminated by a weak bulb in the aft cabin, slumped over with his hands in the bilge. He looked dreadful, a ghostly shade of green. There was a moment of silence before he managed a brief response to my outburst.

"The joys of yachting," he muttered.

That alone nearly cured me of my seasickness.

Twenty minutes later, when the bilge was empty and the floorboards back in place, I began to feel better. I surveyed the cabin with a flashlight. Cooking utensils, books, wet clothes, and sail bags were strewn everywhere. The idea of sleep in such a place was clearly out of the question, so I climbed into a set of yellow foul-weather gear and on bare feet made my way through the small aft hatchway that led to fresh air, and the gathering storm.

The first thing I noticed as I stepped into the cockpit was the powerful rush of wind. This invisible force buffeted my upper body from all sides so that I had to brace my feet and hold onto the cockpit coaming for balance. I was suddenly made tense and alert by the change in the weather. The short choppy seas of early evening had grown into an expanse of heaving waves covered in a thick silvery foam. I watched as terrific gusts blew the crests of the waves into the air, creating a foamy layer of froth that settled uneasily onto the surrounding seas. The twin deck lights shone down from the spreaders and lit up the circle of wild waves that surrounded the little boat.

As *Clea* pitched and rolled her way into the storm, rain and salt spray pelted the deck. For a moment my sense of scale became distorted. The yacht shrank to the size of a plastic boat in a bathtub tempest, with the overhead nozzle showering down rain. This childhood memory of bathtub storms disappeared when I took my turn at the helm at 3 A.M. I had just settled myself behind the wheel when the bow plunged into the heavy seas and a powerful jolt reverberated along the entire length of the boat. Moments later a horizontal blast of stinging salt and foam hit me full in the face, filling my eyes and nose with water. I blinked to clear my vision, and the heavy smell of the sea clung to my cheeks and lips. Suzanne was too sick to share our watch, and Robert, exhausted by taking both his own and Ellen's watch, had gone below deck to wedge himself into a bunk and hope for sleep as the waves hammered the hull and decks. Georgik was not due to come on deck until daybreak, so I sat alone at the wheel and watched with growing anxiety as the seas became steeper.

Several hours earlier the decision had been made to abandon our intended course. We changed our heading from northwest to north, and ran downwind with the storm. I could feel the uneasy motions of the boat as it moved through the heavy seas, but I realized there was little I could do to improve our situation. After fastening my safety harness to the steering post, I braced my bare feet against the sides of the cockpit and went for a wild ride, the sea thundering beneath the keel and sweeping over the deck. My hands grasped the wooden spokes of the wheel to steer, but the continual strain on my arms was such that I found it necessary to support my elbows with my knees.

Exhilaration turned to terror when *Clea* began to surf down the face of twenty-foot breaking waves. I took the waves at a slight angle to avoid burying the bow and pitchpoling the boat. Pitchpoling is the nautical equivalent of a somersault — a maneuver I was not keen on learning in a forty-two-foot sailboat in the middle of the night.

Peaked waves passed beneath the boat and flung the stern into the air with so much force that I became weightless as I was lifted out of my seat and into a half-standing position. I had never been in a situation like this, and I found the combination of lack of control and lack of experience to be completely unnerving. Later, when I eventually got the feel of the seas, I regained my sense of security, switched off the deck lights, and sailed in near darkness. A yellow glow from the gimballed compass binnacle illuminated the cockpit, but I could see little else.

By 4 A.M. the regular pattern of cross swells was apparent, and from the confusion of gusts that encircled the boat I had learned to sense the direction of the prevailing winds. Earlier I found it necessary to check the compass constantly to stay on course, but with practice I discovered that I could steer by the feel of the wind on my face. Later, when I found it possible to sail with my eyes closed, I knew my fear had passed. Without sight I became more aware of the sounds. The rigging hummed a distinctive whistling tune under high tension, and the seas emitted a throaty roar that no longer seemed threatening. Warm and dry beneath my foul-weather gear, I listened to the heavy Dacron staysail as it jibed erratically, wrenching itself from port to starboard with a powerful popping and fluttering.

Then a new sound caught my attention. Something had splintered and snapped on the foredeck. Pieces of wood flew by me and disappeared in the darkness. I switched on the deck lights and could see that one of the port-side lifeline stanchions had been ripped out of the deck. It must have become entangled in the staysail sheet and been sheared off when the wind grabbed the sail and threw it to starboard. I couldn't leave the wheel, and there was nothing to do but let the stanchion beat itself on the deck until Georgik came to relieve me at dawn.

The stars became visible for brief moments, but in my exhaus-

tion the night sky appeared to have gone mad. I had become so
familiar with the heaving motion of the sea that the boat felt
nearly stationary as the stars raced crazily from one horizon to
the other. The first time I witnessed this phenomenon I watched
dumbly, unable to understand why the stars had come loose
from the sky and were reeling in huge, perfect arcs. It was almost
with relief that I discovered it was my mind and not the heavens
that had come unstuck.

Out of this fantastic sky a sea bird appeared. As it drew near,
it tucked its wings and angled at the boat in a steep dive. Clearly,
it could not survive the beating in the air for much longer, and
the chance arrival of *Clea* meant the possibility of safety. Jostled
by the winds, it missed the deck and was thrown upward into the
blackness by a powerful gust. The exhausted bird reappeared
moments later, somersaulting through the air from left to
right in a second dive. The high winds and the uncertain movements of the boat made the deck a difficult target, and the bird
flashed by as a torrent of wind-blown spray filled the air. When
my eyes had cleared, it was gone. Moments later a black-and-
white feathered blur crash-landed in the cockpit with a loud
thud.

The bird lay on its side near the aft hatch for so long that I
thought it had broken its neck, but eventually it stood up,
hopped onto the seat, and waddled over to where I sat. I was
delighted at this surprise arrival, and also heartened by the prospect of having a companion for the night. I made no attempt to
approach the bird. I didn't want it to become alarmed and fly
away. In the face of the storm we shared a common fate. It
seemed friendly and trusting, and had the slightly comical habit
of holding its wings at right angles to its body in a peculiar
spread-wing posture. It watched the churning seas with no apparent interest while I began to feel protective.

As we sailed on I began to think of what it would be like to
touch the bird, to run my hand along its back and smooth the
feathers with my fingers. Would it make a move away from me,
or would it come closer for comfort? I felt such affinity with the

little creature that I carefully reached out to consummate the friendship. The bird didn't budge until my fingers were about nine inches away. Then it emitted a low, guttural croak and attacked. I received a rain of pecks to the back of my hand that were so sudden and so vicious that by the time I managed to jerk my hand away, the attack was over.

Embarrassed and mortified by the bird's reaction, I felt my heart race from fright as I looked at the broken skin over my knuckles, where the blood welled up briefly before being washed away in the spray-filled air. The salt stung my wounds, and I was humiliated by my stupidity. My first instinct was to wring the bird's neck and heave it overboard, but even in my state of shock I realized that the incident was my fault. What wild bird would trust a human being under any circumstances? This one had been attracted by the safety of the boat, not by my companionship. Having established its territory, it didn't move from its spot on the cockpit seat, and I made no further attempts to touch the creature.

The gray sky lifted to reveal a quietening sea littered with sargasso weed; yet there remained a lingering sense of excitement from having driven through the tempestuous night seas. The wind was still gusting, but the breaking waves had vanished, leaving behind deep, smooth troughs between the ten-foot swells. The storm had passed, and I felt a sense of exhilaration born from our lucky survival as we were carried gently over the wave crests and down into the deep hollows in a series of easy fluid motions.

By the time Georgik came on deck to take the wheel at six, the bird had disappeared. Georgik clipped his harness to one of the two parallel lifelines that ran the length of the boat, and I went forward to secure the broken stanchion, which now rested on the deck. Returning to the cockpit, I sorted through our meager selection of cassettes and came up with two possibilities: Strauss and Ravel.

"Georgik, my friend, a waltz or 'Pavane for a Dead Princess' to commemorate the passing of the tempest?"

"A waltz, please," he replied.

The opening passage of the Vienna Philharmonic's playing of the "Blue Danube" filled the cockpit. We sat in silence, absorbed by the sound of the music and the spectacle of the powerful seas. The lifting and falling motion of the boat seemed to go well with the music, and we played the piece several times before shutting off the tape player. I went below deck and after a brief search located the teakettle in the jumble of pots. With great difficulty, I managed to boil water and mix enough powdered milk for two cups of café au lait spiced with cardamom. The foam was blown off the cups the moment I came on deck, but I knew Georgik would be delighted with my surprise. He took a sip, and smiled to himself as we fell silent to watch the sea change colors in the gathering light.

Dawn at sea was a miracle that happened every day. I had volunteered for the three-to-six watch in order to see the sun rise. Georgik shared my feelings. The transformation from night to day: there is no other sight that captures so well the feelings of birth, renewal, and hope.

We had been blown off course during the night, and in the early light we could see how dangerously close we had come to the coast. From less than two miles offshore we caught our first sight of North Yemen. A whitewashed, beehive-shaped structure stood by itself above a long yellow sand beach. The beach separated the blue-green seas from the gray sky, and a diffuse light filtered down from above. A light wind protected us from the heat that we could see radiating from the sand. No human figures were visible, no vegetation, only flat, featureless land.

We picked our way through the maze of light green shoals and coral patches, sailing up the west coast of Kamaran Island before altering course for Uqban Island, which lay fifteen miles farther out to sea. By three o'clock in the afternoon we had entered the lagoon of Uqban, where we intended to repair the damage to the boat and rest for the night. The anchor splashed through the glassy surface, and 150 feet of half-inch galvanized chain clattered over the bow before disappearing into the deep blue water. The boat drifted backward with the momentum, the anchor grabbed in five fathoms of water, and we swung to in the lee of a small, rocky island. There was a quick cleanup below deck and then a dinner of grilled cheese sandwiches and a salad of shredded cabbage, grated carrots, and vinaigrette, followed by a bottle and a half of Johnny Walker Scotch. The sun set during dinner, leaving the boat riding gently at anchor in the darkened lagoon.

The alcohol and the relief from the anxiety of the previous twenty-four hours took effect, and soon the two couples climbed beneath their blankets and into each other's arms. I lay on my bunk in the main cabin and dropped into oblivion to the sounds escaping from the fore and aft cabins: "Mon petit . . . oh oui, oui, mon petit" from the forepeak, and "Oh God . . . yes, yes . . . my God . . . oh my God!" from the captain's quarters. The evening supplications eventually subsided, and the interior of the boat fell quiet. We slept.

Outside, a light breeze rippled the surface of the water. Clouds built up over the sea, and the wind began to grow in strength. Ocean swells flowed over the reef, moved across the surface of the lagoon, and started to play with the boat. With each successive wave the bow raised and lowered, gently at first, until the movement of the seas grew more pronounced. I had not let out enough chain for rough weather, and some time after midnight the anchor lost its grip on the sand-and-broken-coral bottom, a mere thirty feet beneath the keel. In the darkness the boat turned sideways to the wind and moved into deeper water.

At one o'clock in the morning a steady breeze blew across the deck. The main cabin was filled with cool air. A boat normally turns to face the wind or waves when at anchor, but the wind continued to blow steadily across the deck. The breeze woke me up. With my eyes still closed, I noted the direction of the air and waited for the bow to come into the wind. Half a minute passed with no change, and I realized something was wrong. Fully awake, I sat up and waited for a few more seconds to be sure. Then I pulled on a pair of shorts and a T-shirt and went on deck. I couldn't see a thing beyond twenty feet. In a state of confusion, I climbed into the cockpit to check the compass heading. We were facing west, the anchor chain was at right angles to our port side, and the wind was from the south. I put a lead line over the side to check the depth and discovered that we were in nine fathoms of water. These facts left little doubt as to our predicament. We were drifting blindly across the lagoon, with little chance of reaching open water to face the approaching storm. The entrance to the lagoon was less than a hundred yards wide — easily negotiable by day, but impossible to get through in the dark with a heavy sea running. We were trapped.

I woke up Captain Riley, and soon the rest of the crew came on deck. Georgik and I let out the second bow anchor and several hundred feet of chain, but the boat continued to drift. We started the motor, but ten horsepower was not nearly enough to make way against the waves that continued to push us toward the unseen line of breakers. The hollow, thundering sound of the surf grew louder and soon drowned out the puny engine. As we waited in vain for the anchors to take hold, I likened the experience to rubber rafting a couple of hundred yards above Niagara Falls in the middle of the night without paddles. We quickly lost ground to the storm as Captain Riley kept muttering, "We're drifting...we're drifting..."

The beach, now visible in the beam of our searchlight, appeared a hundred yards astern as we were driven closer to it by the wind and waves. The result seemed inevitable. I couldn't understand why the anchors weren't holding. One hundred yards decreased to seventy-five, then fifty, and finally the stern was nearly even with the crests of the breaking waves that swept onto the beach. The helpless terror and anxiety we felt in the previous night's storm had returned. We waited for the first impact, but then a miraculous thing happened: the anchors grabbed, and we came to an abrupt halt no more than thirty yards from the beach, with the surf only a few yards astern.

"That'll hold!" Captain Riley exclaimed, as if his statement had something to do with the event. Then, for reasons that I have never understood, he shut down the engine, as if we had just tied up at the St. Francis Yacht Club in San Francisco and were preparing to step onto the jetty and catch a cab into town for dinner.

With the engine running there was less strain on the anchors, and thus a greater chance that we could keep the boat off the beach. Stunned by the necessity to act, no one offered a word of protest.

The anchors held for twenty minutes. There was little to say. Time passed, the surf thundered behind us, and we awaited the inevitable. When the bow finally lifted up high on a wave, the anchors let go for the last time. We drifted backward, and the boat came down with a tremendous jolt as the keel hit the beach.

Not waiting for instructions, Georgik and I raced for the dinghy, threw it overboard attached by a line, unshackled fifty feet of anchor chain, and fed it into the dinghy, along with two hundred feet of mooring line. *Clea* began to heel over slightly, and the breakers smacked her hull with such devastating power that we lost our footing on deck. Georgik cut the fifty-pound fisherman anchor loose from the stern and lowered it into the dinghy. I waited for a pause between the waves, then began to row into the lagoon. It was dark, and I rowed directly into the wind, keeping the glow of the deck lights dead astern as I made way slowly against the waves. The others braced themselves on deck as Georgik paid out the line. Two hundred feet offshore I threw the anchor and chain overboard. They disappeared with hardly a sound. By the time I returned to the boat, Georgik had winched the anchor line tight amidship in hopes of preventing *Clea* from being forced onto the beach any farther. I was soaked, but there was no sensation of cold, or pain from my hands, where the skin had been rubbed raw by the rope and oars.

But this last effort was useless. I watched the final scene. The anchor line parted with a loud *crack! Clea* rolled onto her side and was driven into the shallows.

In the lee of the hull was a quiet patch of water where we spent the next forty-five minutes unloading the boat with the dinghy. We took ashore water, food, blankets, pillows, dry clothes, and personal belongings that seemed important at the time: passports, money, and a distress radio. I waded through the surf with the others, half hoping the boat would somehow slip back into deep water. But it was much too late for miracles. We wandered into the wind-blown sand hills above the beach, where we wrapped ourselves up in a mess of blankets to wait for morning. My eyes, teeth, hair, and ears were filled with sand and dried sea salt as we nestled beneath a stiff green canvas tarp. The wind blew throughout the night. It was not until dawn that I could hear the cry of sea birds above the beach.

My first glimpse from beneath the tarp was not encouraging. During the night the tide had receded. *Clea* was now hopelessly stranded above the shoreline. There was no denying the fact: we had definitely arrived in North Yemen.

2

Le Grand Pique-nique

JUST AFTER DAWN we climbed from beneath the canvas tarp and wandered around the yacht. Uncertain of what to do next, we climbed aboard, but very little was said as we started to rummage through the cabins, which now lay tilted at a permanent forty-five-degree angle. We unloaded the obvious things first: more food and water, then the medicine, signal flares, matches, solar stills (for extracting fresh water from the sea), sleeping mats, more blankets, and a sail to protect us from the sun. We had unexpectedly been cast into exciting new roles, and no one seemed particularly concerned about being rescued immediately. What were uninhabited desert islands made for, anyway?

We set about practicing our new roles with the innocence of children. Struck as we were by the novelty and glamour of our situation, we seemed incapable of rational thought. I'm certain I was not alone in silently concocting stories to tell friends back home. We had been catapulted out of the present, and indulged ourselves in romantic daydreams of desert islands, shipwrecks, men, women, and the adventure to come. We were hopelessly intoxicated by our expectations.

We must have had some sense left, though, because we continued to unload the boat. Essential supplies were piled up on the beach, followed by the necessities of civilized man and woman: first, the four-burner stove and two full cooking-gas cylinders, then the pressure cooker (to conserve water and fuel), the omelette and crepe pans, mango chutney, pappadams, powdered protein supplements, beer, popcorn, herbal teas, Band-Aids, Pillsbury cake mixes, Hershey chocolate bars, back issues of *The New Yorker,* and finally the suntan lotion and beach towels. The last two items must have awakened some primal urges as well, because Suzanne and Georgik soon disappeared.

I came on deck some time later and found Robert and Ellen staring down the beach. I followed their gaze until my eyes came to rest on the trim, taut, naked bodies of Suzanne and Georgik, who lay flat on their backs with arms and legs spread to receive the sun's rays. Their skin glistened with a fresh coat of coconut oil. From a distance I could sense their feeling of absolute bliss.

"Where do they think they are?" I blurted out.

"I don't believe this," replied Ellen. "We are unloading emergency supplies while those fools are sunbathing."

Robert found the right words. *"Suzanne . . . Georgik!"* he yelled out. *"Pas le grand pique-nique! Arrêtez — venez ici!"*

The oiled figures glanced up from their towels and protested. The sun was coming out, they argued, and it would be a lovely morning to spend on the beach. Indeed, the curve of firm white sand set against the shallows of the turquoise lagoon looked inviting, but I found myself calculating how much of our limited supply of water was going to evaporate from their naked bodies. At a quart each day, I figured, they would exhaust their entire ration of water in thirty days and have to start on ours. I was confused at their lack of common sense, but at this point no one was thinking very clearly.

Georgik and Suzanne argued briefly about their right to sunbathe, but in the end they returned to the boat to help transport the tremendous pile of supplies to our new camp, which lay two hundred yards farther down the beach. We formed an exotic-looking procession as we moved in single file along the edge of the water, where three-foot-long sharks moved silently through the shallows. As the gaps between us grew longer, it was easier to appreciate our selection of clothing. Georgik, a short, well-proportioned man with a gorgeous black moustache, wore a wide-brimmed straw hat and a pair of skimpy black underpants. Slender Suzanne, olive-complexioned and radiant, was barefoot in a flowered sarong tied at the waist. Bare-breasted, she carried a basket on her head. Captain Riley, our blond, lanky leader, wore a baggy pair of khaki trousers that looked like clown pants and a blue wash-and-wear shirt, frayed at the collar and button-less. Ellen, an attractive woman with fine features and curly brown hair, had selected a sensible pair of Levi jeans and a navy blue singlet. For the occasion, I chose a faded green-and-gold-striped rugby shirt splattered with blue paint, a plaid sarong, and a large green cotton dishtowel, which I wrapped around my head. We completed the move after eight leisurely trips up and down the beach. Then we rested. The stove was set up in the wind shadow of the eight-foot coral overhang, and Suzanne boiled water for tea.

After we established camp, we took an inventory of supplies. We had food for at least forty-five days and water for thirty days, allowing one quart of water per person per day, as I had guessed. We soon discovered that the two brand-new solar stills that sup-posedly yielded two quarts of fresh water from sea water on a sunny day could in fact produce only half a cup of undrinkable brine each day. Likewise, the distress radio didn't work. We dug latrines and garbage pits, and established rules to conserve body moisture. No sunbathing or unnecessary walking in the sun without clothing was allowed.

At the southern end of the island, about four and a half miles distant, an unmanned lighthouse was marked on the chart. We had seen its double flash of light at ten-second intervals the pre-vious evening. The next day, after breakfast, the men, armed with vise grips, a hacksaw, and a large hammer, marched south beneath a blazing sun. What we lost in body moisture was par-tially compensated for by our sense of self-importance. We were protecting the female of the species. This exploratory walk was a job for one, but none of the men wanted to be excluded from this heroic task. While we were out playing search party, the women were guarding the camp. With luck they might have lunch ready when we returned. It was astonishing how quickly we shed our "progressive" views and fell into traditional gender roles.

Late that morning we arrived at the cylindrical, whitewashed lighthouse, which was at the edge of a raised coral plateau, about half a mile from the southern tip of the island. We sawed the padlock off the metal door and peered inside. The interior of the forty-foot-tall, five-foot-wide metal cylinder was dark, cool, and smelled of freshly poured concrete. We discovered a set of twelve-volt batteries connected to an automatic switch and wired to a solar panel atop the lighthouse. A quick glance at the wiring revealed that the light was activated when the sun set. During the night it was powered by the batteries, and at dawn it switched off and the batteries were recharged by the solar panel. This was a simple and effective system that required little maintenance.

Looking at the chart of the area earlier, we had noticed that there were several coastal villages that might possibly see the glow from the lighthouse each night, so we decided to disconnect the light in order to attract attention. It seemed reasonable to expect that someone would notice the light was not working. I felt confident that the problem would be reported and that we would be picked up within two or three days. Meanwhile, we arranged to take turns going to the lighthouse each night to signal any ships that might pass by, not just to attract attention but also to warn ships away from the nearby reefs. Everyone was satisfied with this plan, so we returned to share the news with the women back at camp.

On the return journey we took a cursory look at the island. At the halfway point a narrow stretch of sand nearly divided the island into two parts. We surprised ten pelicans at the edge of a salty pond but saw no other life. I found myself wondering what pelicans taste like. Would they be too large to roast in our oven? Could I actually kill one of these beautiful birds?

Robert broke into my food dreams. "Look! Sails — eight sails from the east!" he exclaimed.

It was a beautiful sight: eight lateen sails bearing down on the island. Our elation at the prospect of being rescued quickly passed when Georgik voiced a fear we all felt: "What if they are not friendly?"

We covered the remaining two miles over broken ground at a run, and when we arrived at the beach camp twenty minutes later, we found Ellen and Suzanne standing at the edge of the water, looking at the sails nervously. The cluster of sails closed in on the island rapidly, and Robert, Ellen, and I went to meet them. Sailing in close formation, the eight dhows came right up to the edge of the northern beach. Each boat lowered a man over the side. These men waded to shore laden with rusted anchors, which they set into the beach above the high-water mark. There were about fifty black men aboard the dhows. The three of us stood on the beach, but no one gestured to us, and we felt increasingly vulnerable. I realized the importance of making friends quickly.

The first men ashore were soon joined by others. Robert, Ellen, and I walked toward them to exchange greetings. *"As-salaam aleikum . . . as-salaam aleikum"* (Peace be with you), we muttered.

"Wa aleikum as-salaam" (And upon you be peace), several men replied.

We shook hands, distributed cigarettes, and smiled anxiously. Many of the men wore wristwatches around their biceps and striped boxer shorts on their heads. They didn't look too threatening, but we spoke almost no Arabic, and our uncertainty must have been evident. The men surrounded us, and within minutes Robert and Ellen had lost their nerve.

"Don't let them know what our situation is," whispered Ellen.

"I'm afraid that's unavoidable," I said with a laugh. We had no other choice than to put ourselves at their mercy.

Unexpectedly, and much to my alarm, Robert and Ellen announced to me, and indirectly to the newcomers, that they were going back to camp. Too stunned to question or stop them, I soon found myself alone on a beach ten thousand miles from home with fifty non–English-speaking African men and a pocketbook Arabic-English dictionary. I hardly knew where to begin.

"*Amreekee,*" I said, pointing to myself.

There was no response.

I unrolled a chart of the area and put my finger on the holy city of Mecca. "*Mecca . . . haj. Mecca quiess.*" (Mecca . . . the pilgrimage. Mecca is good.)

Still no response. The men continued to stare at me.

Lively group, I thought. I thumbed through the dictionary and found the words for *storm, boat,* and *broken.* I then pointed to *Clea,* just visible a quarter of a mile away. I was trying to establish some basis of understanding so that we might be seen as human beings rather than foreigners or, even worse, privileged tourists, which is exactly what we were.

The men spoke briefly as one of them reached for the dictionary. I couldn't tell what they were thinking, but then Suzanne and Georgik arrived. Suzanne had dressed up for the occasion. She wore a gauzelike tie-dye blouse that was so transparent and revealing that each man's gaze, along with my own, shifted from the dictionary to her breasts.

"Suzanne," I stuttered, "could you please go back to camp and get dressed?"

"Why?" she asked. Her tone suggested that I was trying to exclude her from the meeting.

"Look, I can't explain now, but we don't know who these men are, and their idea of nudity is a bare arm."

"Georgik will protect me."

"With what, may I ask?"

They considered this, and then, having gotten the message, left. The men watched Suzanne's nicely shaped bottom as she walked away.

The man with the dictionary put his finger on a word and held it out for me to read. I saw his finger next to the word *help.* He then pointed in the direction of the boat.

Help? Did they want to help us with the boat? I was confused, but the blood rushed to my face and I laughed when I realized what the man was trying to tell me. They *were* offering to help. "*Quiess*," I said, smiling. Everyone smiled, and we took turns with the dictionary, trying to tell stories. We had communicated.

This was just the start, but I was very relieved. I remained cautious, however, and when I returned to camp I told the others what I had learned. The men on the dhows were from Eritrea, in Ethiopia. They seemed friendly, but despite their apparent good intentions, we decided to keep watch that night.

Later in the afternoon, several Eritreans came to look at the boat and our camp. They admired the sturdy construction of the yacht, then indicated that they would help get it off the beach. Through gestures, they showed us that the beach dropped off steeply into the lagoon and that all that had to be done was to dig a narrow channel by hand and wait for the high tide. They were optimistic, but the boat weighed seven tons, and the success of this plan seemed a remote possibility.

Surprisingly, Captain Riley was adamant about the Eritreans not touching *Clea*. When I asked why not, he told me it was none of my concern. I thanked the men for their offer and explained as best I could that the captain didn't want their help. They must have been offended and confused. They didn't understand. Neither did I, but I had my suspicions.

The only thing that seemed to keep Robert and Ellen together was the fact that although Ellen owned *Clea,* she didn't know how to sail. She needed Robert to operate the yacht, but there could be little doubt that they had grown tired of their sailing adventure, their relationship, and the financial burden of *Clea*. The shipwreck could not have been intentional, but it provided a convenient solution to their problems. All things considered, I could hardly avoid the evil thought crossing my mind that their seeming reluctance to get *Clea* off the beach was, just maybe, being stimulated by the possibility of a favorable insurance settlement.

I had lived in Asia and the Middle East for seven years and thought more like an Asian than a Westerner. My companions had been away from home only a few months at most, which partially explained why our behavior and responses to events were so different. Perplexed by Georgik and Suzanne's seeming oblivion to our situation and Robert and Ellen's constant quarreling, I felt myself detach from my shipmates and gravitate toward the men in the dhows, who waited patiently for the winds to blow from the east so they could return to their homes along the Red Sea coast of Eritrea. I visited these men every day and observed them closely during their six days on the island.

One afternoon I brought a small parcel of palm sugar to them. As a young boy paddled me out to a dhow in a very unstable dugout canoe, I overbalanced and we capsized, much to the delight of everyone watching. I managed to keep the sticky dark-brown jaggery from getting wet as I swam the rest of the way to the boat. I was handed a dry sarong, and as I changed out of my wet clothes, another man wrapped me in a blanket. I was surprised to see Panasonic and Sony tape players, as well as hundreds of tins of tomato paste from Italy, in the dhow. The men put on a tape of Afar music, which had a distinctive reggae sound created on homemade instruments and steel drums. Later I asked them where they were going, and they explained the Red Sea trade, using the dictionary and sign language to convey their story.

One of the most ancient lines of supply to Eritrea has been across the Red Sea, and the goat and sheep trade with North Yemen and Saudi Arabia is still practiced. Although North Yemen officials collect a small gratuity to look the other way, they are sympathetic to their Moslem brothers from Africa. Small fleets of six to ten forty-foot dhows smuggle the animals to North Yemen and return with flour, fabric, rice, tinned tomato paste, tape recorders, and other consumer durables that are not available or are very expensive in Eritrea because of the ongoing civil war in Ethiopia.

"You go to all this trouble just to buy flour, dates, soup, and tape players?" I asked them, thumbing for words in the dictionary.

One of the men chuckled and then reached into a three-foot-long packing crate buried in a jumble of tinned peaches. He pulled out a plastic bag, untied the top, and handed me a brand-new Kalashnikov. This was an AK-47, the Russian assault rifle. Capable of firing six hundred rounds in one minute, it is the favorite weapon of the tribal people in Yemen and can be purchased nearly anywhere in the country. The rifle in my hands was still coated with a film of packing grease to protect it from the salt air.

The men on the boats were from the northern Ethiopian provinces of Eritrea and Tigre, the centers of the secessionist movement opposed to the Marxist-Leninist government of President Mengistu Haile Mariam in Addis Ababa. As another man pulled back a tarp to reveal several similar wooden crates, I realized we were sitting on an arsenal of weapons destined for the guerrilla fighters. I was struck by a sobering thought. These rifles are highly accurate up to 440 yards; if the Eritreans had wanted to, they could have sat in their boats and fired into our camp. Needless to say, I was grateful for the friendship I had established with these men.

On our fifth day on the island, following a discussion with my shipmates, I tried to convince the Eritreans to take us to the mainland. They expressed a willingness to help, but because of their lack of water and their desire to see their families, they graciously refused. Their return to Yemen would have been complicated by further bribes to the police and army; but more important, they could not risk being found with the weapons. With the unpredictable weather, it might take several more days before they got the right winds. They could take us to Eritrea, but not to Yemen. Having survived a storm only six days earlier, none of us was interested in crossing the Red Sea in one of their fragile open boats.

The Eritreans had offered to get our boat off the beach, and we had refused. When they offered to take us to the African coast, no one wanted to go. These responses indicated to them that we were content to sit on the island and wait. It wasn't possible to pick and choose favors with these people. Nor was it reasonable to expect them to understand our impatience, which is what we were suffering from. We had sufficient food and water. From their perspective, they were not abandoning us at all. They believed in fate, and were leaving us in the good hands of Allah. What was an extra week or month on this island to people who spent most of their lives waiting?

When the Eritreans had gone, I gravitated toward Suzanne, whose creative, childlike attitude in the face of our predicament was refreshing. Like many French women, she knew what to do when confronted with food and a kitchen. It made little difference that our kitchen was on the beach and had neither walls nor ceiling. To help create a sense of order, she introduced the ritual of afternoon tea. It was a way to mark the passing of time.

We fluctuated between conserving our limited supplies and playing at being shipwrecked, and it was during one of these playful moments that Suzanne taught me how to make proper crepes. "The first one is always bad," she explained. "Throw it away. Not too much milk — it is better with water, to make a thin crepe." We made crepes *au beurre sucré, au citron,* and with orange marmalade and raspberry and apricot jam.

Soon we moved on to other desserts. Suzanne taught me the secrets of tarte Tatin and pâte sablée, and I showed her how to make cinnamon rolls and rum balls. For the rolls I used sea water rather than fresh water, and the results were fragrant, chewy, and delicious. What a delight to become lost in the pleasure of kneading dough, grinding up sticks of cinnamon and cardamom pods, and grating nutmeg. We rolled out the dough with an empty Johnny Walker bottle and combined the fillings, substituting jaggery for regular brown sugar. After slicing the roll, we placed the spiral segments into a buttered army mess kit that was half round in shape and hinged on a pair of twelve-inch metal handles. I let the dough rise and then cooked the rolls on top of the stove for ten minutes on either side. They came out caramelized and much more delectable than those baked in an oven.

Sea gulls marched up and down the beach in front of our camp at tea time, waiting for bits of crepes and cinnamon rolls. We didn't give this food away frivolously: our plan was to get the birds accustomed to taking food from us. I thought it likely we could catch a sea gull with a baited hook if the need arose.

Flies, rats, and mosquitos started to arrive in greater numbers, and Ellen took to sleeping in the inflated rubber dinghy in order to keep the rats from getting tangled in her hair at night. During this time my sympathies began to go out to Georgik and Suzanne, who seemed to be adjusting to life on the island with spirit and imagination. They were relaxed and easy to be with.

As the only single person, I had much more time to myself than the others. I began to relish the solitude and took to exploring the island. Every day the sea would bring new gifts. I found a rare nautilus cowrie shell and started to observe the sea life along the coast more closely. One morning, before sunrise, I watched four giant manta rays that measured approximately twelve feet from fin tip to fin tip. They appeared to be feeding as they worked their way along the edge of the rocky shore at the base of the cliffs, far below me. Sleek fish flashed through schools of smaller silvery green fish, and green sea turtles were visible as they moved lazily through the clear water. I made my way down a rocky slope just south of the camp, surprising two pelicans preening on the beach. Startled by my sudden appearance, they flew off, and I continued on to where the beach ended at a natural eight-foot-high overhang worn into the cliff by the waves. The walkway was exposed only at low tide. Its cool, damp shade beckoned me to explore further.

The floor of this passageway was smooth and still damp from the receding tide. Snails and limpets lined the nearby tidal pools; hermit crabs sunned themselves in clusters on the rocks. A cool breeze blew down this half-tunnel, and the shade extended out onto the turquoise water, where multicolored coral gardens were visible just below the surface. Beyond the line of shade, the sea dazzled my eyes with pinpoints of sparkling brightness. Delicate lapping sounds of wavelets on the smooth worn coral echoed in the passageway, and a thick atmosphere of evaporating sea water filled the sluggish air.

Going farther, I came into the sunlight for a moment and then re-entered the pillarless arcade, where a mossy green carpet, cool beneath my bare feet, provided luxurious walking. Porous dark-purple rock contrasted with the wet green carpet, and the walls and ceiling were filled with odd bits of coral fragments and seashells. A sea hawk screeched at my approach, then flew to a more private vantage point. Darkened grottoes with immaculate inclined sand floors, still wet from the tide, appeared every fifty yards or so, and I ventured on in search of new sights and sensations. I had discovered a hidden world that existed only at low tide. The place was perfect for barefoot walking, so my pace continued to slow as I became more and more enchanted by the beauty of the sheltered shoreline. Chirping sand birds flashed away from their rocky perches; miniature red crabs, hiding in the shallow rock pools, brandished their tiny claws and stood poised for sideways flight. Offshore, a black shape cruised by just beneath the surface of the blue-green water. I recognized the distinctive winged shape of a tremendous manta ray, peacefully feeding thirty feet from where I stood.

As I walked, the scattered clouds created unexpected color changes on the surface of the lagoon. The only sounds were of the wind, the tinkling waves, and my own breath. At one point the near silence was broken by the manta ray's jumping into the air and landing flat on its back. It hit the water with a surprisingly loud *smack* before continuing its peaceful glide. I ambled on. Several more turns brought me to a small beach accessible only at low tide or from the sea. I stepped out onto the fine warm sand, into the sunlight. After pausing to allow my eyes to adjust to the light, I followed the high-water mark, looking through the debris for anything interesting. There were large cuttlefish bones, a light bulb (General Electric, 40 watt), an empty liquor bottle (without message), and sheets of translucent, yellow-brown turtle shell. I dipped a hand-sized piece into the shallows and then held it to the light to look at the rich blend of colors.

I had continued down the beach for no more than a few steps when suddenly I was jolted out of my reverie by the sight of fresh prints in the sand. I was instantly tense and alert. These were not human footprints but the unmistakable parallel tracks of a sea turtle. I followed them up the beach for about a hundred feet, where I found the nest. Crouching down, I carefully pulled back handfuls of sand to reveal the first Ping Pong ball–sized egg. There were more than one hundred altogether. I carefully removed a dozen, then re-covered the nest. Judging from the texture and dampness of the sand, I knew the eggs had been laid the previous night. I was extremely relieved to discover that the island was not barren. It was offering us food, and I was thrilled by this realization. I tucked the precious eggs into the front of my sarong and returned to camp to share the news of my discovery.

The response back at camp was typical of the polarization in our thinking. The Parisians were becoming more Parisian, and the Californians more Californian. Suzanne's response was "Omelettes! We can try making omelettes. Maybe with tinned *jambon* or cheese." Instinctively she was concocting delicious breakfasts for us in her mind as Georgik savored the imaginary flavors.

Robert's response was equally predictable: "Don't you realize that green sea turtles are an endangered species?"

I was beginning to feel like an endangered species myself.

The days passed. Late one afternoon the sky turned the sea from purple to blue-black. A southerly wind freshened, and to the west the horizon was illuminated by a progression of pastel pinks and reds. The sunset passed swiftly, and the land became indistinguishable from the surrounding seas. As the island was lost in darkness, my attention was drawn upward to the emerging stars, which sprinkled the night sky and created a sense of immense distance.

We had taken turns coming to the lighthouse every night for the previous nine nights on the off chance that someone might come to check why the light had stopped flashing. With my back against the cold cement base, shielded from the wind, I waited with a loaded flare gun, a quartz halogen lamp, a box of red-and-white hand flares, and a Bic lighter. I paused to reflect on the insignificance of the little island and the frailty of its human inhabitants, but I had difficulty exploring these thoughts because I was excruciatingly uncomfortable sitting in the dark, trying to stay awake in case something happened.

It was half an hour before midnight when I was startled by the red port light of a cargo ship, which suddenly appeared without warning from behind Kamaran Island. Changing course, it headed in my direction, toward the southern tip of Uqban Island, making way slowly and uncertainly because the lighthouse wasn't working. (To attract attention, I had disconnected the light before sunset.) When the ship was about three miles away, I pulled the trigger and a flare arched high into the darkness, exploding with a brilliant red flash of burning phosphorous that slowly trailed to the ground. The stillness of the night had been shattered. I waited expectantly for a response. I flashed S O S with the searchlight, then YACHT AGROUND, YACHT AGROUND. Even as I flashed the sequence of dots and dashes, I realized the minuscule chance of a helmsman in these waters understanding Morse code or English.

Nothing happened for a few moments, but then the freighter appeared to slow down, as if waiting for a sign. The ship was dead abeam the island and moving very slowly. The green starboard light shone clearly, and I could just make out the silhouette of a person framed in the opened doorway of the wheelhouse. With less than a mile separating us, I could see the man looking in my direction. Using my lighter, I ignited a twenty-thousand-candlepower handheld flare and waved it in a huge arc at the end of an eight-foot stick. The flare should have been visible for more than twenty miles, but there was still no response. I was incredulous. Certainly the people on board could see the flare. What were they waiting for? Why weren't they signaling back? Then the ship began to make way toward the southwest, and I panicked.

"No! Come back! *Come back!*" I screamed into the wind. In desperation I loaded and shot off the rest of the arsenal. The colorful red-and-white explosions crackled, fizzed, whooshed, and boomed through the night sky as the ship departed. The sight of this fireworks display must have been spectacular from offshore. My night vision was wrecked, and afterimages flashed before my eyes each time I blinked. Why had the ship slowed down but not stopped? Consumed by frustration and anger, I felt helpless. The terrible, unspoken fear of never being rescued took hold of me, and I felt momentarily paralyzed by anxiety.

We had all been responding to stress in unexpected ways. As the anxiety lessened slightly, I found myself overwhelmed by the urge to take off my clothes. A bitterly cold wind whipped across the island as I stripped off my foul-weather jacket, my shirt, and then my pants. I flung them in a pile and stood naked, facing the wind. My skin and muscles tightened in the brisk air, and goose bumps stood out on my flesh. But at the same time I was filled with an animal-like, sensual warmth that radiated from inside me. I had absolutely no sensation of being cold or feeling foolish. Exhilarated by my irrational outburst, I felt as if I were thumbing my nose at the ship, the wind, and my fate.

The panic and sense of helplessness vanished, and I laughed out loud as I wondered what had compelled me to behave so oddly. *I'm losing my mind,* I concluded as I went in search of my clothes. I got dressed, stumbling around blindly, tripping over the still smoldering, acrid flare casings. I sat down at the base of the lighthouse to console myself with my blanket, some hard-boiled turtle eggs, a chocolate bar, and the shining stars.

The rest of that night, jagged rocks, the wind, and scavenging rats kept me from sleep, and before dawn I reconnected the lighthouse wiring and began the two-hour walk back to our beach camp. During the trip, I thought about our stay on the island and the swings of mood between complacency and anxiety. What were we so worried about? There was food, water, fire, and a warm place to sleep. All we had to do was control our impatience — an agonizing task for people accustomed to getting results when results were needed. We had been convinced that our silly attempts to attract attention would lead to our rescue, but the futility of our efforts was becoming increasingly obvious. We may have been near a minor Red Sea shipping lane, yet none of the freighters that approached the island had responded to our signals.

To pass time, Georgik and I decided to rig the dinghy with sails. There was some possibility that we could sail to the coast if our food ran out, and meanwhile we could take day trips on the lagoon. The design and construction of the mast and sails provided an excellent diversion. After making a preliminary drawing, we settled on a versatile gaff rig with a jib and a genoa sail. Because the prevailing winds were from the north at that time of year, we needed a keel in case we had to sail into the wind, so we bolted a five-foot by twenty-eight-inch plywood keel to the dinghy's floorboards. We then stood waist deep in the lagoon, holding the boat sideways to the wind and waves to find the center of lateral resistance. This was to help us calculate where to place the mast and sails so that the dinghy would have a slight weather helm. We cut the mast from a vertical-grain spruce boat pole, originally used to pick up mooring buoys. I constructed a sturdy rudder with a hinged tiller and then started on the rigging. Georgik and I made hardwood cleats and fair-leads and set up a pair of running backstays.

After we measured out a set of sails following a sketch drawn to scale, Georgik went to work with the hand-cranked sewing machine from the yacht. He selected a light yellow Ripstop nylon from an old parachute for the headsails and a blue striped plastic-mesh fabric for the mainsail. We pounded brass grommets into the head, tack, and clew of each sail and stitched reef points into the main. We worked quickly and efficiently, with very little conversation. As we measured and cut the sail material, we grew enthusiastic. Georgik sewed late into the night, with the aid of two flickering hurricane lamps, and after two days of intense work we were ready for the trial run.

A five-knot wind was blowing directly onto the beach from the south as we inflated the dinghy with a foot-operated bellows pump. Georgik climbed in first. I shoved off from the beach. The wind was strong, and we began a starboard beam reach to the east with a single reef in the main. Picking up speed, we came about and soon passed the camp, only twenty yards offshore. We sailed on for a few minutes before tacking again. I pointed higher into the wind to test our drift and was delighted to find that the ungainly-looking dinghy could sail at a forty-five-degree angle to the wind without noticeably losing ground. We tacked into the middle of the lagoon, sailing at a respectable three to four knots, with Georgik on the windward side for ballast. On the down-wind leg we sailed wing and wing, with the mainsail to starboard and the nicely shaped genoa to port. Georgik and I were proud of our work, and exhilarated to be able to move over the water with such ease. The wake bubbled astern, and after thirty minutes we sailed back to the beach to celebrate. The keel would have to be moved forward a bit to balance the steering, but apart from that the dinghy sailed well.

That evening, Suzanne and Georgik set off to spend the night at the lighthouse to watch for ships. Gratified by the success of our project, I slept well. Shortly after dawn they returned from their vigil, frightened.

"We heard voices last night. There were voices in the night."

Robert asked them to explain.

"From the base of the cliffs below the lighthouse — men speaking Arabic. We heard them at three A.M. We don't want to stay here any longer."

"Maybe it was the wind you heard," suggested Ellen.

"No, we heard voices in the night," came the emphatic reply.

Suzanne had been sleeping at the base of the lighthouse when Georgik started to see what he described as hundreds of lights in the water. He was cold and tired, and in his exhausted state he thought boatloads of men were coming to attack us. He woke Suzanne, and they ran from the lighthouse. At dawn they slowed down, and the panic left them. By the time they reached the salt marsh where the pelicans lived, Georgik and Suzanne were feeling better.

The shock of the experience seemed to make them unusually self-revealing once they were safely back in camp. They described how their fear had subsided as the sun appeared, and they explained how attached they were to the island. "Being here is like a dream," Suzanne said. "A beautiful dream. One that everyone has at some time in their life. To be truly alone and free . . . I love that dream." The days following the shipwreck had obviously strengthened their feelings for each other. "Our souvenir from this time," Suzanne continued, "is the memory of our happiness."

But their experience made me realize that the dismantling of the lighthouse could not have gone undetected for so many days. I looked across the island and wondered if we were being watched at night. And if so, for how long, and by whom? We searched the beaches for footprints or other signs but found nothing. Nonetheless, the incident created a strong sense of vulnerability in us all. I continued my walks, but they became tinged with unease. I began to carry a knife. The wonderful sense of solitude and peace that I had once enjoyed during those walks vanished as I started to look for signs of other human beings. We began to keep a night watch at camp, and that evening no one went to the lighthouse. A brass kerosene lamp from the ship burned as we read or wrote in our notebooks. We were strangely subdued by our fear of unknown people coming in the night.

There had never been much privacy on the boat, and it was no different on the beach. Later that night I could hear Georgik and Suzanne making love, but this time the sounds seemed to blend naturally with the wind and the lapping waves that flowed onto the beach. I looked up at the stars and thought of how each of us dealt with his or her feelings of dread. I internalized my feelings as much as possible, whereas the two lovers could find comfort in each other's arms. This thought filled me with loneliness. Some time later I could see Georgik's and Suzanne's silhouettes at the water's edge. They were washing themselves in the shallows.

They spoke quietly, and I could hear water falling from their bodies. I was struck by the tenderness and natural beauty of the two naked figures quietly refreshing themselves at the edge of the warm sea.

We spent the following day in constant anticipation. Our gaze was directed out to sea, as if at any moment something promising might appear. The island had somehow become infected by our fear and had lost its magic. Nothing appeared on the horizon that day, and two hours before sunset Robert and Ellen went to keep watch at the lighthouse. After dinner Georgik, Suzanne, and I sat on the beach and talked.

Our easy conversation was interrupted by the appearance of a freighter, which was approaching the island. Its deck lights passed to the south of the lighthouse and disappeared behind the headland. We watched as Robert and Ellen's three bright red-and-white pistol flares shot into the air. They were quite noticeable from where we sat, but looked silly and out of place. Who would understand the meaning of distress flares on such a remote island? It was as if we had placed all our hopes in a commercial airliner's responding to flashes from a signal mirror. How foolish to expect a ship to stop for us. Our distress radio was broken, the solar stills didn't work, and our food supplies were dwindling. We had sixteen days of water left. The realization that we might not be rescued put us in poor spirits. Why hadn't we been more careful, or more resourceful? Why hadn't we sailed to the African coast with the Eritreans? Our constant expectation of being rescued "tomorrow" had made us careless.

That evening the last romantic notions about our situation fell away. We longed to be taken from the island. *Le grand pique-nique* had come to an end.

3

A Palace for
Mr. Buona Notte

SEVERAL TIMES A DAY I scanned the surrounding sea. This
was more out of habit than anything else, but one morning as my
eyes followed the distant blue horizon they fastened on a minuscule shape that had not been visible fifteen minutes earlier. I
watched the shape become a sail, a small blue-and-white lateen
sail. I was almost afraid to blink in case the vision disappeared.
But the sail grew larger. Two weeks was a long time to be abandoned by the universe, but the sight of the sail and the prospect
of salvation left me strangely unmoved. I was peacefully resigned
to my fate. Did it matter if the little boat stopped at the island?
Where could it possibly take us? I reached for the plastic water
bottle at my side and took a drink. Hot, dry sand filled the spaces
between my fingers and toes.

The sail and sea began to shimmer in the early morning heat. I
left the shade of the cliffs and walked north, wandering through
the heat waves until I arrived at a distant beach. Sitting down in
the bushes above the high-tide mark, I watched the boat approach. As it drew near I could distinguish five black men sitting
near the stern. The topsides of the rough wooden hull were
painted a dull red. White lime antifouling paint was visible above
the waterline. In the lee of the island the sail came down, the boat

drifted up into the wind, and a man made his way through the shallows to place an anchor high on the beach. After setting it, he knelt on the beach and touched his head to the sand, thanking Allah. I stood up and walked toward him. White powdery sand was stuck to his forehead and nose as he looked up and noticed me, but his blank gaze revealed nothing. I could detect neither surprise nor alarm from his expression or his movements.

The other men waded through the shallows, and Robert and Ellen joined me. We handed out cigarettes and shook hands. These people were also Eritreans. There were three men named Mohammed, a young boy, Ahmed, and an old man referred to as Mr. Buona Notte because he had memorized those two words of Italian as a child. The men were barefoot and dressed in plaid cotton sarongs. Simple wraps of fabric covered their heads, and their fingers were adorned with faceted red and blue glass gemstones fixed into imitation gold settings. Their slight builds belied an exceptional strength and agility that became evident only when they worked. This group seemed very friendly. Judging from their appearance, they also seemed very poor. I pointed to words in the dictionary once again, gestured toward *Clea*, and again used sign language to tell our story.

"*Al-hamdu-lillah!*" (Praise the Lord!) they exclaimed in turn when they heard the tale of the shipwreck. "Fourteen days on this waterless island?" They indicated the number of days on their fingers to make sure of the count. Despite their shortage of food, Idrise, the first man who had come on the island, unobtrusively waded back to his boat and returned with half their remaining stores — a double handful of precious dates. He apologized for the grains of sand and the poor quality. Looking at his thin wrists and forearms, I was stunned by the magnificence of his gesture. I thanked him, and indicated that we had food and would like to invite them to come eat with us.

It was at about the time I was shooting flares from the lighthouse and running around naked in the middle of the night that a storm off the Eritrean coast scattered a fleet of eight small sailing craft carrying goats to North Yemen. Idrise's forty-foot open boat with its distinctive blue-and-white sail had been blown off course for five days. By the time the storm had passed, the goats were dying of starvation. Every day one or more would die and the men would throw another carcass into the warm, languid sea. Their drinking water was nearly gone, and it must have seemed like they were aboard a death ship, sailing toward the edge of the world. On the morning these men caught sight of Uqban Island, they had been at sea for nine days. A soft westerly wind and the slow roll of the ocean swells carried the boat toward the island. Soon the men could rest and the goats would be able to feed on a particular species of bush that grew on the sand hills of the island.

The men carried the goats ashore, counting them as they did so, and then let them graze. The young boy, dressed in a long ivory-colored shawl and a pair of ragged blue cotton drill shorts, tended the animals with a thin sapling. He and the goats filtered into the sand hills and were soon lost from sight. Idrise, who had been shy at first, eventually revealed that he could speak English — merchant seaman's English. "We have come to save you," he announced, as if his sole purpose for visiting the island had suddenly become clear to him. "Allah has sent us, and we will take you from the island." We didn't quite know where these men were going, but we were not willing to let another opportunity escape us, so we immediately accepted his offer.

At midday the Eritreans came to our camp to eat. We offered them water to wash their hands, and then we all sat down to a meal of rice, lentils, tinned fruit, curried fish, and tea. The rice and lentils were served from a communal plate, and we ate with our fingers. After lunch Idrise surprised us by announcing that he had been to Japan and Europe and had visited New York City for one day. A black taxicab driver in Manhattan called him "little brother" and later cheated him of $40. Idrise laughed as he recalled the incident.

Mr. Buona Notte picked up a magazine that had come from the yacht. I think it was *Better Homes and Gardens*. Thumbing through the colorful pages, he stopped at a full-page advertisement for a modern kitchen. Idrise told me that the man wanted to know whose palace it was. I told them it wasn't a palace but rather a household kitchen in America. They were transfixed by the opulence of such a cooking area. I pointed out the hot and cold faucets, sink, refrigerator, garbage compactor, dishwasher, food processor, toaster, and other accessories essential to Western eating habits. Idrise translated my description of each appliance, but in the end the Eritreans were still confused by one thing. They wanted to know where one could kill a goat in such a place. I thought about the question for a moment, and then pointed to the breakfast alcove with the flowered wallpaper and curtains. The men were satisfied.

We drank more tea, and Idrise talked about his experiences in the West: "Here [in Eritrea] a man eats at six o'clock in the morning — he eats only rice — and at six o'clock in the night he eats again. He eats more rice. We have dates, goats, tea, small tins of fish, plus flour for fire bread. In America or Europe the people can eat anytime they want. They eat this, they eat that . . . they eat hamburger, and everything whenever they want. They eat all day long, and some of them get fat like this." He stretched out his arms. "Here we can only eat for living, but in my home we have some animals, one pig, and can drink camel's milk. No problem . . . have plenty food, but only eating sometime." He laughed.

After all the midnight vigils at the lighthouse and attempts to repair the distress radio, it seemed fitting that an open boat full of goats and five Eritreans should rescue us. I couldn't think of a better way to go. We made arrangements for the men to take us from the island the next morning.

A pattern of scattered cloud shadows crossed the island as we walked along the shore to where the yacht lay on her side. Robert asked Idrise what he and his companions wanted from the boat. The men replied that they didn't have any money to pay for anything. We explained that we would like to give them a gift in return for taking us off the island. As they still hesitated, Robert located the brand-new Dacron genoa sail and handed it to them, along with several hundred feet of rope and a selection of hand tools. The men were so dumbfounded with surprise and gratitude that they stood rooted to the sand, staring at their gifts.

Loaded down with this treasure, they returned to their beach, a half-mile from our camp. They collected a huge pile of gnarled roots and dried shrubs just before sunset, and I could see the flames of their campfire throughout the night.

A peach-colored predawn light found us busy at the task of burying our possessions in the sand. The goat smugglers could not risk taking us directly to the authorities, and it was understood that once we arrived on the mainland, we would have to walk for help. Because it was unclear how far we might have to walk, we decided, for reasons of safety, to carry food and water but little else. I didn't know how long it might be before I returned to the island, so I wrapped the rest of my belongings in Dacron sail bags, making two parcels. The larger one contained extra clothing, sarongs, blankets, a selection of books, seashells, and a shaving kit. The smaller, more valuable parcel contained maps as well as seven years of travel journals. I kept the notebooks separate because they fit snugly into a purple Dacron bag that had once been used for holding sail ties aboard *Clea*. As an extra precaution, I dug my hole deep, placing the bags three feet down. I filled in a foot of dry sand, then dumped the previous two days' garbage on top, covering this with a small amount of sand in order to make the hole look like a continuation of our rubbish dump. The others dug shallow holes, thinking it highly unlikely that anyone would come to the island in our absence.

While we were busy digging, I could see Idrise and his friends in the distance, rounding up the goats and carrying them on their shoulders to the boat. We walked to the Eritreans' camp with our small bags containing bottles of water and enough food for two days. The last goat was brought aboard, the anchor was stowed, and the boat gradually drifted backward with the wind. We had left everything behind: the camp, the yacht, our sailing dinghy, and our beautiful beach kitchen. As we moved away from the island, Suzanne noticed me looking at *Clea* and read my thoughts. "It is like leaving an old friend behind," she said.

Despite our repeated inquiries, we weren't yet exactly sure whether we were going to Kamaran Island or the mainland, but it didn't seem to matter. The important thing was that we were on the move again. Infinite possibilities seemed to open up as we surrendered control of our situation.

There was a beautiful simplicity to the Eritreans' boat. The classic lateen sail was made from white flour sacks patched with blue plastic-mesh bags from fertilizer that had been donated to Ethiopia by the Canadian government. The rigging consisted of one combination backstay-boom halyard with a single-purchase handmade pulley, one shroud, and the mainsheet. The hull planks had been polished smooth by countless goats and were clinched to tree-branch ribs with steel nail fasteners. A forty-four-gallon steel drum held fresh water (from the yacht), and another half-drum near the mast served as the galley. A communal knife was used for rope work and cooking. Few other possessions were visible — a flashlight near the helmsman, odd lengths of frayed rope, a weathered nylon fishing line, but little else. No blankets or food, but each man carried a small pouch of dried leaves and a tobacco paste mixture. They occasionally dipped into the pouches with their fingers and placed a pinch of the stuff inside their lower lips.

The ten of us sat crowded together on the small aft steering platform, which extended over the stern. We overlooked a floating goat corral that filled the boat. Because the boat leaked and the goats urinated and defecated constantly, the bottom required bailing every twenty minutes. The smell of the animals was powerful, and I was glad not to be sailing into the wind. On a beam reach we managed approximately two knots an hour. The men executed three lazy tacks all day to cover the fifteen miles from Uqban Island to the uninhabited northern tip of Kamaran Island. During the journey, two white sails were sighted to the north. I saw one torpid flying fish, but nothing else. It seemed unlikely that our rubber sailboat could have managed the same trip.

Eight hours after we had clambered on board, the goat boat anchored just west of Douglas Point on Kamaran Island. We five white passengers disembarked and waded ashore to spend the night on the island; there wasn't room for all of us to sleep on the boat. We were drowsy from the wind and sun, and as we sat on the beach a freighter passed within three hundred yards of the shore. The ship looked huge and totally out of place behind the Eritrean boat. It might as well have been fifty miles away; we made no attempt to signal to the people on board. Squatting in the sand, we ate a dinner of tinned peaches, dried apples, and processed cheese. Idrise and the other men looked comfortable on their boat as we searched for shelter on the flat beach. A strong warm breeze was blowing, so I dug a shallow trench in the lee of a low bush to keep out of the wind, then settled in for the evening. After I wrapped my upper body and head in a sarong to keep out the sand, I put my head on my little bag of food and water and soon fell asleep.

By dawn the temperature had dropped and the wind had swung around to the south. This meant the Eritreans would have to wait for the wind to change before taking us any closer to Kamaran harbor, which lay another fifteen miles down the east coast of the island. This was where we wanted to go, but we might have to wait as long as two more days before the winds were favorable. Our desire to go with the circumstances was terribly short-lived, and in typical Western fashion we became impatient and decided to walk across the sand dunes. Idrise strongly advised us against this decision, but when he saw that we were determined to go, he pointed into the desert and said that there was a North Yemen Army outpost seven miles to the south. We said goodbye and left as dawn broke, with two quarts of water each, a compass, a bag of dried fruit, and an approximate route penciled onto our chart to indicate the way to the army camp.

A cold wind buffeted us head-on as we walked across the sand. We encountered camel footprints, followed the edge of a mangrove swamp, and walked up and down sand dunes that grew bigger and more disorientating with each step. The heat arrived without warning, but we had no choice but to hurry on, in fear of being caught in the sand at midday with so little water. What fools we were. We should have listened to Idrise; now it was too late to change our minds. If we turned back, there was no guarantee the boat would still be at the beach.

We continued south, gauging distance by our pace, which we

estimated at two miles an hour, and agreeing that for safety we should stay within sight of each other. But soon our group stretched out to over a mile in length. For periods I lost sight of the others in the wind-blown sand. We stopped to rest and re-group every hour, and incredibly, after the second rest stop Georgik and Suzanne announced that their water was gone.

"Why didn't you sip it slowly?" Ellen asked.

"We were thirsty," came the obvious reply.

We shared water and walked on. There was nothing but sand and rocks in every direction.

After more than four hours of walking we spotted the army outpost, a distant boxlike structure that sat atop a low hill rising out of a vast flat plain, which shimmered in the midday heat. With the last of our water gone, we hesitated only briefly before starting across this last obstacle. As we approached the hill, a strange sight became visible through the waves of heat. On the summit I could see men dressed in white skirts jumping up and down. What the hell were they up to?

We stepped through strands of rusted barbed wire and climbed a slight slope that formed the base of the hill. Completely oblivious to the possibility of land mines or other nasty devices, we crested the summit and surprised a soldier sitting on a rock. He was in casual dress — a white, pleated, knee-length skirt, black leather shoes without socks, a polyester sport coat, and a pink shirt buttoned at the neck. The handle of a jambia, the traditional curved dagger, protruded from the center of his embroidered waistband at a suggestive angle.

Clearly, nothing could have been further from this man's mind than our unexpected arrival. He leapt to his feet with remarkable speed, picked up his Kalashnikov, then, realizing the unfriendliness of this gesture, put the weapon down, reconsidered his position as a soldier on duty, and picked it up again, being careful not to point it at us. We all stood there, uncertain what to do.

"*Keif halak?*" (How are you?) I ventured.

"*Al-hamdu-lillah!*" (Praise the Lord!) cried the skirted soldier. He slung the assault rifle over his shoulder, shook our hands enthusiastically, and invited us in for tea.

The jumping men turned out to be Yemeni soldiers enjoying a game of volleyball in the middle of the desert. The court had been set up between a sandbagged field gun and the concrete blockhouse. Joining us in the blockhouse, the players did everything they could to make us comfortable. Were we hungry? Thirsty? We had just broken years of boredom for these men. It was not surprising that they were eager to show their gratitude.

We had arrived from the open desert without food or water, two of us were barefoot, and Suzanne was crying with relief. When she pulled the flowered scarf from her face, I could see damp lines below her eyes where the tears had flowed down her smooth, dusty cheeks. It was obvious that something extraordinary had happened to us. The soldiers knew that there was absolutely nothing to the north of this outpost. So where had we come from? We must have generated a great deal of suspicion as well as sympathy in the minds of these men. Their confusion was evident, but they remained hospitable and friendly, even though conversation was impossible without the dictionary that we had absentmindedly left on Uqban Island. We drank hot, sweet tea before they took us by truck to army headquarters in the old British residency that overlooked Kamaran harbor.

There Major Abdul Rahman introduced himself and made us welcome. He also gave us lunch: more goat — half a carcass, draped over a bed of rice on a serving platter nearly a yard wide. Oval loaves of warm, chewy, golden brown flatbread came with a fiery paste of ground red chilis and a dish of gray, doughy wheat paste that enclosed a reservoir of fat-and-marrow soup. To accompany the meal there were warm bottles of Coca-Cola. The lunch was delicious and the hospitality reassuring.

Several hours later we were handed what looked and tasted like hedge trimmings. This was qat, a mildly intoxicating leaf. We chewed, time passed, and when we were all feeling relaxed and cozy, the major announced that we were under house arrest. We surrendered our passports, handed over our money, and spent the next ten days waiting as the army looked into the possibility that we were Soviet spies from Eritrea.

· · ·

Longing for company, the major softened the shock of his announcement with several bottles of White Horse whiskey, and he accepted us as his personal guests pending the outcome of the investigation. Later in the first day an interrogator took statements from us, and the next morning Robert, Georgik, and I returned to Uqban to show the major the yacht in order to verify our story of the shipwreck. Three speedy fishing boats were commandeered from Makram, a small fishing settlement on the west coast of Kamaran, and the return to Uqban took less than two hours.

When we entered the lagoon from the southeast, we immediately saw black shapes swarming over the yacht: looters were already at work. As we reached the beach, three soldiers leapt into the knee-deep water and charged ashore. They were two hundred yards from the looters when they leveled their weapons and began shooting. Loud bursts of automatic gunfire echoed down the beach. We yelled for them to stop, frantically insisting that there was nothing of value on *Clea*, but the major indicated that these were merely warning shots to scare the looters away. I was relieved to see the men on the sailboat fleeing to the other side of the island, where a large motor-powered dhow was waiting for them. They staggered into the sand hills, bent double beneath the weight of tremendous loads. I wondered how these men had arrived so soon after our departure. We had spent two weeks on the island without seeing anyone except the Eritreans, yet suddenly dozens of men were climbing all over the yacht.

Our camp had been demolished. The looters' priorities were obvious: all the food was gone, as were the bedding and gas bottles. The stove was left standing, with the oven door open. It was interesting to note that two of the buried bags had been dug up. This confirmed my earlier suspicions that we had been watched during our stay on the island. I thought back to the night Georgik and Suzanne had heard voices. I suspected the looters were the same men, and felt relieved that they had had the courtesy to wait for our departure before helping themselves to our belongings. I could see that someone had dug down to the layer of garbage in my hole but had gone no further. My things were safe for the time being, but I was uncertain of the major's intentions, so while the others excavated their valuables, I decided to leave mine buried.

When I arrived at *Clea,* Major Abdul Rahman was walking around the area, carefully examining the piles of neatly sorted booty. He inspected the snipped battery cables and the half-removed screws that secured the compass to the binnacle. The remaining anchor chain had been pulled out of the locker, and the engine bolts had been cut off with a hacksaw. Sail bags were stuffed with ropes, miscellaneous tools, and plumbing fittings from below deck. Following the confusion of gunfire, Robert had gleefully invited the major to take everything. The man hardly needed prompting. He continued to survey the scene for several minutes before speaking. "What you can carry is yours," he explained in a detached voice. "The rest is mine."

He didn't have to elaborate. We understood perfectly, and no one responded to his statement. Like the looters twenty minutes earlier, we saw the major's point: his men had the guns. The fishermen who had brought us to the island had initially been jubilant at the thought of sharing such a prize, but they too fell silent when they realized they would get nothing. *Clea* was the major's plum.

The fishing boats were brought from down the beach and then loaded with the most portable and valuable articles. While this was going on, my uncertainty concerning our fate at the hands of Major Abdul Rahman began to dissipate. Realizing that we had no control, I grew strangely resigned to the situation. The soldiers continued sorting through the booty, and I returned to the camp to dig up my belongings. The gunfire and the chaotic scene of looting had unnerved me, and I felt confused and distracted as I pulled my bag from beneath the garbage. Dry sand immediately filled the hole as the bag came free. Not until we were well away from the island, with no possibility of turning back, did I look into the sail bag and realize I had left the smaller one behind. At the time, the notebooks seemed like a minor loss. We had been rescued, and my mind was overwhelmed with a sense of relief. Ten years would pass before I felt the need to return to the island to search for those lost pages.

4

Going Home

DURING OUR CAPTIVITY on Kamaran Island I became even more resigned to our circumstances and began to take an interest in the country. I was gradually introduced to the Yemeni people through daily contact with our guards and their families, who treated us more like house guests than prisoners. I enjoyed one soldier, Ahmed, who had a fair command of English, in particular. We talked about qat. Thursday (the day we arrived) is traditionally the day to chew, so when I noticed the soldiers gathering on Friday afternoon with armloads of qat, I asked Ahmed why they were going to chew again.

"It is like this," he explained. "Do you see that small, white, domed shrine?"

"The one standing by itself to the west of town?" I asked, looking out the window.

"Yes, that is the one. It is a saint's tomb, and today we will chew to celebrate the saint's birthday."

"I understand."

Saturday a similar scene developed. Once again the soldiers arrived with their long bundles of qat wrapped in newspaper and plastic.

"Ahmed, why do the men chew today?"

"We chew to celebrate the day after the saint's birthday," he replied.

"And tomorrow? What will be the occasion? Will you celebrate two days after the saint's birthday?"

"Yes, exactly!" He laughed. "And you will join us, please."

The afternoon qat-chewing ritual continued throughout our stay, and I began to develop a taste for the bitter leaves. Qat is the Yemeni version of afternoon tea, the most obvious difference being that instead of sipping an infusion of leaves, you put the leaves in your mouth and chew them. Ahmed called qat the great social equalizer, and this certainly fit with my observations. For several hours on most afternoons the major, the lower-ranking soldiers, and one or more of the suspected Soviet spies would contentedly chew foliage and smile at one another. I could not join in the conversation, but it was a delightful way to pass time as we waited for our release.

We couldn't leave the grounds of the residency during our stay, but qat was brought fresh from the mainland. It was evidently part of our room and board, and may have been in exchange for the items the major had stolen from us. For ten days we chewed leaves, ate goat, and drank whiskey. All things considered, it was a very civilized arrangement.

The whiskey provided the major with an opportunity to practice his English. Most nights, after a few drinks, he would fearlessly launch himself into Arabic thoughts for which he had no English sentences. He managed to make himself understood, largely because the theme never varied. He spent these evenings concocting different versions of how he had saved us. Each story was intended to enhance his own role in the adventure and to cover up his failure to respond to our distress signals, which must have been clearly visible from his front verandah.

One evening the major told us the story of how he had planned a midnight commando raid on Uqban Island. "The attack was planned! One hundred by one hundred chance!" he slurred, pounding the wooden tabletop with his fist. A fine layer of dust puffed ten inches into the air before settling on the glasses. Our forearms were stuck to the table with perspiration. "The orders were written!" he continued. "We did not know you were our brothers — *we would have killed you!* The shore guns were trained on the island. The troops were made ready. We thought someone was directing a bombing raid on Kamaran Island!"

The major sloshed more whiskey into the glasses, then sat back with arms crossed and eyeballs askew. The man seemed lost in youthful dreams of a distinguished military career that had never happened. Had he gone bonkers at this desert outpost? Had he planned to utilize the local fishing fleet for the invasion? And what shore guns was he referring to? It seemed as if he had Uqban Island confused with Dunkirk or Normandy.

It seemed reasonable to assume that the major had seen or been notified of the flares from the lighthouse. He was probably confused by the unusual sight and couldn't decide what to do. I later learned through the port authorities in Hodeida that several of the freighters had reported our distress signals to the harbor-master at Salif, the nearest mainland port, but there had been nothing he could do to help us. He could not obtain clearance to send the government launch to investigate. Port authorities later claimed that our rescue was further complicated because Uqban is in a highly sensitive military zone. Rumors that Russian gunboats from Ethiopia were hiding near the offshore islands were enough to keep commercial shipping well away from the area.

I grew tired of the major's nightly war stories. One of them told of a Russian MIG strafing Idrise's boatload of goats. These tales were unbelievable, and the entertainment value soon wore off. I devoted my time to writing while the events on the island were still fresh in my mind. I spent the days by myself or talking to Ahmed about the remote villages that lay hidden in the mountains of North Yemen. My initial interest in the region was stimulated by his descriptions of towering fortresses constructed from hand-hewn stone and mountain citadels with crumbling mud-brick battlements. Ahmed brought these fairytale castles to life by talking about the people who lived in them. He had grown up in Manakha, one of the most strategic mountain villages guarding the western approach to the fabulous capital, San'a. He told me about the beehives he had kept on the terraced mountainsides as a young boy, and described the excitement that was generated when the first bicycle was brought to town. I was captivated, and became interested in visiting the places he talked about.

After ten days on Kamaran Island, we were free to go. Two soldiers took us to the mainland in a military launch. The journey from Kamaran harbor to Salif took thirty minutes. Driving south to Hodeida with our army escort, we picked up a young Peace Corps volunteer who was hitchhiking at sunset. He worked in Hodeida and had rented a crumbling old house built by a Turkish merchant more than a century earlier. The house was conveniently located near the city markets, and the young man generously offered us a room. We stayed for five days, spending much of that time cleaning the house. The American lived in a state of squalor that an Eritrean goat smuggler would have found intolerable. After the pristine conditions on Uqban Island, I found the household filth unbearable. The climate of Hodeida was unpleasant as well, and I decided to leave the hot coastal plain as soon as possible.

The first morning in Hodeida, Georgik and Suzanne went to the French Bank of Indochina to inquire about having money cabled from Paris. While explaining their predicament to a teller, the manager, who was from Lyon, overheard their story of the shipwreck. He was delighted by the tale and took them to lunch. After listening to the entire story, he provided them with an apartment and introductions to friends in Hodeida, and, without being asked, arranged for a modest loan that would allow them not only to get home but to take their time doing so.

On hearing this, I looked forward to going to the U.S. embassy in San'a. I had approximately $350 in traveler's checks, which was not enough to get me back to the United States. I didn't want to risk the possibility of cabled money going astray, and so for the first time in seven years of travel I felt the genuine need to ask for a favor from the diplomatic corps. I wanted a small loan. Five hundred dollars would be enough to get me to New York.

Georgik and Suzanne moved into their apartment the next

day. We exchanged addresses and said goodbye. They wisely took this opportunity to free themselves from the group, and as time passed, I grew to envy their quick decision.

Three more days went by before the Yemeni Department of Immigration finally issued us two-week tourist visas. I walked out of the office with my passport and was immediately caught up in a flurry of airborne litter. Wind-whipped plastic bags, cardboard, and unidentified flying particles of colorful paper swirled about me like autumn leaves as I walked toward the marketplace. The streets of Hodeida were a trampled, multicolored collage of imported packaging. The town seemed to be disappearing beneath a tide of labels, cartons, cardboard advertising, and a small fortune in flattened aluminum soft-drink cans. Because it was dry and fresh, however, the street litter did not have the offensive smell of Western household garbage. Moving through the laneways was like being in a perpetual ticker tape parade. The market stalls were hung with plastic gewgaws of every color and description. Squeaky children's toys and blaring portable tape players of immense proportions competed for the viewer's attention with the hand-pulled carts and gridlocked, honking traffic. Like a plague of desert locusts, the storm of consumer goods had descended on the old marketplace.

I continued into the market, where I caught sight of stern Yemeni men seated in ancient barber chairs on the sidewalk as razor-wielding barbers fussed over them. Pausing by one of these streetside chairs, I listened uneasily to the slow rasping sound of sharpened steel moving over the skin to produce irregularly shaped but perfectly shining orbs.

On the morning of our fifth day in Hodeida, Robert, Ellen, and I took a shared taxi to San'a. The driver managed to stuff ten passengers into his Peugeot 504 station wagon before we departed. En route we stopped for tea and gas . . . lunch, prayers, qat, more tea and more prayers, fresh lime juice . . . more qat, a flat tire, water for the radiator, and frequently to pee at the side of the road. Every fifteen to twenty miles an army checkpost appeared, where we were stopped at gunpoint and asked to show our travel permits and passports. After a spectacularly uncomfortable and scenic five-hour drive through a high mountain range dotted with the fortified stone towers of medieval-looking villages, we arrived at a broad plain surrounded by more mountains. In the center of this plain was San'a, an ancient city still partially enclosed by mud-brick battlements.

We made a long, winding descent, entered the city, and found our way to Al Qa, the old Jewish quarter, which lay outside the city walls, just to the west of the *sailah,* the seasonal riverbed that runs through San'a from north to south. We had been given the address of Carolyn Ross, an American nurse, who graciously put us up during our stay. She lived with several other aid workers in a traditional Yemeni tower house. The five floors were connected by a steep spiral staircase, and we were shown to separate rooms on one of the upper floors.

I had not eaten all day, and by the time we arrived I was hungry. I asked Carolyn where I could find a local restaurant that served typical Yemeni food.

"Something authentic?" she inquired.

"Yes, a place that doesn't cater to Western visitors," I requested.

"I don't know how traditional you are willing to get, but there is a place nearby that should still be serving lunch." She smiled as she handed me a small sketch map that indicated a series of laneways leading to the restaurant. "There's no signboard on the building, so keep an eye out for the bread sellers."

I went in search of the place and fifteen minutes later arrived in front of a Yemeni restaurant. Colorfully veiled women were in the street, selling stacks of steaming, crusty flatbread from baskets balanced on their heads. Male customers, with the warm bread already folded under their arms like newspapers, were clustered outside a blue, wood-framed doorway set into a mud-brick wall. I bought my bread and waited with the others. A dozen disheveled men were suddenly disgorged from the doorway, the waiting crowd surged forward, and I was carried into darkness by the momentum of the surrounding bodies.

Blinded by the rising heat and smoke billowing up the stairway, I descended slick, foot-worn stone steps and entered an inferno. It was difficult to move freely in the crush of bodies, and I was immediately damp with sweat. Flames from ferociously hot earthen ovens shot into the main room and illuminated a writhing throng of lunch guests and kitchen staff. Following the example of those around me, I climbed over the tables and steaming ceramic dishes until finally I managed to wedge myself between two heavily armed strangers. With hand gestures these men instructed me in the technique of throwing wads of paper at the waiter to attract his attention. The floor was littered with little balls of paper. I struck the man between the shoulder blades on my second throw, and he nodded vaguely in my direction. He was soon at my table, yelling something in Arabic.

"Saltah!" I yelled back, following Carolyn's instructions. I motioned to my mouth with my fingers for emphasis. My companions chortled roughly, and the man disappeared into the confusion of bodies and airborne paper balls. There was no menu, and only one dish: saltah, a spicy potato, garlic, and mutton stew covered in a green froth called hulba, a sauce made from whipped fenugreek paste. The stew was served in earthenware pots so hot they left circular burn marks on the scarred tabletops. There wasn't room for everyone to be seated, and many men were squatting on the tables with their shoes on as they helped themselves from large, steaming communal pots.

The waiter fought his way back to my table and set down three identical bowls. I took the pot nearest me and ate with my fingers, using small pieces of bread like an edible spoon. The meal was delicious, but Carolyn had seriously understated the rustic charm and unpretentious service. I hadn't been prepared for a meal in such a place, and as I ate, I understood the meaning of her smile when she made her recommendation.

I was charged with energy by the time I finished. This was partly due to the high concentration of chilis in the saltah, but also the result of the excited conversations and pandemonium around me. Uneaten bread was left on the table or handed to fellow diners. After finishing my lunch, I staggered back over the table and washed my hands in a basin next to the stairs. A soiled terry-cloth hand towel hung on the wall, but I preferred to wipe my hands on the seat of my pants. I paid the equivalent of two American dollars before allowing myself to be carried by the rising tide of bodies up the stairs and back to daylight, air, and the relative calm of the traffic-jammed streets. If that was a typical Yemeni meal, I told myself, I could well understand why people chewed qat in the afternoon. It seemed reasonable to resort to euphoric substances in order to quiet the mind and body after such an experience.

On the horizon, a towering wall of dust approached the city. This was a sandstorm blowing off the Empty Quarter — the Rub'al-Khali, an immense desert that lies far to the east. I returned to the house in Al Qa, and soon the sun was obscured by the advancing curtain of fine reddish dust. I didn't go for a walk in the afternoon and stayed up late that night drinking tea with Carolyn. She told me about her work as a midwife in San'a, and I talked about my weeks on Uqban and Kamaran islands. Thick auburn curls fell to her shoulders, and as our conversation progressed I found myself attracted by her humor and intelligence. Carolyn was also very pretty, and after the stress of being on the island, it was a pleasure to lose myself in her good company.

When it was time to go to bed, she brought extra blankets to my room, along with a candle and matches. She closed the door quietly on her way out. Before falling asleep, I lay on my back and looked up at the ceiling ten feet above me. The entire room was neatly plastered with a layer of white gypsum that nicely caught the light of my bedside candle. The ceiling beams were spaced about three feet apart and were roughly rectangular in cross section. None of the beams were straight, and they appeared to be fashioned from slender trees, eight to ten inches in diameter. In the course of spanning the room, these hand-hewn beams meandered in slow, graceful curves. The smooth coating of plaster flowed over the beams and down the walls in such a way as to give the impression that the room had been carved from a single block of soft white chalk. The ceiling undulated in accordance with the random course of each individual beam, and by candlelight the general appearance of the room was very pleasing. The interplay of shadows on the stark white surfaces made it difficult to distinguish where architecture ended and sculpture began. The beautifully irregular wall surfaces were dictated by the whim of the builders and the nature of the materials used. No attempt had been made to create straight lines or perfectly flat surfaces, and the overall feel of the space was harmonious, functional, warm, and sensual — the precise qualities of an ideal bedroom. I slept well that night.

When I awoke it was not yet light, but somewhere in the distance I heard the crackle of static from a poor-quality loudspeaker. There was silence once again before a booming voice rolled across the darkened city as the morning call to prayer began. From a second and more distant minaret another voice called out. A multitude of amplified voices soon filled the morning stillness, and I sat up to listen to the mesmerizing, incomprehensible words as they drifted back and forth across the sleeping city.

I wanted to watch the sunrise, so I pulled on a pair of pants and started up the spiral staircase that led to the roof. As I ascended the wide stone steps, I was bathed in the rich aroma of freshly baked bread from the kitchen on the ground floor. In semidarkness I felt my way upward along the cool walls, and soon arrived at a low wooden door. I lifted its hand-forged catch and emerged onto a section of flat roof that was surrounded by a masonry wall four feet high. Moving to the edge of the roof, I set my hands on the mud-brick wall and looked across the darkened city.

At first there were only random pinpoints of light and vague rectangular shapes. The call to prayer finished, and as the air began to warm, a soft morning light filtered into the awakening city. Shadows became noticeable, and I caught my breath as the jumble of towering earth-colored buildings became visible. My first impression was that during the night I had fallen back in time and awakened in the midst of a fairy-tale world from my childhood. I looked out at a gingerbread fantasy in which every surface was adorned with mad geometric designs, covered in squiggles of white cake icing. Each facade blended into the next, and the thousands of whitewashed, irregular window frames, the low-relief zigzag friezes, and the openwork in the stone walls grew indistinct in the middle distance until they finally melted into the buff-colored mountains beyond the city walls.

The splendor of San'a could not be taken in at a glance. Each visual morsel deserved careful attention. Among the first architectural details to catch my eye were the roof finials. The most distinctive of these adornments had a stepped, saw-toothed pattern that was most striking when seen from the street. The rows of white zigzag shapes appeared to be interlocked with the sky. I have since been told that this is to insure that heaven and earth are joined. Watching this first sunrise over the city, I understood perfectly well the symbolism of oneness expressed by the finials. I had been unprepared for this sensation of attachment. No one had warned me about the allure of San'a, and in my surprise, I was caught off balance — seduced without a struggle. The magical, otherworldly beauty of the city took hold of me, and I didn't resist.

Nearby, I could see delicate gypsum tracery of brilliantly colored stained glass fanlights, while in the distance white minarets thrust above the skyline to bathe in the first pinkish glow of dawn. Protruding discreetly from among the cluster of buildings were the white nippled domes of the Ottoman mosques. Observing these sights, I couldn't help but amuse myself with thoughts of how the austere Islamic faith could allow such sensuous religious architecture.

As households began to stir, black swallows darted over the rooftops and ghostly white clouds of smoke from breakfast fires floated through the confusion of buildings. The smell of burning wood and charcoal drifted past me, and deep in the twisting passageways dark figures moved slowly.

Despite the high technical skill evident in the exterior stonework, I was surprised at the apparent lack of pretense. There were no ostentatious displays of wealth or style. Perhaps these expressions were confined to the interior of the houses. San'a had a unified look, but I'm not certain why this should be so, because closer observation revealed chaos rather than order. The structures were similar but at the same time unique in their range of unexpected variations on a theme. On the facade of a nearby building I counted twenty-three windows. Of those windows, three were similar. The other twenty were so completely irregular, and placed in such random fashion, that it was impossible to determine their precise function, let alone establish where one floor began or ended. If there had been an original plan for any of these buildings, it escaped my notice. The millions of mud bricks and hand-cut stones appeared to have been placed by individual whim. I was looking at something eternal, ageless, and precious — a place where I could leave myself far behind. The city of San'a was a spectacular living monument to the playful genius of the Yemeni builders.

I felt optimistic about my arrival in San'a, and the following afternoon Robert, Ellen, and I went to the U.S. embassy to report the shipwreck and the loss of most of our belongings. I had already been warned about the possible delays in transferring money to Yemen, but I must have been dreaming when I imagined I might get help from the embassy. That afternoon we were introduced to American diplomatic hospitality. We waited for more than an hour beneath the arrogant gaze of a Marine guard seated behind bulletproof glass. I never saw the man blink nor heard him say a thing other than "Yes sir" and "No sir." When the consular official finally made his appearance, he breezed into the reception area and immediately pointed out that the embassy was normally closed on Friday (the holy day). He then informed us that we had interrupted him at an "official diplomatic luncheon." He actually managed to make me feel guilty for not coordinating my problem to suit his mealtimes.

With a condescending indifference that I still remember with astonishment, he asked what we wanted. Looking at this man's ample midsection, striped silk tie, starched collar, immaculate fingernails, and perfectly shined shoes, I recalled the turtle eggs I had eaten on Uqban Island and calculated how many more I might have had to eat if the Eritreans had not showed us a generosity this man would never have considered, much less offered. He recited a poorly memorized statement outlining our rights as American citizens and the responsibilities of the embassy. As he spoke, I was given the impression that several dozen American citizens were shipwrecked each week in Yemen and the over-worked staff was just going to have to draw the line somewhere. We were not offered as much as a glass of water, and assistance was limited to showing us to the door and pointing vaguely in the direction of the country's only international-class hotel. Three nights in that hotel would have exhausted my remaining funds.

We returned the following day to file our report, but by then I wasn't in the mood to ask for favors or a loan from these em-ployees of the United States government. They would have in-sisted on keeping my passport and flying me directly home on an expensive flight. Neither one of these conditions appealed to me, and I decided to take my chances with the generosity of the Yem-eni people.

My remaining $300 in traveler's checks could have lasted me for several weeks in Yemen, but I decided to leave San'a as soon as possible. The least expensive flight to Europe was around $250, and so I spent the following days visiting the airline offices, asking for a discounted flight out of Yemen. If this wasn't possi-ble, I suggested flying now with the promise of sending a check later. I tried Royal Jordanian, Alitalia, Air France, Ethiopian Air, Aeroflot, and others. Not surprisingly, only one airline was vaguely interested.

I visited the office of Syrian Air twice and established a good rapport with Mr. Rashid, the manager. Robert and Ellen, who had plenty of money, were intrigued by the possibility of free air-line tickets, and persuaded me to let them join me on my third visit. Foolishly, I let them come along. We were served thick, sweet coffee from a polished brass tray, and they sat in on the end of a delicate discussion that had lasted for several hours over the previous two days.

"This is a very good story, you know, and we would like to help you," Mr. Rashid told me. "There are always empty seats on our flights to Damascus, and I think we can make some ar-rangements." This, I felt, was the prelude to a generous offer. I tried not to reveal my eagerness or desperation and merely nodded in order to let him continue. He asked me to tell him once again how we had been taken from the island in a boatload of goats. This portion of the story struck him as extremely funny. I think he delighted in trying to imagine himself in a similar situation.

We both enjoyed our little game of drawing out the conversation with as much suspense as possible. Given the situation, the tone of the conversation, and my understanding of hospitality in the Middle East and Asia, I felt extremely confident that the manager would simply surprise us with an offer of complimentary tickets. In return, I would refuse, and offer to make at least a partial payment. Mr. Rashid would exclaim that this was out of the question, and point out that he knew I simply did not have the funds. What was important for him to be able to convey was the fact that he wanted to help. We were not to question the extent of his assistance. This exchange would increase the pleasure for both of us, and at the same time emphasize his generosity and my gratitude.

We were in no rush to conclude our talk, but as we chatted I could sense Robert's growing impatience and desire to participate in the exchange. The thought of his getting involved filled me with dread, so I tried to bring the negotiations to an end. I had gone over the details of my financial situation with Mr. Rashid earlier, but I sensed that before his final surrender he wanted one last measure of drama. I must be left in doubt until the end. I listened to his words but took the meaning from his eyes. I felt certain he was going to help us.

"How much of the full fare can you afford?" he asked.

In my mind I formed an answer. I would go over the complications of having money cabled, the scene at the embassy, and my genuine need. I would also express my thanks for any small favor he could provide. This would give Mr. Rashid his opening.

Unfortunately, I never had the chance to express my thoughts, because at that precise moment Captain Riley saw his opportunity. "We can pay two hundred and twenty-five dollars!" he blurted out.

I don't know how he arrived at that amount, or what his intentions could have been, because his comment completely contradicted my entire story at the crucial moment. I stiffened in my seat, totally mystified. Mr. Rashid stared at me in a state of similar confusion. Moments earlier, all had seemed clear. We had established trust, and the subtle exchange had been fluid and full of grace. I had claimed destitution, but now there seemed to be extra funds available. How could I explain to Mr. Rashid that for personal reasons I didn't want to ask Ellen for a loan? How could I excuse the fact that Robert and Ellen actually didn't need his help? Whatever was going on in his mind, it was obvious that the mood had been broken. I felt the manager withdraw. I was ashamed. Mr. Rashid was stripped of the pleasure of his generous offer, and felt betrayed. I was deprived of my credibility, and the airline ticket.

It was an uncomfortable situation, which I only added to by apologizing, blushing, and walking out the door, with the other two Americans following. I was furious, but once on the street all I could say to Robert was "Thanks, genius!" I didn't wait for a reply but turned to walk to the office of Air Yemenia, the domestic carrier. I didn't know for certain if it had planes that flew out of the country, but this was the last airline. Perhaps someone in the office could help me.

I seated myself at a desk opposite Mr. Yusuf al-Iriyani, the manager of Air Yemenia. Tea was brought, and I started to present my well-practiced story. No more than a minute passed before Mr. al-Iriyani set the official army report aside and said, "What can I do to help you?"

"Well, there's more to the story," I replied, wanting him to hear me out before saying no.

"It's not necessary — I believe you need help. What can I do?"

Mr. al-Iriyani began to smile. He realized how surprised I was at his trust in me but concealed any acknowledgment of this. He believed my story and understood my problem. Mr. al-Iriyani was remarkable for his rare blend of thoughtfulness and efficiency.

"We fly as far as Cairo, so the ticket from San'a to Cairo is no problem. Cairo to Athens is around fifty-four U.S. dollars. From there you are on your own."

I offered to send him payment later, but he refused.

"Don't worry, the airline will survive. But I want you to promise me one thing."

"What is that?" I asked, slightly stunned by the unexpected turn of events.

"The next time you see someone in need, I want you to pass on this favor. It was given to me, and now it is yours."

I was remarkably touched by this wise response to the situation. Rarely does one receive such valuable life lessons in an airline office. I immediately agreed to his condition. Mr. al-Iriyani wanted to know who else was with me on the sailboat. I mentioned Robert's and Ellen's names, and the following day, when I returned, I was handed three ticket folders.

"What are the two extras for?" I asked, without opening the tickets.

"For your companions," he said with a smile.

"Yes . . . for my companions," I replied dryly.

Two days later I was sitting in a plane at the end of the runway of San'a's international airport. I could finally relax. Vibrations from the engines lulled me into a pleasant state, and I thought back to a night on the Red Sea when the stars became unstuck from the heavens and I rode down the face of giant waves covered in silvery foam. There was the vision of Idrise's blue-and-white sail on the horizon and the sight of an exhausted sea bird tumbling out of a fantastic night sky to sit with me until dawn. In my mind I was walking along the cliffs of Uqban Island when the plane began to move down the runway. As it gathered speed, I realized that a seven-year journey had come to an end. I was on my way home.

A Sackful of Locusts

San'a, North Yemen, 1988

I STEPPED ONTO THE RUNWAY at 3:30 A.M. wondering how I would get into town and where I would stay. Armed guards who had surrounded the aircraft were now shuttling passengers into a bus to take us to the darkened terminal. Between the immigration desk and the customs checkpoint I was approached by a short man with black curly hair protruding from the bottom of a skullcap. I could hear him talking, but took little notice of what he was saying. I was exhausted. Waiting beside the conveyor belt for my bag, I observed the man's dress as he approached, in turn, each of the foreign men who had been on the flight. He wore a black sport coat over what appeared to be a powder-blue cotton nightgown. Girdling his waist was a three-inch-wide belt of purple velvet richly embroidered with gold and silver threads. Shoved behind the belt was his jambia, a wicked-looking ten-inch curved dagger in a green leather sheath. The man wore black leather shoes without socks. He looked like all the taxi drivers pressed behind the metal barricade as they waited for passengers. He wandered back to me and repeated the same unintelligible phrase. I looked around once more for my bag.

"Meester Hereek?" I finally understood him to say.

"What?" My voice squeaked its amazement.

"You are Meester Hereek?"

"Yes."

"Your car is waiting."

I hadn't ordered a car, but the man was insistent. When I offered my bag to be inspected at customs, the man at my side dismissed the uniformed officials and armed guards with an impatient wave of one hand. Everyone smiled courteously. Who could this fellow be?

We drove into the night.

"Our destination?" I inquired.

"To Queen of Sheba Hotel," he replied.

I asked who was paying for such luxurious accommodation, thinking that he might be hustling clients in return for the usual remuneration.

"Do not worry . . . you are welcome to Yemen," my escort reassured me. He patted my knee and smiled while indicating obliquely that the room and car were to be provided without charge. I was confused.

The smiling man in the blue nightgown introduced himself as Mohammed Aziz Alaghbari. He had been sent by Yusuf al-Iriyani, the former manager of Air Yemenia who in 1978 had helped me leave the country. Now Mohammed was to be my *murafiq* — my protector, driver, and traveling companion. "I will take you where you want to go," he assured me.

How could Mr. al-Iriyani know that I was returning to Yemen after ten years? I still don't know, but I remembered enough about the country from my first visit not to ask. There is no such thing as knowing "the real story" in Yemen. There are far too many versions from which to choose. Motivations vary; mystery remains a constant.

Mohammed left me at the front desk of the hotel, promising to return late that afternoon. After lying on my bed for an hour, I realized that sleep was impossible and decided to go for a walk.

Light filtered into the city. The upper stories of a thousand-year-old stone building were touched by the predawn glow. A lead-colored light spread through the chilly depths of darkened passageways paved with blue-gray stone. The twisting laneways were nearly deserted, but as I moved through the shadows I could smell the smoke from household breakfast fires. I passed two soldiers with Kalashnikovs slung over their shoulders. The men were shivering beneath the hoods of their olive-green over-coats as they crouched beside a miserable-looking fire of card-board boxes and plastic bottles. I moved further into the city, where rows of veiled women were selling loaves of steamy bread from cloth-lined tea chests. The wooden chests were covered with blankets to retain the heat. The freshly baked bread gave off a delicious aroma of barley and sorghum flour. I bought one of the five-inch-wide loaves and sat down in a streetside teashop to sip a thick foamy drink made from ground coffee husks and sweetened condensed milk. A crushed green cardamom pod floated on the surface. The sun was rising.

A man approached. Dressed in a beige sport coat over a full-length orange terry-cloth bathrobe, he performed an extraordi-nary dance in the street. He twirled with arms outstretched and his palms opened to the morning sky. Like a dervish he continued to turn, and as he did so he began to sing and smile in the dusty road littered with refuse. At first I thought he was crazy; then it occurred to me that he might be merely happy. I couldn't under-stand his song, but as he drew near I could see his eyes — wild and unblinking black orbs that saw a world I could never imag-ine. A single white dove flew overhead, displaying a pinkish hue beneath its wings.

A young daredevil wearing a skindiver's mask darted out of a lane astride a carpeted bicycle. He peddled furiously past the dancing man without paying him the least bit of attention before disappearing into a narrow alleyway pinched between two build-ings. Like a phantom, the cyclist seemed to vanish into the mud-brick walls. A hint of dust hung in the air to reassure me that I had not imagined the scene.

I enjoyed the view from my table, and it was nice to feel so comfortably dislocated in a strange city. I wondered if I was the only one relishing the bizarre sights, but when I looked around the tables to gauge other people's reactions, I realized that the sight of me drinking a cup of coffee and eating a piece of bread was infinitely more provocative than carpeted bicycles or twirling madmen singing in the street at sunrise. I cleared my throat self-consciously as I attempted to become inconspicuous through nonchalance. I dug into my pants pocket for a letter. The man continued his song to the sky as I smoothed the stiff page on the table.

Months earlier, a friend in New York had given me the name of a Mr. Martin Plimsole, an English instructor at the Bristol Language Institute in San'a. I had heard through our mutual friend that Mr. Plimsole had been living in Yemen for six years. He spoke the San'ani dialect perfectly and had read Arabic at Cambridge. I had returned to Yemen to search for the journals I had buried on Uqban Island ten years earlier, and I somehow thought Mr. Plimsole might be able to help. I had written to him at once. It was a rather formal letter, introducing myself and briefly explaining the shipwreck in 1978 and my plans to revisit the island. He had been described as an ethnographic walker, so I took the opportunity to suggest we might go on a walk in the mountains during my stay. I envisioned a kindly middle-aged man who favored gray herringbone blazers and wool gabardine slacks cut generously at the waist — perhaps the sort of outdoorsman who might take along a tin box containing a set of hairbrushes, binoculars, and a silver butter knife for spreading gentleman's relish on dry biscuits imported from England. If there was a shop in San'a selling Wilkin and Sons apricot preserves, Martin Plimsole would know the place.

I was gratified to hear from him within three weeks of posting my original letter, but I wasn't quite sure what to make of his reply.

Dear Eric,

Many thanks for your letter. I was away in Spain for a few weeks. I visited Galicia where people are so melancholy . . . then on to León where they are also melancholy. I traveled to Portugal and found the people there even more melancholy. The friend I was with thought he was going to die so we left the day before the Great Fire of Lisbon — having eaten and drunk far more than was good for us. I spent a few days in Cairo, where people thought my Arabic hilarious. I found the Egyptians anything but melancholy. The cafés there serve a hot milky drink with nuts in, which is ambrosial. I rowed around the Nile in the sunset, and listened to a tape of readings by Benjamin Zephaniah, an English Rastafarian poet, in the City of the Dead under the shadow of the Qait Bey mosque. It's beginning to get cold in San'a, which always makes me want to go on walks. PM is right in recommending Jabal Bura. I once went walking there, climbing the last part of the mountain with my nose on a level with a donkey's farting fundament. A Bura burro. There's a strange bit of forest along the way — loud with the cries of baboons. What I'm trying to say is I should love to go on a trip with you. You asked what you could bring. A piece of cheese would be nice, and a supply of cigarette bangers. The sort that you put in a cigarette and blow up the end.

Hope to see you soon,

Martin

I refolded the letter and returned it to my pocket. Rastafarian poets? Flatulating fundaments? What sort of man might he be? And the cigarette bangers, what were they for? I had been concerned about practicalities such as proper footwear, medication for chloroquine-resistant strains of malaria, and whether I would need an umbrella. But having put these matters aside, I found myself taking an immediate liking to Mr. Martin Plimsole.

By the time I left the teashop, the man had stopped twirling. He sat upon a pile of rock rubble at the side of an alleyway. One of the female vendors had offered him a loaf of bread, and he chewed contentedly on the crust.

Leaving this scene behind, I walked for several minutes before losing my way in the maze of dust-laden back streets. I didn't mind being lost, because I had no particular destination in mind. My intention was to continue walking through the old city of San'a until I was tired enough to sleep. The thirty-hour plane journey from New York to Yemen had taken me beyond mere exhaustion. I floated on a cloud of adrenal vapor, bleary-eyed, yet hopelessly wide awake and full of anticipation. I had been wandering through the empty city since before daylight, when the call to prayer had dislodged all true believers from their warm sleeping places. By the time the night watchmen in the grain suq had ceased calling to one another, it was light enough for me to begin picking out architectural details as well as less obvious distinguishing features of the city. The garbage struck me as remarkable. The discarded paper packaging reminded me of the storms of litter that had filled the streets of Hodeida in 1978.

I stopped to look at a section of roadway strewn with trash. The colorful expanse of flattened litter that lay before me revealed all there was to know about Yemeni brand loyalties. Imbedded in the surface of the road was a blue polka-dot pattern made up of discarded lids of Nivea skin cream containers. Labels from Dutch Lady evaporated milk cans displayed pastoral scenes from nineteenth-century Holland, and Topaz Brand double-edged razor blades protruding from the compressed debris made barefoot walking inadvisable. Red-blue-and-silver bottle caps carrying the Pepsi-Cola logo in Arabic script sprinkled the ground like discarded coinage, and judging from the cans, Portuguese sardines in tomato sauce were clearly less popular than fava beans from China. Gazing at the flattened, dried body of a pigeon that had become amalgamated with a padded bra bearing fresh tire marks, I became self-conscious. Plastic bags bounded past me like tumbleweed as I continued walking. Farther down the lane I glanced back to see a blanketed figure looking at the ground that I had so meticulously examined moments earlier.

Yemen, as I correctly guessed, is a country of imports. My opinion was supported by the evidence underfoot. An astute wholesaler or small goods merchant could devise an entire marketing strategy for specific neighborhoods merely by checking the surface of the roadways. So intent was I on uncovering the traces of my past that no object or thought seemed too insignificant. Even the litter spoke to me that first morning. I wandered aimlessly, searching for deeper meanings. The commonest sights held my attention. Weeks later I was to stride over this same garbage without giving it a second thought. It would gradually disappear through familiarity.

Children were making their way to school as men returned from the markets with bundles of fresh vegetables and clear plastic bags full of red meat. I fell in step behind five men carrying identical towels with pink, yellow, green, and blue stripes under their arms. They entered an open doorway set in a whitewashed stone wall, and I followed. Warm, moist air blew over my face and forearms as I stepped into the dim light. This was the entrance to a *hammam*, a public bathhouse. Once inside, the men turned to the left and immediately disappeared. Quickening my pace, I followed them down a short corridor that opened onto a domed room. An empty stone fountain dominated the middle of the floor. As I paused to allow my eyes to adjust to the light, the men moved farther into the shadows, and were soon lost in the steam and darkness. I heard a wooden door open and close but saw no movement. The thick stone walls gave off a damp earthy smell and amplified the sounds of male voices and splashing water from the inner rooms. I felt like an intruder as I stood in the partial light beneath the dome.

I stepped back onto the street and walked to the rear of the bathhouse. Sensing my curiosity, an attendant, bared to the waist, showed me the fires below ground level. The stone floors and water reservoirs of the bathhouse were heated directly by a slow fire. Fresh cow skulls, assorted animal bones, and hides were used for fuel. Horns gave the most heat, the man told me. Fuel lay in heaps near the arched openings to the furnaces. In the jumbled piles I could see skulls, bones, discarded clothes, old rubber thongs, leather shoes, and worn-out truck tires. The attendant tapped one of the tires and then gave me the thumbs-up sign to indicate that tires burn well. Little smoke was escaping from the roof vents, which caused me to wonder if the frightful smell of burning rubber and hides entered the bathhouse.

As I wandered farther, a pair of window shutters creaked open high above me. Lifting my gaze, I saw a cobalt sky framed by the familiar mud-brick facades frosted like gingerbread with gypsum plaster. They looked like the result of child's play — handmade and ageless. A woman's bare arm appeared from a darkened window and hung a caged gray parrot in a patch of sunlight. The arm withdrew, and I continued walking.

By seven o'clock I was standing in front of a man selling locusts. He was seated on a brick behind a blanket covered with a three-foot-high mound of reddish brown insects. Demonstrating how to eat them, the man first pinched off the wings and discarded them, then popped the body and legs of the locust into his mouth. I tried one. It tasted like crunchy, smoked milk powder. The locust was good, although it might have been even better lightly salted.

The locust seller, pleased that I had eaten one of the insects, spoke to me in English. "We consider the locust to be a delicacy, but a ram's head is preferred to a sackful of locusts."

I told him that neither ram's heads nor locusts were readily available in my country.

"Correct!" he replied knowingly. "In Amreekee you eat the hot dog, the hamburger, and the potato chip."

In yet another narrow laneway, with just enough room for two loaded camels to pass, a horn began to blare. A vehicle was approaching. The pedestrians backed against stone walls as the honking vehicle moved forward. Three veiled women faced me from the opposite side of the lane. The car advanced, passing between us, and as it did so a protruding fragment of chrome trim caught hold of my trousers just to the left of my zipper. I heard the sound of ripping fabric before I knew what was happening. When the dust cleared, I inspected the damage. My skin was untouched, but the entire upper section of my left pant leg was torn open to reveal most of my thigh. I couldn't see the women's faces, but they obviously enjoyed the sight of my naked leg. They didn't point, but the movements beneath their veils betrayed their convulsive laughter.

The prospect of having to walk across an entire city full of veiled women with my thigh exposed suddenly made me feel tremendously weary. I paid a man on a motor scooter the equivalent of $1.50 plus a sackful of locusts to take me back to my room. The morning had been well spent. It was time to sleep.

6

Motoring with
Mohammed

THE FOLLOWING AFTERNOON I found my way to the Bristol
Language Institute, where I was disappointed to learn that Martin Plimsole was visiting friends in Jordan. He would not be returning to San'a for another week, so I decided to begin my
search for the journals without him. The next morning Mohammed picked me up promptly at 6 A.M. to take me to the
coast. My plans were mindlessly simple: first we would drive
from San'a to Hodeida, then make our way north to Al-Luhayyah, the coastal village nearest Uqban. In Al-Luhayyah we
would hire a boat to take us out to the island, where I would dig
up the journals. The following day we could take a leisurely drive
south along the shore of the Red Sea as far as Hodeida. A late-
afternoon drive through the mountains would have us back in
San'a before dinnertime.

It was on the second day of our journey, while motoring north
from Hodeida, that we drove into a towering wall of dust. The
heat was terrible. Hot wind riddled the car with a hail of grit as
the sun disappeared. We could no longer see the road. Plastic
bags flew at us like a lost squadron of dehydrated kamikaze jel-
lyfish. The windshield wipers were soon fouled with the bags,
making it impossible to continue. Mohammed, showing the

same calm assurance he had when he picked me up at the airport four days earlier, eased the car to the side of the road to wait for the storm to pass. I checked the temperature inside the car. Forty-eight degrees Celsius (118°F) — two degrees hotter than the day before. We were on the Tihama, a fifty-mile-wide coastal plain renowned for its debilitating climate and featureless landscape. Five major wadis, or seasonal riverbeds, cross the Tihama from east to west. We were somewhere south of Wadi Mawr. I reached into the back seat for the water bottle, but found it empty. The hot plastic stuck to my sweaty palm. I felt dizzy, and hot air filled my lungs. Stupefied by the heat, I collapsed against the door of the passenger seat, a damp, torpid lump.

There is a great wind called *shamal* that blows from the north across the Arabian Peninsula during the months of December and January, as well as May and June. The sand-laden wind can block out the sun and bring down aircraft by clogging the air intake to the engines. Vehicles have been stripped of their paint in these storms. I asked Mohammed if the storm we were in was a *shamal*.

"No, this is only garbage — it is nothing," he answered, fastening his black-and-white-checked *kaffiyeh* around his face to keep the fine dust out of his mouth and nose. "It will pass," he added, his voice muffled.

As we waited for the storm to clear, I thought about Mohammed's reactions to events. Few situations seemed to affect him in predictable ways. The previous night, on our way from San'a to the coast, we had stayed in a hotel in Manakha. Late in the afternoon I had been standing on the roof enjoying the spectacle of rising mist billowing up the mountainside and flowing between the tall stone buildings when gunfire erupted in a nearby laneway. Two long bursts — thirty shots or more. From where I stood I could tell the direction of the shots, but the narrowness of the lane made it impossible to see the gunman. People on adjoining rooftops smiled knowingly at each other. No one seemed alarmed. I retreated down several flights of stairs to where I found Mohammed nibbling at a fresh bundle of qat. I asked him what had happened, but he seemed unconcerned.

"It is nothing, only gunfire."

I explained that gunfire, especially automatic-weapon fire in populated areas, was a cause of grave concern where I came from. I asked if something might be wrong.

"A child has been born," he replied, placing a leaf of qat into his mouth and chewing contentedly.

I asked how he could be sure of this theory.

"By listening to the rhythm of the bursts. The short bursts are the deadly ones. It was the husband shooting. The gunfire makes the wife and child happy, and announces the birth to the village." His slow smile told me to relax.

When the storm of plastic bags had subsided, Mohammed pulled onto the road once again, and we continued north. We got as far as the signpost indicating the turnoff to Al-Luhayyah before being stopped by a Land Cruiser full of soldiers. Two of the men seated in the back carried rocket-propelled grenade launchers, while a third stood poised behind a fifty-caliber machine gun mounted on a tripod. Their expressions made me reconsider my plan to wander off the main roads without proper travel documents.

To go anywhere in Yemen one must first obtain a *tasrih*, a road permit, that specifies exactly where one can travel. Border areas, certain archeological sites, oil fields, and tribal lands not under government control are off limits. Thinking that I could go where I pleased, I had picked up a permit in San'a that allowed me to visit the major cities and villages along the main roads. Unfortunately, I didn't realize that the Red Sea coast and islands north of Hodeida were in a highly restricted military area. There were vague rumors that the Palestine Liberation Organization had a training camp on one of the islands and that Russian military supplies were off-loaded somewhere near Salif, but neither of these possibilities, nor the fact of our proximity to the terminus of the Hunt Oil pipeline near Kamaran Island, sank in until we were confronted by the soldiers in the Land Cruiser.

This encounter with the military was our first opportunity to talk our way out of a difficult situation.

"Where is your road permit for the coast?" one soldier asked us.

"Well, I don't have one . . ." I started to explain, with Mohammed translating, but I got no further. Two minutes later Mohammed and I were heading back in the direction from which we had just come.

Not knowing what else to do, I visited the local Lloyds of London agent at the Hodeida Shipping and Transport Company. Kenneth Beadle, the manager — a ruddy-faced Scot with a ginger-colored beard — crushed my hand in greeting. He was dressed in a crisp white shirt with short sleeves and double-pleated shorts in blue drill, which had been ironed by an expert. Freckled kneecaps and golden hair covered the gap between the bottom of the shorts and the tops of his white knee socks. Kind enough to interrupt his work to look up the original insurance claim for *Clea,* he opened the thin file, and as I suspected, there had been no salvage. No one had been sent out to conduct a survey, and there were no photos or other records. He suggested that the boat might still be on the island or being used by the local fishermen.

Mohammed and I checked the fishing port south of the city center, but no one had seen a boat that fitted *Clea*'s description or knew the story of the shipwreck. Using a series of remote back roads, we again attempted to drive north of Hodeida to talk with people in the fishing villages of Ibn Abbas and Khawbah, but had no luck. Once again we were turned back at an army checkpost that guarded the coast. Not wishing to pass the night in the dreadful humidity of Hodeida, we made our way down a coastal track as far as Wadi Rumman before turning inland to join up with the main paved highway.

We continued south toward Zabid on a black asphalt road flanked by light brown sand dunes perfectly proportioned in every way. Not a twig was visible on the trackless expanse of shimmering sand. Eventually we came upon a man dressed in a white robe hiked up to the knees. He was carrying an axe over his shoulder as he strode, with long purposeful steps, over the sand dunes, and he presented a strange sight in the heat of the day, carrying neither water nor an umbrella. I asked Mohammed what the man with the axe might be doing.

"He is collecting wood."

"But there is no wood to collect," I innocently remarked.

"It is not important," Mohammed replied. I didn't pursue the subject.

An hour later a similar exchange occurred as we drove into the market town of Bayt al-Faqih. In front of the police station, a crowd of men had gathered to look at a body lying motionless at the base of the front steps.

"What is happening, Mohammed?"

"Nothing."

"Nothing?"

"It is only a dead man. I will show you the suq. We will buy *khadi* for our wives to perfume their hair. Then we will look at the sheep."

Khadi is the sweet-scented flower of the pandanus palm (*Pandanus odoratissimus*), which is cultivated along most wadis of the western escarpment. Women place the cluster of tiny flowers in their hair beneath a piece of fabric or plastic for a few hours. *Khadi* gives the hair a wonderful scent, which I immediately recognized from the fragrance of the fresh flowers.

I appreciated learning about the pandanus flowers, but Mohammed and I were having difficulty sharing most of our other interests. What I viewed as remarkable, he saw as commonplace. A dead man in the street or a lone woodsman in the desert did not stimulate his thoughts. Likewise, he was perplexed as to why I wanted to find a sailboat that had been wrecked ten years earlier. I hadn't owned the boat, so what was the purpose of my search? He realized that I was looking for something and that he had been hired to assist me in any way possible, but regardless of where I wanted to go, we somehow always ended up looking at sheep.

Mohammed took advantage of our journey to compare the price of village sheep to those in San'a. Id al-Adha, the Feast of the Sacrifice, was still months away, and he planned to fatten three or four sheep on the concrete balcony of his apartment in San'a. He would keep one of the animals for himself. The others he planned to sell at a profit.

"And what will your neighbors say when they see sheep on your balcony?" I asked.

"Nothing," he replied. "I am getting this idea from them three years ago."

There were many things to see in Zabid: a citadel from the Ottoman occupation, the maze of covered passageways through the seedy marketplace, and the decorative brick facades hidden within the courtyards of private houses. Since before the twelfth century Zabid has been known as a center of Koranic studies, specializing in the Shafi'i school of Islam. The city has prospered through grants and donations sent from throughout the Sunnite world, and private libraries containing rare manuscripts are found in family homes as well as in the many mosques and religious schools. But I saw none of these things. Instead, Mohammed and I looked at sheep. We pinched and slapped their flanks, nudged them with our toes, and lifted the smelly creatures to check their weight as Mohammed discussed prices.

I had wanted to inspect a rare twelfth-century *minbar* (pulpit) in the Asha'ir Mosque that had been specially made for readings of the Hadith (*Traditions of the Prophet*). More than twelve hundred years of history lay waiting for me in Zabid, but I found myself helping Mohammed force the reluctant rear end of a sheep into the back seat of his car. I reminded him that we would not be returning to San'a for another two days.

"What is two days to a sheep?" he replied.

The following morning Mohammed bought two smaller sheep in the village of Hays. That made a party of five, two people in the front seat and three sheep in the back. Mohammed had enough livestock for his balcony. I didn't want to seem presumptuous, but since it was I who had flown ten thousand miles to search the coast of Yemen, I suggested that we drive south to the Eritrean refugee camp at Al-Khawkhah. I wanted to talk to the people who lived there on the off chance that someone might know of the men who had rescued me from Uqban Island.

When we arrived at the camp, two policemen were talking to a group of angry Eritreans. Mohammed, overhearing the conversation, told me that an Eritrean woman had been raped by Yemeni soldiers. While this discussion was going on, a young man came up and introduced himself as Tibo. He spoke Arabic and Afar fluently and communicated well in English. As he took us on a tour, he described daily life and explained why the camp had been established.

Less than one hundred miles to the west, he reminded us, across the Red Sea, lay Ethiopia, one of several countries to be devastated by civil war and the worst drought in recent African history. Strategically located above the Horn of Africa and overlooking the southern entrance to the Red Sea, Ethiopia is in a favorable geographical position to receive aid from Western countries.

As a response to the drought, the United States, Canada, Great Britain, France, and other countries set out, in 1984, to "save the children." The plan included the children of the northern provinces of Eritrea and Tigre, the centers of the secessionist guerrilla movement. There were the usual distribution problems, geographical as well as political. Although grain, high-protein biscuits, and milk drinks were airlifted to Ethiopian cities by British and U.S. military cargo planes, the poor rural areas, especially those sympathetic to the guerrillas, were receiving little, if any, food. Britain offered to parachute food and supplies directly into the stricken areas, but the Ethiopian government said that the bags of grain might break. Armed truck convoys transporting food from the cities to selected distribution centers further insured that none of the food fell into the wrong stomachs. Tibo explained that this selective starvation by the Ethiopian government had encouraged people to make their way across the Red Sea to refugee camps like the one at Al-Khawkhah.

The community was divided into three sections: the housing area, the school and boys' quarter, and the clinic. About fifty children lived in the boys' quarter. Some were orphans, but many of the boys' parents lived in Eritrea. Tibo, like the others, had three meals a day consisting of a steamed flatbread called *injera* eaten with a soup made from tinned tomato paste, pepper, flour, water, and chilis. The people drank water or weak tea. They had lived on this diet for seven years.

The clinic at the camp was funded by the United Nations. Local Yemenis came to take advantage of the free medicine and treatment, which may or may not have been in keeping with the original plan, but the arrangement helped make the camp more acceptable to the surrounding villagers. In any case, the Eritreans were in no position to object. Like the other five to ten thousand refugees in Yemen, the people of Al-Khawkhah camp soon discovered they had few rights, as the African and Western aid organizations moved in to control their lives.

The representative of the Eritrean Liberation Front (ELF) who ran the camp was half Yemeni and half Eritrean. The international aid organizers distrusted one another but were united in their hatred for this man, who they claimed was embezzling funds. A power struggle had developed between the ELF representative and Oxfam, the British aid organization, each of whom used the threat of National Security (secret police) intervention to blunt the other's efforts. The Eritreans were aware of their precarious situation and went to great efforts to smooth any possible difficulties between the rival aid organizations. These attempts to please everyone left the refugees with little control over the running of the camp. It was humiliating, but Tibo claimed that the people remained grateful as well as optimistic. They had a safe place to live.

The men could not work in town, but were allowed to practice subsistence fishing if they had the approval of the local sheik. Some had been able to make their way to Saudi Arabia, where they could save enough money to get their families out of the camp. These men might be gone for years, and many never returned. Most, however, remained in the camp. The women made straw mats and sold goats. The transport of goats across the Red Sea, as practiced in 1978, was still in evidence but had fallen into decline. Starting in 1983, the boat trade had been restricted by both the Saudi Arabian and Yemeni governments, in order to encourage domestic livestock production.

The uncontrolled flow of Eritreans into Yemen was also viewed as a problem. Who qualified for refugee status? No passports or other identity papers were available for Eritreans leaving Ethiopia. These people managed to get to Yemen either by walking overland to the Sudan or by sailing across the Red Sea in open boats. The official Yemeni policy toward them was friendly but unclear. They were generously provided with a place to live, but as the camp was set up they could not integrate with Yemeni society. The young Eritrean boys excelled at the local schools, and I understood why: education provided them with the only opportunity to leave the camp.

I asked Tibo about the rumor that local soldiers had raped one of the camp women.

"I cannot say. It has happened before. There is nothing we can do about these things. Life will not change for us in this place. It is better we find a life elsewhere. We dream of going home, to our own country."

In Yemen it is the custom for a man to buy his wife. The money is given in trust for the woman. The average price for a Yemeni woman is between 20,000 and 40,000 riyals ($2000–$4000). In Al-Khawkhah, poor Yemeni men, or those seeking an additional wife, were coming to the camp to arrange marriages for considerably less than the going rate. In Eritrea this is not the practice, but what were the alternatives for a young woman in the camp? Once outside, she was in a better position to change her life and help her family financially.

Returning to the car, I showed Tibo and the group of men who had joined us on our walk several photos of Idrise and the others who had rescued me from Uqban. They looked at the photos carefully, but could not identify the men. A policeman came over and talked to Mohammed. The investigation into the alleged rape was creating an ugly scene, and my presence was not appreciated. I was politely asked to leave the camp before sundown — preferably sooner. This suited Mohammed, who would have been mortified to pass the night there. For him, three sheep in the back seat of the car was nothing compared to a night in a refugee camp. I felt quite the opposite.

A man carrying a sackful of onions hitched a ride with us to his home, which lay a mile or so from the camp. Ibrahim had been having little success selling his onions to the Eritreans. He invited us into his tumbledown reed hut patched with plastic sheet and cardboard, a dwelling that was modest even by Tihama standards. When I accepted his invitation to spend the night, I noticed Mohammed rolling his eyes toward the sky. "Allah!" he declared.

Ibrahim, like millions of other Yemeni men, had gone to work in the Gulf states during the oil boom of the 1970s. He had saved money and now had his own business selling produce and sundry items to the outlying communities near Al-Khawkhah. His operation consisted of buying a mixed donkeyload of tomatoes, onions, cigarettes, dried fish, and plastic trinkets at the weekly market on the main road, then making the rounds of the family compounds, selling two tomatoes here, an onion there, between market days. Ibrahim was his own boss, but little else could be said in favor of his enterprise. Much of the business was done on credit.

We sat about on tall bed frames strung with hemp rope. A wall of battered oil drums filled with sand provided a windbreak, protecting us from the hot afternoon breeze. Dry and wrinkled with age, Ibrahim's wife looked as if she had grown out of the ground. She was tired, and it was clear that she had spent a lifetime arguing with her husband. Ibrahim had not provided her with the comforts of life, and there were no children. She killed a chicken for us, but when she asked her husband to contribute an onion to the meal, he hesitated.

"Don't you have one of your own?" he mumbled.

"No," she replied.

Handing his wife the smallest onion he could find in the sack, Ibrahim made no secret of the fact that the onion given that night would mean less business for him the following day.

After dinner he produced a small television set from a cardboard box wrapped in cloth. Beneath the night sky, he connected the television to a car battery he kept in a separate box. A dozen people from the surrounding huts drifted over to watch an Egyptian soap opera followed by a military parade. Mohammed tethered the sheep to a palm tree, and we slept on cots beneath the stars.

We had failed to reach the fishing villages on the northern coast or collect information about the fate of the sailboat, but rather than return to San'a directly, I asked Mohammed to make a detour. We drove south from Al-Khawkhah, then east into the mountains, toward the village of Yafrus. Stories from various sources indicated that Yafrus had been a center of mysticism for more than fifteen hundred years. The tradition had been passed from the Jews to the Christians and finally to the Moslems. The present-day mosque had been built near the ruins of a synagogue dating from the third century.

In San'a I had met Dr. Obruk, an effusive Turkish scholar visiting from Ankara. He claimed that Yafrus was the original home of the Cabala, an occult theosophy practiced by rabbis and medieval Christians as well as some contemporary followers. The Cabalists believed that through a secret mystical interpretation of each letter and word of the scriptures, one could gain access to the divine mysteries.

Yafrus was also known as a center for healing. Sufi pharmacists collected herbs, bark, and other substances from the countryside to sell at the mosque. Medicines for the stomach, urinary tract, and kidneys were available, as were burn ointments and a special salve for gunshot wounds.

The mosque that now stands was constructed five hundred years ago in honor of Ahmed Ibn'Alwan, who lived in Yafrus during the Rasulid period, from 1229 to 1454, a time of vigorous artistic and cultural development in Yemen. A Sufi scholar and poet, Ahmed Ibn'Alwan wrote numerous books on Islamic mysticism and Sunni law. Having enjoyed the pursuit of pleasure and vice in his youth, he spent his later years in meditation and study.

Mohammed and I turned off the main road and started up a gravel track leading to Yafrus. Entering the whitewashed courtyard of the mosque, I noticed a man in leg irons hobbling toward the ablution tank. The people of Yafrus had confined this man to the mosque, hoping to cure him of his madness. It turned out he had been there four months, but he seemed happy enough with his situation. I had heard stories that mystics from the area were known to beat themselves with chains, but I saw no chains apart from the ones on the man's ankles.

Mohammed showed extreme reluctance to inquire about flagellants. "These things are from the past. They are not important," he insisted.

"But they are important to me," I stressed.

Mohammed had become increasingly uncomfortable and useless as a translator, but when we approached a *qadi* (judge) outside the mosque, he did ask questions about the flagellating mystics for me. I was encouraged by the holy man's long, thoughtful, impassioned responses in Arabic, but Mohammed translated his comments simply as "Yes, he agrees," or "No, he cannot say why."

Correctly sensing that he had failed me, Mohammed stopped at the side of the road to show me what he called the Yemeni chewing-gum tree (*Ficus vasta*). He pounded the bark away from a small area with a rock, and white, milky sap appeared. The sap dries in the sun for a day before someone peels it off. I pulled off an old piece and tried it. The elastic substance was similar to chewing gum in texture, although the flavor was more akin to that of a rubber band. The tree we stopped to look at was visited frequently. Scars covered the trunk as high as a child's reach, and suitable rocks for pounding the bark lay at its base.

The following morning we visited the suq of Ta'izz. Mohammed had more shopping to do for his wife before our return to San'a. The marketplace within the old city walls was not large enough to get lost in, but instead of wandering on my own, I decided to follow Mohammed as he walked from one vendor to the next. He had grown up in Ta'izz and knew many of the shopkeepers from his childhood.

Veiled women with imported stainless steel knives squatted on the curbsides, peeling prickly pears for the morning shoppers.

Stacks of puffy golden fried bread steamed on tall countertops as wheelbarrows full of cabbages, apples, grapes, and bananas rumbled over the rough ground. The bananas were nestled on flat pieces of cardboard to prevent the skins from becoming bruised from the jostling. More wheelbarrows maneuvered through the impossibly narrow and twisting streets. In the shade of wide umbrellas lay piles of green and red tomatoes, green chili peppers, purple onions, yellow mangoes, russet sweet potatoes, and carefully constructed pyramids of green limes. Folding tables were covered with blue-and-white plastic thongs from Taiwan.

The cool morning air held a multitude of fragrances, and the pungent, sweet, musky smells of cooked food reminded me that I had not yet eaten. Small boys cautiously worked their way through the crowd of male shoppers. Balanced on tin cans atop the boys' heads were fiery terra-cotta bowls of saltah, which the boys steadied with folded pieces of cardboard to protect their fingers. The newspaper sellers, the dust, the early-morning light, the crowds of coffee drinkers engaged in thoughtful silence, the jangle of animal bells, and the smell of harness leather and donkey shit put me in a pleasant mood.

A line of stunningly beautiful women entered a lane and passed within a few feet of me. Their perfume filled my nose as well as my imagination. Unveiled, these women moved through the suq as if they owned every brick and pavingstone in the place. Mohammed told me that they were from Jabal Sabir and had come to sell qat in the marketplace. These mountain women are renowned for being the most ferocious bargainers in the country, but this reputation is largely offset by their great beauty. With their turmeric-colored cheeks, eyes lined with kohl, and long sprigs of sweet-smelling basil draped seductively over their ears, they looked inviting.

"Don't stare!" hissed Mohammed.

The pharmacists in Ta'izz sold a type of wood that looked familiar to me. They called it *oud,* which simply means wood in Arabic. Little chips of it were displayed in large glass apothecary jars. Fingering a piece, I recognized it as *gaharu,* a type of aloes found in the tropical forests of Southeast Asia. *Oud* produces a thick, sweet scent when burned over charcoal. In Yemen, small ceramic braziers of it are frequently used to perfume men's clothing, beards, and underarms during important qat chews or weddings. The guests wave the smoke onto themselves with their hands.

Driving north from Ta'izz, Mohammed stopped to buy qat. He bought an extra bundle for me to try. I began to pick the leaves and chew. The sheep in the back seat bleated, and their dry pellets of shit littered the floor. Before long the qat began to take effect, and we settled in for the long drive back to San'a. To pass the time, Mohammed told me the story of Rashid and Safia. He spoke for more than an hour, pausing only long enough to stuff more leaves in his mouth.

Rashid was fifteen years old when he fell in love with Safia, a girl from the village of Raydah. She was named after the Prophet's daughter, and by her eleventh year she already bore the signs of exceptional beauty. One day Rashid went with his father to ask permission to marry Safia. The girl's father said, "I agree to the marriage, but you must pay me one hundred thousand riyals as a bride price, plus a Toyota Land Cruiser." This was an impossible sum, but Safia was a lovely girl, and Rashid, in the flush of young manhood, was determined to have her as his wife.

He set off for the oil fields of Saudi Arabia, where he labored for fifteen years, living simply and sending money back to his brother to put in the bank. He sent letters to Safia via his brother. She lived with her family and waited for her fiancé to return. Safia's beauty and reputation grew as the years passed. She loved Rashid and adored the attention her suitor brought her.

By 1976, Rashid was ready to return to Yemen. He bought a Toyota Land Cruiser and began his return journey with 300,000 riyals in cash. During the long drive across the desert between Riyadh and Najran in Saudi Arabia, he began to think about his promises as a young man. Certainly the bride price was too high. Perhaps the father would reconsider. Rashid could use the truck to help him start his new life in Raydah.

He arrived at the village, and soon after that a big welcoming party was held for him by the men. A few days later Rashid and his father went to the house of Safia's family. Rashid had not seen Safia in fifteen years, and he was stunned by her beauty. When the men discussed details of the marriage, he announced, "I would like the marriage to be arranged immediately. What are the terms?"

"As we originally agreed," replied the father.

"But certainly the price is too high," Rashid began.

"If it is too high, look elsewhere for a wife."

"Arrange the marriage," said Rashid, "but on the understanding that you and your family will never ask for anything more from me. The one hundred thousand riyals I will give you is much more than enough for the wedding gifts, the goats, qat, clothing, gold jewelry, and marriage party."

The girl's father agreed to ask for nothing more if Rashid would pay the promised sum. Rashid's father bore witness to the man's words.

"And the Toyota?" the future father-in-law asked.

"All right," said Rashid. "Here are the keys."

The wedding took place. The marriage was happily consummated, and Rashid and his new wife began their life together after fifteen years of waiting. The story of their patience and devotion had spread to the most remote villages in the area. The father-in-law boasted of the handsome price he had received for his daughter. Safia, in turn, was thrilled at having commanded such attention. The wedding had been a wonder. No woman in the region had ever generated so much admiration and envy.

Safia was a good wife, and Rashid began looking for ways to invest his remaining money. He first bought a secondhand truck to transport goods between San'a and Raydah, but it broke down continually, and he finally sold the vehicle at a loss. He then bought a freezer in San'a and had it transported to the village. He became one of the first sellers of frozen French chickens in Raydah. The business turned a modest profit, which pleased Rashid, because most of his savings had been spent on the wedding and setting up house. It was not easy for him to adjust to married life after years as a single man in the oil fields.

Not long after the wedding, Safia's mother began nagging her.

She wanted gifts and money from Rashid. At first Safia refused, reminding her mother of the promise not to ask for such things. But the mother continued to pressure her. "He has so much — he has worked in Saudi Arabia for fifteen years!" the mother exclaimed.

Rashid and his wife were happy together, and it was time for a family. Safia was soon pregnant. With a baby on the way, she had less strength to argue with her mother. Rashid loved his wife, and when she finally confided in him he was not angry. He decided to make a small gesture. The first gifts were insignificant and for the mother only. Later, Safia's father and brothers demanded gifts as well, and Rashid's remaining capital began to disappear.

Tensions developed between Rashid and Safia. They argued. After four months, the money was gone and payments were due on the freezer. Rashid had to borrow money from his father. The savings from fifteen years of labor had been spent. Now Rashid had only his frozen chickens. He argued bitterly with his wife one night and struck her with his open hand. Safia went to sleep in her father's house, which, under Islamic law, was her right.

Three days later Rashid's father went to ask for his son's wife. "My son lost his temper — they had words in their own home. It is not your concern. I ask you for my son's wife."

Safia's father refused to return his daughter. Rashid was humiliated. The entire village had followed these events keenly, and everyone knew the full extent of his sacrifice. He loved Safia, but the shame he felt was unbearable.

Four more days passed before Rashid snapped a clip of bullets into his father's Kalashnikov and went to reclaim his wife. He knocked on the door, but there was no response. The Toyota — his Toyota — was proudly parked beside the house. Rashid knocked again, this time with force. "Open the door!" he called out.

Rashid's father-in-law appeared behind the metal bars of a ground-floor window. "What do you want here?" he jeered.

"Nothing unreasonable — I only want my wife. Let me in so I can talk to her. If I have done wrong, we can still reach an understanding. Let me in," he repeated.

"You will not have your wife. Go home."

"So be it," muttered Rashid. He leveled his rifle and without another word fired three bullets into his father-in-law's chest. The man was dead on his feet. He slumped to the floor, out of sight. Rashid shot the front-door lock to pieces, then kicked in the door. The mother-in-law ran to investigate the commotion and was cut down by another burst of gunfire.

The final tragedy approached. Safia appeared. When she saw the bodies of her parents riddled with bullet holes, she screamed. Rashid, overcome with emotion, cried, "You are my wife, I worked fifteen years for you! Your family has taken everything from me. I am a fool. You would not come with me!" Completely out of his mind, he shot his wife dead and then fled to Saudi Arabia.

Mohammed still received occasional letters from Rashid, who was planning to work in Saudi Arabia until 1992. He was painting houses and office buildings in Jidda to cover his blood debt. One day he would have enough money to come back and settle in the country of his birth. Enough time would have passed so that Safia's relatives would not demand his life; instead, the Islamic court in San'a would decide how much he must pay Safia's family to compensate them for the death of one man and two women. The death of the father would set Rashid back at least 320,000 riyals; the mother and daughter would come to an additional 150,000 riyals each — nearly $50,000 altogether. He had also lost his Toyota Land Cruiser. I found it a strange irony that even after death, his wife's family continued to milk him of his earnings.

According to Mohammed, Rashid had no immediate plans to remarry. "Because of stories like this, we southerners don't like to marry girls from the north. There are too many problems," he joked.

I wasn't amused. It was a disturbing story, and far more complex than a simple case of injured male pride or random domestic violence. My sympathies were with Safia, but I didn't see how else Rashid could have responded in the Yemeni village setting. Given the sequence of events, tragedy seemed inevitable.

• • •

The journey to the coast had been a success for Mohammed. He had the sheep, several rounds of his wife's favorite smoked cheese from her hometown, Ta'izz, pandanus flowers for her hair, *bakhour* to perfume her skirts, and a set of ceramic coffee bowls from the village of Hays. He would receive a warm welcome. By comparison, I had little to show for my efforts.

"Tell me," Mohammed asked as I stepped from his car, "are these sheep not fine?"

"The sheep? They are not important," I joked, using his favorite expression.

"A sheep for Id al-Adha is not important?" he exclaimed. "And what do you know of sheep?"

"Not much," I said to myself as I watched him drive off. Standing in the dust at the side of the road, I realized that although I had discovered next to nothing about how I might return to Uqban Island, I had learned a great deal about the futility of single-minded effort. Visions of a serendipitous journey through Yemen and toward my journals began to fade. Even at this early stage of my search, it was clear that if I were to achieve my goal, it would not be in a linear fashion. There were going to be complications.

Apart from Martin Plimsole, no one in the country had a very clear idea of why I had come back to Yemen or even what I was really searching for. Realizing this, I suddenly felt a great affinity with the woodcutter I had seen walking across the sand dunes in the heat of the day. He was looking for wood on a treeless plain; I was searching for notebooks that lay buried on a desert island somewhere over the horizon. We were on similar missions.

7

New Customer Welcome

LATE ONE MORNING, five days after returning to San'a, I found myself watching two Yemeni boys playing a game of darts near Bab Shu'ub, the northern gateway to the old city. The boys had made their darts from discarded syringes. Chicken feathers were attached to the plungers to improve the balance and flight, and the darts thudded into a piece of white Styrofoam with surprising accuracy.

Other street games were in progress. I could hear the distinctive *clack-clack-clack-clack-clack* of the devil's balls, a game that was played with two smooth plastic balls fastened to either end of a twelve-inch cord. Midway along the cord was a metal ring, through which a player put his middle or index finger. The boys manipulated the cords in such a way that the balls described matching arcs as they struck each other above and below the hand. The object of the game was to keep your balls clacking louder and longer than anyone else's. It was not difficult to imagine where the term "the devil's balls" came from. The toy, clearly a curse from Satan, was tremendously popular, and the frantic clacking could be heard in every neighborhood.

Another boy had made a windmill-like propeller from the split neck of a plastic water bottle. As he ran or faced the wind, it spun rapidly in front of his face on a short length of wire attached to a cardboard headband. With head down and arms held out like airplane wings, the boy shuffled his bare feet excitedly and then blasted off. He banked right into an alleyway and disappeared on an unknown mission.

I was passing the time watching these games as I waited for Martin Plimsole. It was twenty minutes later than we had arranged to meet, and I was beginning to think he wasn't coming when I noticed a bicycle weaving its way uncertainly down a congested laneway. A thin, fair-skinned man clung to the handlebars of the rickety-looking three-speed as the front wheel jerked from side to side to avoid potholes, pedestrians, and the hulks of wrecked cars. Although the bell rang out, the crowd paid no attention. The man pumped his knees awkwardly, trying to maintain balance at slow speed as he aimed for open areas that invariably closed at his approach. He seemed constantly on the verge of a collision, but each time he saved himself at the final moment. It was obviously not his first bicycle ride through the old city. He wore a cream-colored sport coat (of Hungarian manufacture, as I later learned) and a fine white cotton shirt without its detachable collar. His pant legs, tucked into a pair of well-worn green socks, were lightly soiled with chain grease. The mudguards rattled and the bell sounded one last time as the cyclist came to a halt just beside me. It was Mr. Plimsole, out of breath.

"Hello there! Awfully sorry I'm late." We shook hands as he continued talking. "Bit of a problem at the Bristol Language Institute. We had a man, actually a flasher, wandering about. A Saudi, I'd guess, from the description. Not a flasher by our standards, mind you, but he was frightening the female teachers. He kept leaping out of the bushes and displaying his open hand. Across the palm he had written I WANT WOMAN with a ballpoint pen. Bit of a laugh, really, but we did have to call the guard. Anyway, that's why I'm late. Are you hungry?"

We sat in a local café that served a fiery minced lamb stew fragrant with the aroma of cumin, fresh coriander, garlic, and a fenugreek paste called hulba. We ate the bubbling stew from a blackened terra-cotta pot, using pieces of golden-brown flat-bread known as mulouj. Hulba is customarily eaten during the noon meal because Yemenis believe it softens the stomach lining and enhances the effect of qat later in the day. "Hulba opens the way for the qat" is a well-known expression.

When I handed Martin the cigarette bangers he had asked for, he chuckled to himself, but pocketed the small tins without comment. He asked me about the shipwreck, and then I told him about my recent journey along the coast with Mohammed. He found the story amusing.

"You must find a Yemeni with influential friends. It is the only way to get things done here," he told me. "In order to return to Uqban Island, you must first get permission from the National Security Police — not an easy task, I assure you. For some reason the Yemenis are very sensitive about the coast near Saudi Arabia. I can't risk getting involved directly, but I will see if I can find someone to help you."

We went on to talk about various aspects of Martin's life in Yemen over the previous six years. I was surprised at his age: he was in his late twenties. As our conversation progressed, I realized I was in the presence of a true original. Martin was one of those rare individuals who had found his place on earth. He owned a house in Kent and was unmistakably British, but there was little doubt that Yemen was his home. His good humor and quiet confidence attracted me immediately. Despite his knowledge of the people and the country, he was completely without pretense. I spoke almost no Arabic, yet he was perfectly willing to accommodate me in any way he could. I found it remarkable that a man of his experience would be so open with a perfect stranger. It is far more common for a person in his position to hoard knowledge, occasionally doling it out to a privileged few.

I soon discovered that Martin and I shared a similar sense of the absurd, and that day at lunch our friendship began. Before leaving the café we set a date to go for a walk in the mountains, in four weeks' time. Then Martin invited me to chew qat with some of his Yemeni students. We walked to a nearby qat suq. Although I barely knew enough Arabic to count to ten, I decided to buy my own. Martin advised me on price and quality before drifting off to make his own purchase.

I approached a vendor seated on the ground, a man surrounded by eight other men. Some of them were buying, while others, like myself, were merely comparing prices. The vendor transacted at least four deals at once. People crowded around him, so that I had trouble following the negotiations. I watched money and qat change hands several times before stepping forward to select a *rubta* (bunch) of the leaves.

"*Kam riyal?*" (How many riyals?) I asked. The vendor made a gesture with his fingers that I didn't understand.

"Sixty riyals he is asking," a man at my side explained. "How many are you wanting?"

I indicated that I wanted two *rubtas,* but at 40 riyals each. The English speaker yelled something at the vendor. The vendor shook his head, and then held up four fingers and drew his right index finger across the middle of his left index finger. Four and a half fingers indicated a price of 45 riyals.

"*Tammam, sadiq?*" (All right, my friend?) the vendor inquired, stuffing one man's purchase into a plastic bag before turning to engage yet another buyer. Stacks of worn bills passed from hand to hand. The money was bent double and then counted out with surprising speed. Hundreds of vendors up and down the street were busy conducting similar transactions. I agreed to the price, but as I handed over the money an onlooker complained loudly.

"*Hatha agal min asar al-hagigi!*" (That is less than the real price!) Earlier he had paid a higher price for a similar quantity from the same vendor.

"*Ma shi! Tarheeb liz zaboon,*" the vendor replied. Everyone laughed, including the disgruntled man, who walked away, satisfied with the explanation. I asked the English speaker what the vendor had said.

"He say, 'New customer welcome.'"

I found Martin arguing loudly with a man sitting in the shade of his truck surrounded by dampened burlap sacks full of qat.

"Buy this qat!" the man yelled.

"Why should I?" Martin replied. "It is much too expensive."

"Buy it because it is the best!"

"How so?"

"It will make you fuck well and conceive a son. What more do you want? Here, take two bunches."

Martin laughed and took a closer look at the qat. After deciding that the quality was in keeping with the price, he told the vendor that he was unmarried and not ready for children but would buy it anyway. A small crowd had gathered to listen to the exchange. For them, the conversation was of far greater interest than the price. Seldom did they have the opportunity to hear a foreigner speak their language so deftly.

We worked our way out of the qat market, Martin pushing his bicycle. Walking to the party, he translated the graffiti scribbled on the stone walls. The first two read THE EYE OF ENVY LEADS TO BLINDNESS and TAKE CARE OF YOUR NEIGHBORS. The third one, DON'T PISS ON THIS WALL, reminded us of our civic responsibilities.

We turned from the street down a low passageway and were soon climbing the stone staircase of an old San'ani tower house. At each landing Martin called out, "Allah! Allah!" This, he explained, was to alert any women on the upper floors that men from outside the family were arriving. The warning allowed the women enough time to cover their faces or step into private rooms.

On an upper floor we were met by Ahmed Ali, one of Martin's students. After exchanging greetings, he ushered us into a white-washed room with windows that admitted light on two sides. The floor was covered with inexpensive red-and-blue oriental carpets. Laid out around the perimeter of the room were padded backrests, elbow bolsters, and mattresses upholstered with red plush and gold piping, on which about ten young men were reclining. They greeted us warmly by shaking our hands and then touching their fingers to their lips, then indicated places for us to sit. Water flavored with incense was brought in a Thermos. A small brazier was passed from one man to the next. I took my turn fanning the sweet smoke onto my clothes and hair. A four-foot-tall water pipe sat in the middle of the floor. Attached to its base was a twenty-foot-long hose, covered with lurid green crochetwork, that ended in a turned hardwood mouthpiece.

Once we were all settled, Martin took a look at my qat, then laughed kindly.

"What's the joke?" I asked him.

"You will have trouble sleeping tonight. That lot you just bought is the sort of qat one buys for long road journeys. It is known as truck driver's qat."

I wasn't sure what to expect. I hadn't chewed in a formal setting in more than ten years, but I knew from my reading that poetry, music, and dancing often accompanies traditional qat parties. Observing the television set, video player, and soccer pictures hung on the walls, I somehow doubted there would be any religious poetry or tribal dancing with daggers that afternoon. As Martin's students passed the hose of the water pipe to one another, they first politely turned the mouthpiece downward. When it was my turn, I took a puff. The sweet, cool smoke was soothing.

Martin explained that each qat session is different, though there are certain rituals that have developed over the past several hundred years. Cool drinking water and soft drinks are usually set in front of each guest, as the leaves make one thirsty. Several spittoons are set about the room. After the initial excitement and anticipation of the afternoon dies down, people begin to chew in earnest. Twigs and branches are often thrown across the room to friends as gifts. The chewed leaves are stored in one's cheek as new leaves are packed in; the distended cheek of an experienced chewer could probably accommodate a regulation-size billiard ball. The green mush between the teeth is not attractive, and the taste is bitter.

The group passes through different psychological phases, which vary with the quality of the qat, the occasion, and the mood of those present. People relax during the first stage of chewing, which may last two hours or more. Qat sessions serve many purposes, but most important, they help create a sense of unity among the chewers. People come together as equals during the daily sessions and discuss important issues concerning family, business, or politics. Seating is arbitrary, and most of the conversations are open to anyone present.

The entire session may last anywhere from three to six hours. At first, thoughts are stimulated and conversation dominates. At the ideal qat session, Martin explained, each person contributes what he can — jokes, poems, stories, or music. After two or three hours, the qat quiets the tongue and thoughts turn inward. This state of quietude should arrive shortly before sunset, a time commonly referred to as Solomon's hour.

During the transition to this more reflective state, *oud* music is often played by one of the guests. The *oud* is a Middle Eastern stringed instrument similar to the European lute. The music is intended to bond the listeners further and to enhance the communal feelings. Love themes, some of them quite erotic, are common in the lyrics, but the music itself is intended to induce a dreamy state and transport the listener.

To overcome the excess of thinking and to change the communal mood, men will sometimes dance. Others become talkative. Arguments are not uncommon toward the end of the session, as the sense of unity continues to disintegrate. An hour or so after sunset, the men spit out the leaves and quietly depart. This procedure of losing oneself in an ever-changing group of individuals is repeated each afternoon, and is a powerful socializing force in Yemen.

Classic qat sessions are rare these days, and my afternoon with Martin and his students was consumed by the telling of bawdy stories, followed by a discussion of Yemeni love lyrics and a videotape showing the highlights of the 1986 World Cup soccer finals. I remember Saleem, one of the older students, telling a story that involved a play on words. The word *sinayenee* (literally, "little tooth") is a Yemeni family name; it is also a child's term for penis.

There was once a young widow who lived in the mountains. She cultivated a small plot of land to support herself. One day she discovered that one of her stone walls had been moved. Her neighbor, a man by the name of Sinayenee, had trespassed a distance of one cubit [the length of the forearm, approximately eighteen inches] onto her property in order to dig a well. A second neighbor examined the wall and agreed that the widow's claim was legitimate. A dispute arose over land and water rights. The three neighbors went to the sheik of the village for a hearing. The widow and Sinayenee, the accused well-digger, told their stories. The second neighbor spoke last. In front of the assembled men of the village, he confirmed that Sinayenee — the man, but meaning his penis — had penetrated the widow's property (suggesting her private parts) to a depth of one cubit. "And she is complaining?" exclaimed the sheik. Everyone laughed, but the widow won the judgment.

"Ahhh . . . qat," remarked Ahmed Ali. "It is a paradise of the mind."

Similar stories continued for more than an hour. The qat started to loosen my thoughts, and I felt a sense of well-being radiating from my chest. The effect of the leaves was negligible, as the conversation seemed to create a momentum of its own. Martin and the others fell into a discussion of popular Yemeni love songs, but in the hands of these second-year English students the romantic mood was lost entirely. I recall the following lines: "The sounds of your footsteps are like notes of the music walking up a stairway of my hearing organ" and "Open your buttons and share your beauty . . . he who grasps your pomegranates [breasts?] needs nothing else. Come here, and don't be stingy with your saliva."

As the young men continued to discuss pomegranates, I asked Mohammed, the unmarried youth seated next to me, to describe the ideal Yemeni woman. His immediate reply suggested that he had given serious thought to the subject.

"She must be beautiful, delicate, honorable, patient, and clean in spirit and self. A woman should combine sweetness, strength, and beauty in all their aspects."

This thoughtful reply caught me off guard, and as I mulled over his response, Mohammed was drawn into another discussion and the conversation passed me by. Ahmed Ali slid a videocassette into the machine, and we watched World Cup soccer until sunset. By then the leaves had most certainly taken their subtle effect. I have never had any interest in soccer, but that afternoon I watched every move of the Argentinian star Maradona as he befuddled one player after the next. Everything seemed soft, especially my head. The incense-flavored water flowed down my throat and cooled my stomach. I tried without success to imagine myself as a young student chewing leaves with one of my schoolteachers under similar circumstances.

The stars were out when Martin and I stepped onto the street. I thanked him for the invitation and wished him luck on his night ride across the old city. Mounting his bicycle unsteadily, he disappeared into the shadows. Moments later I heard a muffled cry, followed by what sounded like a bicycle going into a ditch filled with discarded tin cans and plastic bottles.

Standing perfectly still, enjoying the night air, I realized that I must have entered the final stage of the qat experience, when all thoughts turn inward and one's sense of fellowship dissipates. Instead of investigating the sound, I turned and walked off into the darkness, laughing to myself. Days passed before I saw Martin again. His bicycle had survived the crash; his Hungarian sport coat had not.

8

Najiba

CURTAINS STIRRED behind the dusty pane of an upper-story window as a hand withdrew from sight. A potted geranium sat on the window ledge, warming itself in the sun, while I stood knee-deep in a layer of cold night air that lingered in the shaded alleyway. Next to me stood Pascal Marechaux, the French architect and photographer, whom I had met the previous week. He had brought me to the mud-brick house in San'a where a French-woman, Najiba, lived with her Yemeni husband and twelve dogs. Pascal was delivering a bag of oranges, as he often did, and I had come to listen to the old woman's stories.

The instant Pascal called out from the front gate, a horrible chorus of barking dogs erupted from the far side of the wooden fence. The knotholes in the planks had been nailed over with tin-can lids. A woman yelled at the dogs in Arabic, and at once the animals fell silent. Moments later Najiba stepped through the gate, bringing with her the smell of dog hair and dust. She could no longer invite visitors into her home because of her invalid husband and the dogs, but she was willing to speak to us in the alleyway for a short while.

Najiba was unsteady on her feet and bent over with age. She was not feeling well that morning. She had broken her leg recently and could walk only with great difficulty. Her dry, yellowed hair was unbrushed and blew stiffly in the breeze. Behind her tired smile I could sense the exhaustion of a long and difficult life. Pascal translated from the French as she spoke.

"It is sometimes painful to talk about the old Yemen," she began. "There was this feeling of terrible isolation. Beautiful and complete isolation. It was frightening at first. The country was of another world. Arriving in San'a for the first time, I felt like I was walking into a church . . . as if I were seeing a place from my past. You could hear the birds, and the streets were clean. You can't imagine how clean. There were few strangers, and people took care of their neighbors."

As Najiba's thoughts drifted back to a different time, we let her talk without interruption. She had arrived in the country in 1949 with her first Yemeni husband, whom she had met in Paris, where she converted to Islam and took an Arabic name. (Najiba means "the clever one.") They traveled by sea as far as Aden and then looked for a truck heading north. The night before Najiba left Aden, she watched from the street as Englishmen in evening dress waltzed with fair-skinned ladies on a hotel rooftop near Steamer Point. She was leaving behind all that was familiar, and little did she suspect that forty-one years would pass before she saw Paris again.

The waltz music soon passed from Najiba's mind as the battered truck labored its way up Wadi Tuban, a dry riverbed leading into North Yemen from Aden. The road, barely a track, was so rough that she could not look out at the broken landscape. All of her efforts were confined to holding onto the hot metal dashboard and bracing herself against the terrific jolts that bounced her between the driver and her husband. Her feet did not reach the floorboards, and only during the stops when the truck broke down, or at landslides, did she have an opportunity to look at her new country. The dusty journey from Aden to Ta'izz, a distance of one hundred miles, took three days. The driver was experienced, but as the truck negotiated the narrow roads through the mountains, the passengers knew their lives were in the hands of Allah.

When the truck broke down for the final time, Ta'izz was in sight. Najiba and her husband entered the city on foot. She knew no one in Yemen and spoke little Arabic. Her first home, which was built of mud bricks, had no toilet. Despite her Arabic name, she did not feel very clever when confronted by her new household tasks. Cooking over a wood fire, drawing water from deep wells, and grinding flour by hand were skills that did not come easily to a woman of her experience. The Yemeni women helped her as best they could, but it took years for Najiba to adjust to the changes in her life. When she arrived in Yemen, there were no paved roads, nor a postal system. Public executions by sword were not uncommon, and the massive ironclad timber gates to the walled cities were closed from 8 P.M. until sunrise. Najiba had left Paris for a kingdom of donkey trails and feudal lords.

Imam Ahmed, the supreme ruler of Yemen at the time, also lived in Ta'izz. In 1949 his subjects believed he possessed supernatural powers. Looking at his dark, staring eyes, they were convinced that the Imam could read their thoughts. Indeed, his eyes seemed to be everywhere. From his palace he could see far into the narrow laneways of the suq and observe the activities of his people. No thought or action seemed to escape his attention. Najiba credited his extraordinary eyesight to a pair of British Army field glasses; his subjects were unaware of such modern devices.

The Imam cultivated a fear of his psychic powers, and he let it be known he communicated with the spirit world. Servants could hear him talking to the jinn (spirits) when he was alone in his room, but they could not understand what the jinn replied. Imam Ahmed was also known to have a power over poisonous snakes. At night he spoke to his snakes, who told him where to find lost gold and jewelry (usually at the bottom of dry wells). The snakes also warned him of plots against his life. A man with such contacts was not to be trifled with.

As described by Najiba, the single telegraph line strung between Ta'izz and San'a, the two main cities in Yemen at the time, was essential to the running of the country. When people wanted to contact the Imam or make a request, they would send him a telegram. Most of his administrative work was conducted by telegram or with handwritten notes on small pieces of folded paper. The Imam had several counselors and a *qadi* to assist him, and he considered each request carefully before making his judgment. A reply was an acceptance. If he refused, there would be no reply. Nearly everyone respected the Imam, who was generally viewed as a fair but unforgiving father to his people.

Najiba told us of the time she had come in contact with Imam Ahmed in the hospital at Hodeida. "He was a great man!" she exclaimed with feeling. *"Formidable!"*

"How so?" I wanted to know.

The Imam, she explained, was recovering from gunshot wounds after an assassination attempt in 1961. He wanted breakfast, but he could not make the two Catholic sisters understand his request. Still weak from his wounds, he managed to stand up on the bed. The sisters watched in astonishment as the Imam (who weighed close to three hundred pounds) strutted about the mattress, clucking and scratching like a chicken while flapping his one good arm. When they understood his simple pantomime, they burst out laughing. He wanted chicken eggs for his breakfast. Remembering the scene, Najiba laughed as if the incident had taken place that morning.

During my search along the coast with Mohammed, I had visited the Imam's former palace in Ta'izz. The building had been turned into a museum to display the bourgeois comforts enjoyed by the ruler and his family. Contrary to popular stories today, the Imam did not lead a luxurious or happy life. Many rumors detail his lavish and degenerate existence, but the lurid accounts of a despotic morphine addict with an appetite for dancing girls and young boys are largely untrue. The ticket seller at the palace had whispered to me that the Imam had ninety wives, who danced naked for him each night. I doubted the man's story, and looking through the palace, I didn't find a room that would have accommodated half that number of naked women standing buttock to buttock.

From conversations with a former doctor of the Imam's wives, I knew that he did not chew qat or drink alcohol. Sexual excess was also unlikely, as he suffered from impotence after an unsuccessful operation to cure his frequent bouts of hemorrhoids. A European doctor had injected morphine into his lower back to relieve the pain, but the procedure had been bungled, and for the rest of his life Imam Ahmed endured great pain from the waist down, which led to his dependency on morphine. Then there were the assassination attempts and gunshot wounds. The Imam spent the final days of his life in an electric rocking bed, watching his health and his kingdom fall to pieces. According to a French radiologist working in Ta'izz at the time, Imam Ahmed died of a heart attack and not from lingering wounds from the numerous attempts on his life.

Of the supposedly lavish furnishing in the palace, I noted a chipped enamel chamber pot concealed in a wooden box with an upholstered toilet-seat cover. On one of the upper floors I found an English-made electric stove with two spiral heating elements and a grill plate suitable for making toasted cheese sandwiches. There was a collection of Victorian-looking medical instruments that featured a stainless steel corkscrew. Other royal treasures included an Electrolux refrigerator that ran on kerosene, an electric blanket, and a plastic owl clock with eyes that shifted from side to side sixty times per minute. Far from evoking the mystery and architectural splendor of the Alhambra or the sumptuousness of the furnishings in the Topkapi Museum, the Imam's palace, with its collection of fountain pens, toasters, and Bulova wristwatches, brought back memories of my middle-class American childhood in the 1950s. A dust-laden Hostess cupcake wrapper or a Howdy Doody lunchbox would not have been out of place.

Imam Ahmed was the last of a long line of Zaidi rulers in Yemen. The Zaidi dynasty extended back to 897, when Yahya al-Hadi ila'l-Haqq was summoned from Medina to negotiate a peace between the warring Hamdan tribes near the town of Sa'da in northern Yemen. Having settled the dispute, this clever man must have recognized a fertile situation, because he soon had a vision, a message from Allah, in which he saw himself as the ruler of the tribes. He convinced the tribal leaders of his divine mission, and in this way Al-Hadi Yahya, as he was later called, became the first Imam of Yemen. He established his rule based on the Koran and the traditions of the Prophet. For the next thousand years varying parts of Yemen were ruled by the Imams.

It is common knowledge that Imam Ahmed kept most Yemenis in ignorance of the outside world, apparently in an attempt to protect his people from evil. The Imam was a deeply religious man with a paternal love for his subjects. He saw modern life as having no moral values. As the absolute spiritual and political leader of the country, he perceived it as his obligation to shelter his people from the corrupting influences of the West. Imam Ahmed felt he understood the outside world as well as he understood feudal life in Yemen, and he feared the effects development might have on the religious life of his people.

British and American oil companies were maneuvering to get into Yemen as early as the 1930s and 1940s. When Standard Oil offered the Imam $2 million in return for permission to conduct a seismic survey, he told his advisers that oil was the devil's urine, then refused the offer. Two million dollars was a tempting sum, but it was a pittance compared to the cost of getting the oil companies and their governments out of Yemen if things didn't go well.

Secluding Yemen from the twentieth century meant that the Imam's subjects were also deprived of decent health services and modern schooling. The nondevelopment of the country frustrated educated Yemenis, as well as other members of the royal family, who were aware that other countries, especially Egypt, were making the transition from outdated monarchies to modern forms of government. The powerful Shafi'i merchant class from the south was much more interested in developing free enterprise than in maintaining a dynasty based on religious purity and one-man rule.

Najiba followed these changes in Yemeni society with interest but was preoccupied with her own problems. Her husband changed on his return to Yemen, and shortly after they moved to San'a he began to beat her. He would not come home nights and then started to sleep with other women. Najiba was miserable, but without a family or tribal group to back her up, there was little she could do. One morning at breakfast Najiba's husband pounded her to the floor with his fists. It was not the first time, but when he started to jump up and down on her chest for not putting enough sugar in his coffee, she knew it was the end. She fled to the hospital where she worked as a translator. The director provided her with a room, and Claudie Fayein, a respected French doctor, helped care for her. Weeks passed before the bruising on her chest disappeared.

Few foreigners lived in Yemen at this time, and those who did could consider the Imam to be their protector. When Imam Ahmed heard the story of the beating through his fourth wife, who lived in San'a, he immediately sent a telegram to a local judge, who intervened. But the husband was tough. He wouldn't grant a divorce, because he would lose face and access to the money he habitually stole from Najiba's earnings at the hospital. In order to force him to divorce Najiba, the judge threw him into an asylum for the insane and destitute sick. The man was determined to have his way and lasted eight days under frightful conditions before going to pieces. He finally agreed to the divorce and was released.

Instead of returning to France, Najiba, who loved her work at the hospital, stayed in San'a. She remarried in 1956. Her second husband, Mahyoub, was said to be kind, but their life together was also marred by tragedy. Mahyoub wanted a family, but after four years of marriage there was no child. In Yemen a barren woman is looked upon with ridicule, and a husband can rightfully divorce a woman who cannot bear children. Realizing that her husband had to take another wife, Najiba encouraged him to do so, reasoning that the birth of a child by the second woman would save her marriage.

Mahyoub married a divorced woman, who soon became pregnant. Najiba and the second wife did not become friends. The woman stole things from the household and was jealous of Najiba's relationship with their husband. When a baby girl was born, the new wife proved to be a negligent mother. Najiba took care of the child as if it were her own, but it died in her arms before it was three months old. Najiba was shattered.

With the death of the baby, the second marriage lost its purpose. Mahyoub sent the second wife away so that there would once again be peace in the house. Life was quiet for a while, until the second wife, humiliated by her rejection, decided to seek revenge. She went to her sister, who told fortunes beside the curb in the old city. Using a basket of seashells and stones, the two women put a spell on Mahyoub. When Pascal asked what sort of spell, Najiba replied: "Since that day, he has been only a brother to me." Mahyoub never made love to her again.

The second wife married three more times before throwing herself headfirst down a dry well and breaking her neck. Remembering these events, Najiba shrugged her shoulders and laughed. After all, it had happened so long ago. She tottered, and Pascal and I reached out to steady her.

"*Ça va, Najiba?*" Pascal asked.

"*Oui, ça va, mon fils,*" she answered, holding his forearm. She did not look well.

At the end of more than an hour's reminiscing, Najiba stared hard at me and asked what I was doing in Yemen. Pascal told her the story of the shipwreck and of my return to search for my journals. She seemed to soften, as if realizing that I too had fallen under the spell of the country. She understood very well how Yemen can seduce the unsuspecting visitor.

"It is good to come close to danger and death," she eventually said to me. "What you saw out there [in the storm and on the island] made you feel alive. You must hold on to those feelings. One who grows old without such memories has nothing." She took a breath before continuing. "Memories . . . they are our souvenirs from a lifetime of forgetfulness."

Pascal handed Najiba the bag of oranges, and we let her go inside.

9

The Experts

THE DAYS CONTINUED to come and go, and late one morning
Martin asked how I was getting along with my plans to revisit
Uqban Island. His question wasn't one I much enjoyed thinking
about. Like fishing, most activities in Yemen involve an extraordinary amount of waiting around for something to happen, and
after having spent two aimless weeks in the country, I was just
beginning to appreciate what a formidable project I had created
for myself. With the network of army checkposts, random police
roadblocks, required travel permits, prohibited military and
tribal areas, and armed villagers suspicious of a stranger's every
move, I found it impossible to travel freely. This inability to act
independently made long-range planning pointless. I was determined to persevere, but in order to keep my mind clear, it was
essential to start discarding excess baggage. The first thing to go
was my grip on real time, the minutes and seconds by which we
organize our lives. It hadn't taken me long to realize that in a
country where Allah was calling most of the shots, there was little sense in distinguishing between five hours and five weeks.
Most of my time thus far had been spent sitting around confused
and frustrated as I entertained fantasies of digging up my notebooks.

Before trying to reach the coast a second time, I decided to seek out the advice of foreigners who had spent considerable amounts of time in the country. I assumed that their knowledge of how to get things done in Yemen, gleaned from years of experience, would help guide me in the right direction. With this plan in mind, I set out to meet the local experts.

First on my list was Nicholas Arnis, whose primary activity seemed to be walking through San'a carrying a clipboard and a folding chair. Each morning at precisely seven o'clock he set up his chair in front of one of the city's twenty-three public toilets. Every day it was a different toilet. He penciled notes until nine, at which time he folded up his chair and walked home.

"*Malak?*" (What are you doing?) the men would ask as they waved their hands in the air. Nick hardly spoke Arabic and could not explain. Weeks passed as the rumors spread through the marketplace. Early one morning I found him comfortably seated on his chair in front of a public toilet, and I listened to his story.

"None of them believed me when I told them I was conducting a survey."

This was not surprising. Nick was studying the toilet habits of Yemeni men and boys. UNESCO, USAID, and the Peace Corps wanted to renovate a public toilet as part of their contribution to an international effort to preserve the old city of San'a. Since there was enough money and time to renovate only one of the twenty-three facilities, Nick was searching for the one used most frequently.

The Islamic Trust of San'a owned the public toilets but no longer maintained them. They are usually situated near a public garden, a bathhouse, or a mosque. "You can smell them from twenty paces," Nick told me. Approximately thirty paces downwind from where he sat I could see a row of four plastered domes set behind a rough stone wall. This structure was an eight-stall dry-composting toilet, built more than one hundred years earlier. During a lull in the activity I took a quick look inside. No water was available, and the smell of dried urine was overwhelming. On the floor of each stall was a slit in the stonework over which one could squat. Beneath the floor excrement tumbled down an inclined shaft to the collection area behind the building.

Before the introduction of indoor plumbing, Yemeni tower houses had similar squat toilets on each floor, one above the other. Urine was directed to a drain that led to a specially prepared stucco surface on the exterior of the building. Given the height of the buildings (four to six stories) and the hot, dry climate, the liquid evaporated before reaching the ground. The excrement fell to the bottom of a tall airshaft shared by all the toilets. As water is scarce in Yemen, these dry-composting drop toilets were ideally suited to the climate. Only in rural areas are they still in use.

The dried excrement used to be collected from the household and public toilets by men known as *mukharwis,* who would take donkeyloads of the stuff to the public bathhouses to be burned as fuel. The resulting ash was then sold to farmers to spread on their vegetable gardens and fruit orchards. The entire recycling process was self-sustaining and regulated by city officials. Prices were fixed, and there was even a standard unit of measure, *khabshat al-khara,* the basket of shit. Now that discarded truck tires and fossil fuels are more commonly used to heat the bathhouses and there are few drop toilets in use, the *mukharwis* of San'a have no work. These days the excrement from the public toilets is hauled off by trucks to be dumped.

Nick explained all of this with keen interest. Before arriving in Yemen, he had worked in the Environmental Planning Bureau of the Oregon state government. The toilet project was his introduction to the field of international aid.

"Well, look at it this way," he said. "The job has given me an opportunity to meet the people, the average Yemeni. Sitting in places like this puts me in touch with people I would normally never meet." I admired his optimism.

"Don't forget to count me!" one old man called out as he entered the toilets. The time was approaching nine o'clock, and the morning shift was nearly finished.

"People have not always been as helpful as that man," Nick

pointed out. He had begun his work speaking little Arabic. When men spoke to him, he could only smile and shrug his shoulders in response. One of the few questions he understood was *"Aysk ismak?"* (What is your name?)

"Nick," he would reply, gesturing to himself.

"Neek!" many of the men would exclaim with indignation. *Nik,* pronounced "neek," means *fuck* in Arabic. *"Nik nafsak ya makhnuth!"* (Well, fuck yourself, you faggot!) they would yell at him before striding off to a different toilet.

This level of conversation continued for several days, until Nick discovered what his name meant in Arabic. After that he decided to use his nickname, Arnie.

Once the men understood his purpose for loitering near the toilets, they became more helpful — too helpful. They used the toilets more frequently than usual in hopes that their favorite one would be chosen for renovation. Their "help" threw off the statistics, but little could be done to keep the survey a secret. Nick had become a well-known figure throughout the city.

I dared to ask whether toilet paper was used. Nick told me that most of the old men picked up stones to clean themselves with, or used scraps of discarded paper and cardboard off the ground.

"What is the ideal stone?" I asked.

"A smooth one about the size of a golf ball," Nick replied. "Historically, a basket full of stones was left by the toilets. Afterward, the stones were placed in a separate basket, to be cleaned and reused."

I found this story difficult to believe.

Nick's project was funded by UNESCO's Old City Preservation Office, with a small assistance grant from USAID. The Peace Corps would provide construction materials, and the local Yemeni development organization promised to supply the labor. After many months of notetaking and detailed calculations, Nick figured out that the toilets at Hammam Madhab received 1200 to 1500 men per day. The building, which consisted of seven stalls, had a sound structure and was selected for the renovation project. Water faucets would be installed, and the interior walls would be covered with *qadad,* an impervious plaster consisting of crushed pumice, lime, gypsum, and animal fat. The estimated cost was around $35,000 to $50,000. At $5000 to $7000 per stall, the toilets would be the most expensive in Yemen.

But a dispute soon arose over design. The Yemenis wanted *frangi,* European-style toilets, but Nick and the funding organizations felt that the traditional dry-composting toilets would help conserve water. At the estimated 1500 eight-liter flushes a day, Hammam Madhab would use 84,000 liters of water weekly, 336,000 liters monthly, and slightly more than 4 million liters annually. Originally, no water had been used at these toilets.

It was finally decided that because the Yemenis would be responsible for maintaining the toilets, they should be flush. This made some sense because of the disposal problem. More important, the sophisticated flush toilets would represent progress, a milestone in city planning. I wondered how well the stones would flush.

I had heard of a Catholic priest in San'a who carried a confessional booth in the back of his car, and I decided to seek him out next. Unfortunately, he too was unable to offer any practical suggestions on how to obtain permission to visit Uqban, but he was happy to spend an afternoon telling me stories about his work.

Father Philippe grew up in Lille, a city in the industrialized north of France. He attributed his interest in missionary work to the slow-witted textile factory workers who populated his hometown. He couldn't wait to leave the place. "It was a solid-faced town of normal activities and mediocre thoughts," he told me, "not very mystical or spiritual."

As a young man, Father Philippe longed for an active life with religious purpose. Toward that end, he was ordained in 1950 and trained for three years in Tunisia. The people and climate suited him, and for the next thirty-five years he worked in the rural Moslem communities of North Africa. In 1985, at the request of Mother Teresa, he went to North Yemen, where Mother Teresa had previously established three communities: a hospital for the elderly in Hodeida (1971), a leper clinic in Ta'izz (1972), and an orphanage in San'a (1973).

Mother Teresa returned to Yemen in 1985, with a simple request. "She is a bit of a hard woman," remarked Father Philippe. Meeting with President Ali Abdullah Saleh, she pointed out that she could expand her work in Yemen only on the condition that her sisters received spiritual support. Catholic priests would have to be admitted into the country. If this was not possible, many other countries were asking for her help.

"Fortunately, a translator was present to help sweeten her words," Father Philippe explained. Mother Teresa was granted permission to bring three *murshids* (spiritual leaders) to Yemen. Because of his fluency in Arabic and thorough understanding of Islamic culture, Father Philippe was selected as one of them.

The priests worked on a variety of projects. One set up a program to rehabilitate delinquent boys and former criminals. Another distributed food and medicines to poor villages. Father Philippe worked on a wide range of irrigation projects, but like his two associates, he felt that his primary purpose was to minister to the spiritual needs of the Catholic sisters and the Christian community. He conducted Mass in a hall above the City End Supermarket, and it was true that he listened to confessions from within a portable booth constructed by the Filipino congregation of the Catholic church in San'a. The booth and chair folded up and fit in the back seat of Father Philippe's car.

Mother Teresa's leper clinic in Ta'izz was called the City of Light. Outpatients came every day to take their pills, and eighty to ninety patients stayed for one or two months during the first stages of their cure, especially when they had open wounds. The lepers easily hurt themselves, because they had lost all sensation in their fingers and toes. Burns were common. There was a simple operating theater, and when I asked Father Philippe what kinds of operations were being performed, he replied, "Well, they mostly cut off fingers and toes. But the major problem is that the nerves are constricting."

A French doctor who had arrived two years earlier found a

simple way to revitalize the nerve endings by operating on the nearest joint. Father Philippe recounted witnessing one of these operations. "It was very moving. The patient couldn't pick up a pencil, because he couldn't feel it. After the doctor opened up the elbow joint, the man had the good use of his hand." The following week the same man was back. *"Hakim, hakim,"* the man implored, "last week you opened my right elbow and made it better. Before you go today, please operate on my left elbow." To feel pain in his hands gave the man hope.

A village for lepers had been built beside the City of Light. The outpatients who lived there could marry, and the families helped one another build their houses. The men worked in Ta'izz, while the wives and children generally stayed in the village. Because leprosy is not inherited the children were healthy.

I asked Father Philippe why the Catholic Church would set up a mission in a Moslem country if conversion were not one of the primary goals. He admitted that it would be dishonest to say that the ultimate purpose was not to open the Yemenis to the Gospel, but that this must be done freely, through their own thoughts. "We provide help and friendship," he told me. "Conversion is a matter of individual choice." The Catholics did not oblige anyone to believe, nor did they distribute Bibles in an attempt to attract people. Father Philippe described his goal as helping individuals to get free of their own fears and the constraints of their social life. "The object of our work is not to bring in a lot of medicine or to perform baptisms. We want to make the people more aware of their lives — to help them help themselves, in the most appropriate way possible."

In many ways Father Philippe felt he had better communication and understanding with the leaders of his neighborhood mosque than he did with some of the rival Christian churches. He told me what had happened the previous year when he attempted to organize a joint Easter celebration with the Anglicans.

"On the Saturday night before Easter," he said, "we have the long night vigil, with the celebration of fire, readings of the Old Testament, and the celebration of the water. I suggested to the

Anglican bishop that we could adapt this part. He was invited to select passages to read from the Bible. We could have a small party together afterward. Later, the Catholics would go to Mass and the Anglicans could do as they wished."

The bishop was suspicious, however, and would not commit himself. In the end, he explained that the Anglicans were willing to invite the Catholics to join them for a Sunday sunrise service. At 5 A.M. on Easter Sunday, the bishop, along with his congregation and several Filipinos from the Catholic congregation, set out on foot toward Jabal Nuqum, a nearby mountain. The walk ended badly: the interdenominational procession was rounded up at gunpoint by the government security forces that patrol the main roads of San'a from sunset to sunrise. The bishop had forgotten to obtain a permit for the gathering.

"It is a strange thing," Father Philippe pointed out, "a pity, really, that in this country we cannot be more united in front of Islam. The Moslems see us bickering and they are amused. They ask me who is a Baptist, who is an Evangelical, a Presbyterian, a Pentecostal, a Catholic. I try to explain that the differences are similar to those between the Shiites and the Sunnis, but the Moslems are quick to point out that in Yemen the Shiites and the Sunnis, and even the Ismailis, can and do pray in the same mosque. The Christian community in San'a has not set a good example of similar cooperation. The Moslems don't understand how there can be more than one version of the Bible. It suggests to them that Christianity has not been thought out properly, because there is but one version of the Koran. I understand why there is not a great interest in Christianity here. For me, Yemen is a good place to be in touch with the roots of the Arabic world. It is the genuine Islam here. Very tolerant, and very open-minded. Mercy, charity, and compassion — these are the true teachings of Islam. Considering the present political situation in the Middle East, and considering Western media coverage, how many people are aware of these aspects of the Moslem faith?"

"Precious few," I replied.

. . .

Giuseppe Montello had spent most of his eighty-two years near the Red Sea. He was born in Ethiopia before World War I, when the country was still called Abyssinia. After a lifetime of work in Aden and San'a, he thought of Italy as just another foreign country, and he rarely went there to visit relatives. He had brought up his family in Yemen and was still active as an engineering consultant, travel agent, and importer of machine parts. He helped Yemeni families place their children in European schools, and the people referred to him as Sidi, "wise old grandfather." The nickname was appropriate.

Father Philippe gave me Mr. Montello's address, and so one afternoon I took tea with him in his street-level office.

"What does this country produce?" he asked. Then, without giving me an opportunity to respond, he said, "The exports consist of a few sheep, cowhides, and small amount of fresh fish sent to Saudi Arabia. Salt is the one exportable mineral, but it is being extracted by hand, dynamited from the salt flats at Jabal Milh in the northern Tihama. Slabs of salt pried out of the ground with crowbars and then hammered to bits by hand — ridiculous! Is this the way to build a modern economy?

"There are no resources in Yemen, no ways of earning foreign exchange in a country whose economy used to be based on remittances from an army of migrant workers. Two billion dollars a year were being sent into the country. It has now dropped to a third of that figure. As work declines in Saudi Arabia and overseas, the men come home to find no work. They can't compete with Pakistani labor in the Gulf, and at home many of the big development projects are run by foreign governments that import their own skilled labor. The Koreans and Chinese are the best examples of this.

"The ratio of imports to exports is three hundred to one! Appearances have changed, but the simple fact remains: the country produces nothing. Biscuits are manufactured in Yemen, but they are phantom exports — all made from imported ingredients. The money that comes into this country is all spent on imported goods. The cost of living is high in Yemen because everything comes from overseas. Therefore, wages have to be high. Yemeni labor costs are no longer competitive."

I mentioned the recent discovery of oil near Marib.

"You ask about the oil. No one has seen a penny of the oil money! As oil revenues increase, foreign aid decreases. Millions are being spent on defense to protect the oil fields. The oil will only offset the decline in remittances and foreign aid. The anticipated volume of oil was 200,000 barrels per day. So far they are producing 130,000 per day. Nobody knows what the actual reserves are, and now everything in the economy hinges on the oil. Agriculture has suffered because of the years of the migrant workers, in the 1970s and early 1980s. Mountain terraces that took hundreds of years to build have washed away because of lack of maintenance. Agricultural production in 1972 was twice what it is today, with the exception of qat and potatoes. In that year the Yemeni men started a mass migration to find work in the Gulf states and Saudi Arabia. One million, out of a total population of six million, left the country. These other countries were spending their oil money on huge development projects. Those projects are finished now. The men have come home. Who knows what will happen? We pray for the oil."

He poured more tea for both of us, then continued with his story.

"For three years the government has prohibited the import of fruit and vegetables, electronic goods, machinery, autos and trucks. But all these things are available. Half of the imported goods are being smuggled. The Toyota agent is paying the Land Rover dealer not to import spare parts. Cars, especially Mercedes and Peugeots, are driven across the border from Saudi Arabia. No import permits are officially allowed, but at the border the drivers pay the customs officials what they want. With customs papers, one can register the cars. It is not difficult.

"What can one say about Yemeni life? What is today will not be tomorrow. Look at the street. Did you see this in 1978? The honking, the dust, the crush of people, clogged traffic. Simple, honest people from the villages swarming to the city to gawk at the store-window trinkets. When I first came here, water was being delivered in carts pulled by camels. Now all this garbage strewn everywhere. This time of play must come to an end!"

In the face of this, my response seemed weak. "Sounds pretty grim," I said. To change the conversation, I asked Mr. Montello whether he would retire in Italy.

"Retire? Leave Yemen? *Never!* I love this wonderful country. I will work here until I fall to pieces."

Before I got up to leave, Mr. Montello asked me if I was working in San'a. When I told him about the shipwreck and the search for the notebooks, he sat back in his chair, chuckling to himself.

"And may God help you, young man," he muttered, looking out the window.

At times it seemed like the deeper I looked into the foreign community, the further I distanced myself from Yemen. One afternoon, while trying to interview the wives of Hunt Oil workers in the City End Supermarket, I was approached by a trim older man. He wasn't pushing a cart, and I thought he might be the store manager, coming to protect his shoppers.

"You want to know about Yemen?" he said. "Well, you can ask me. These women don't know a thing. They beat a path from the supermarket to the video library upstairs and then back home. Hell, you'll never see them inside the old city. Some three-week expert at the embassy told them that they might get abducted. Never heard such a fool story. No sheik on a white horse would be caught dead with one of them, I'll goodandgoddamn guarantee ya that! By the way, Skip Chandler's the name." He held out his hand to shake. Three of his fingers were missing.

We drove back to his house, which was situated in a walled compound protected by Yemeni soldiers. He wanted to show me his gun collection; I wanted to ask him about the possibility of falsifying road travel permits. We got drunk instead.

"I own a house on Cyprus," he told me. "The people are civilized there. Well, the Greeks and Turks still have some things to sort out, but I'm away from all that. The government's got this scheme called the Resident Retirement Program. You show them a bank statement and a work history and write up a biography for yourself. If they like what they see, you're in. I'm twenty miles from Limassol, one of the most beautiful places I've ever seen. You can have the United States. I've got a house in North Carolina, but I'll give it to my kids from my first wife. I'm married to a Filipino woman now. A beautiful, gentle woman. I love her. Back home they'd call her a nigger. I'll never go back. Hey, I'm doing all the talking! Let's go over to the Mile High Club. I'll introduce you to Bob."

We found Bob unloading cases of beer from the back of a Ford van. He had converted the front porch of his house into a bar known as the Mile High Club. The back of the bar was an expanse of bamboo poles nailed directly to the exterior wall of the house. Polaroid photos of Skip, Bob, and their buddies were pinned to the wall next to currency notes from different countries. Two five-by-seven-inch cards caught my eye. They read "Nine out of ten men who have tried camels prefer women" and "Why are camels called the ships of the desert? Because they're full of Arab semen."

A Willie Nelson tape filled the porch with a truck driver's lament. We drank Pepsi-Cola and Scotch. It was eleven o'clock in the morning. I could detect the rusty, metallic smell of a cast-iron frying pan that had been left half submerged in a sink for several days. Fragments of egg, coffee grounds, and bacon fat probably lined the sink. As the wind shifted, I picked up the odors of cigarette butts, salted peanuts, and empty beer cans. I wasn't surprised when Bob told me he was a single man. He worked in construction.

"That's the swimming pool and tennis court they [the Yemeni government] promised us in the brochure," Bob told me, gesturing toward the dirt-and-stone parking lot surrounded by a border of eucalyptus and casuarina trees. "Yep, the Yemenis are pretty good at finishing things seventy percent." Bob liked to speak in terms of percentages.

I listened to the two men talk. On the surface they appeared to be old hands, seasoned veterans of the expatriate community. But the more I listened, the more I realized that they remained firmly attached to a long-since-vanished segment of American society. They lived in Yemen, though they could have lived any-where; their way of talking and responses to ideas remained squarely in the American middle class of the 1950s. Living museum pieces, they had set themselves adrift socially, and their familiar reference points had faded with time. They considered themselves worldly, but the term was applicable only in the geographical sense, because they didn't seem to connect with their surroundings. Skip had his house and wife in Cyprus, but for Bob and thousands of contract workers leading similar lives across the Middle East and Asia, there was no such thing as home. Isolated by language, insulated by work, and housed behind Cyclone fencing topped with coils of wire, they led the lives of well-paid, tax-exempt, nomadic prisoners. It didn't take long to understand the bravado that masked the loneliness of their lives.

The Mile High Club was a gathering place for these lost souls. By the time I left, the Scotch bottle was empty, Bob was feeling 100 percent, and I had forgotten the purpose of my visit.

At a teahouse located just off Ali Abd al-Mughni Street in San'a, I looked across the table at a man who could not stop talking. He was a friend of Martin's whom I had invited for tea. His name was Edwin Peebles.

"Absolutely *ghastly stuff!*" he exclaimed as he stared into a streaked water glass filled with a steamy, clay-colored liquid. Broken tea leaves floated on the surface of the drink, which had been sweetened with two tablespoons of sugar, mixed with condensed milk, and covered with a fine layer of road dust. A satisfactory beverage, considering the establishment, but hardly Edwin Peebles's idea of a proper cup of tea.

Edwin was from Beaumont, Texas. It was rumored that he had acquired his British accent in Yemen. He had lived in San'a for fifteen years and was employed by the Great Mosque, where he restored page fragments from a recent find of ancient Korans. Edwin had important friends in the government, and I was eager to talk to him about the best way to approach the National Security Police about returning to Uqban Island. Unfortunately, he was in an agitated state that morning and was determined to tell me about the day he reregistered his car.

The incident had taken place a month earlier. The registration papers for the vehicle, he explained, had long since expired, and he had grown tired of slipping bundles of riyals to the police who stopped him. Because Edwin knew the manager of the taxation department in a distant city, he had decided to make a day's outing in the hope of getting the paperwork sorted out quickly and cheaply.

The morning of his journey, he placed several bottles of chilled mineral water on the passenger seat of his car before setting off. The air, he recalled, was heavy with the smell of freshly turned earth as he motored north from San'a. Stopping at a roadside stall, he purchased a small watermelon, then cut neat slices from it with a knife he kept in the glove box for that very purpose. He explained how he had wiped the blade on a tissue and then gazed out at a spectacular view. Mountain walls, textured with tier upon tier of stone terraces, extended from the canyon shadows to purple-black summits, where the silhouettes of stone towers sat in the clouds. Atop jagged promontories, abandoned watchtowers from the Ottoman occupation linked the ruins of forgotten garrisons. Edwin ate half the melon and handed the rest to a passing goatherd. The boy scooped out the sweet red flesh with his fingers. The rind went to the animals, and Edwin drove on.

When he arrived at the tax office, he spent about an hour and a half visiting his friend. They were negotiating a price to register the car when the office suddenly emptied. His friend looked up and said, "Would you like to go to an execution?" Edwin thought the man was joking, but the invitation proved to be genuine.

Edwin didn't think a foreigner would be allowed to go to an execution, but he and his friend joined a gathering crowd of onlookers wending their way through the maze of cobbled streets. They were led to a dingy, dull-colored building made up of small, ill-lit rooms littered with garbage and smelling of urine. This was the local judiciary. They came upon a tall man of about sixty-five years tied up with red plastic rope. He looked confused, as if he didn't know quite where he was going. The rope held his arms behind his back, so that he looked much like a trussed chicken. This was the man who was to be executed. He had just written his last will and testament in a nearby room.

Out of an adjoining room came a small crowd, in the middle of which was a woolly-headed man who also looked a bit dazed. Edwin was introduced to this fellow, who was the executioner. The man had just been to the office to collect his money. The court had had a terrible time finding someone to actually pull the trigger. The man was paid 5000 riyals ($500) to do the job. As Edwin and the woolly-headed executioner shook hands, the man announced that if a foreigner was going to be present, he would like to be paid in American dollars. This was meant as a joke, and everyone laughed, with the exception of the condemned man.

When the room emptied, Edwin and his friend from the taxation office followed a subdued crowd for five minutes to an open area between the grammar school and the hospital. Classes were still in session as 250 people in tribal dress gathered in a rough horseshoe shape. The crowd stood four deep. No one spoke. A billowing mist rolled across the execution ground, obscuring everything except the waiting group of people. One side of the crowd was made up of the condemned man's family, the other half of the family of the man he had shot.

Edwin admitted to feeling quite horrified by the situation. He felt certain he would be sent away at some point. To the contrary, a dozen suited people from the government offices turned up, and instead of sending him away, they formed a line on either side of him. Much taller than the others, he was quite the center of attention. Then the hospital staff arrived: an Egyptian doctor, a Yemeni doctor, and two nurses, one Egyptian, the other Russian. Many of the office workers giggled and joked as a means to relieve the tense atmosphere.

A van arrived from the courthouse. It was huge, like a furniture removal van — completely solid on the sides, with no windows. The man to be executed was guided out of the back and into the middle of the crowd, which faced the van. At that moment one of the white-coated doctors took charge of the proceedings. The condemned man wore a white robe with an unbleached muslin shawl around his shoulders and head. These were taken from him and spread on the ground. He was given ten minutes to say his prayers, which he did upon his knees. When he finished, the crowd stepped forward. Edwin couldn't see the man and so moved to within six feet of where he was kneeling. Curiosity drew him to the scene, but at the last moment he decided he should not be so close. The execution was not for strangers; it was a family affair. Edwin retreated twenty feet, to stand with the dignitaries.

The event had started with a shooting. The condemned man had killed a neighbor following an argument over a stone wall separating two fields of sorghum. While he spent a year in prison, negotiations were carried out between the two families involved. Those who forgive a murderer by letting him pay blood money are highly regarded, but the family of the dead man would not accept money as compensation. They were offered twice the normal amount of 200,000 riyals, but they refused. The Islamic court wanted them to forgive, but the wronged family wanted the man's life.

The doctor helped position the man face down on the ground, then, with a felt-tipped pen, marked the area where the heart was located. The executioner stepped forward with an assault rifle, stood over the prostrate man for a long moment, then fired a short burst through the man's back. It was over in an instant. The doctors had watched the execution as if it had been a normal medical procedure. A stretcher and an ambulance were about ten yards away, to take the dead man immediately to the hospital, and a group of women from his family waited with a white shroud and perfumes, with which they would prepare the body for burial.

The crowd turned to walk away, chatting about their normal concerns as if nothing had happened. Stunned by the event, Edwin Peebles could not move. He had to be led away by his friend.

Judging by both families' reactions, the execution came as a relief. The dispute was settled. The final solution was easier to accept because the executee was old; he had lived his life. It seemed fair that he should die, because the man he had shot was young, with a new wife and small children. If the man had not been executed, a far bloodier confrontation would have erupted between the families, possibly involving many other deaths.

Shaken but in control of himself, Edwin managed to obtain his new car registration later that day. He paid quite a lot more than he had expected, but then, he got more than he had bargained for.

Having finished his story, Edwin got to his feet, shook my hand hurriedly, and marched out the door of the teashop. I never had a chance to ask him about his influential friends or possible contacts in the National Security Police.

In my search for local knowledge, some of the best stories came from the most unlikely sources. One afternoon my attention was drawn to a set of red suspenders stretched tautly over a man's paunch. Tooled into the back of his leather belt was the name Billy. His T-shirt read "Kickin Ass on the Wild Side of Town."

Billy wore a gold Rolex watch on his left wrist. White Reeboks protruded from the cuffs of a pair of Levi 501s, and his baseball cap looked as if it had recently been dry-cleaned. The thumb of his left hand was hooked into a front pocket. The right hand grasped a frosty can of Budweiser beer. His eyes, hidden behind the mirrored lenses of his Ray Ban aviator glasses, seemed to gaze into the middle distance. He wore a look of simmering bovine violence.

"Yeah, this is it!" Billy told me, without shifting the Ray Bans in my direction. "The big day. Everything hinges on this day."

It was the Fourth of July. I was standing in the garden of the American embassy compound in San'a. An announcement came over the loudspeaker that the tug-of-war competition was about to begin. The first event would be men versus women.

"Looks like macho time," Billy told me as he lifted the red-white-and-blue aluminum can to his lips. He must have been twenty-five years old, but he had the corpulent body of a man twice his age.

Ten Hunt Oil workers, along with three United States Marines, had challenged all of the American women to a tug-of-war. One of the Marines sported a pair of the largest ears I have ever seen. They sat at right angles to his head and might have given him trouble in a strong wind. He had no chin, but presumably knew how to kill with his bare hands in four seconds. Mustard was smeared on his white T-shirt.

The barefoot men had been drinking, and when the whistle blew, thirty-five women in ripple-soled jogging shoes promptly pulled them onto their backsides. There was nervous laughter as the men struggled to their feet. I could see Billy working his jaw muscles. To regain his composure, he popped open another beer.

"Hey! I got one for ya," he suddenly blurted out to me. "Yeah, just last year I heard that seven out of ten dogs in Yemen were rabid, and so's I borrowed an M-16 — semiauto — from my buddy. Climbed to the top of the American School and dusted twenty-two of the fuckers till I ran out of ammo. Hell, turned out four of 'em were pets! Real sorry about that. Neighbor's children weren't too happy. Not one little bit! And did y'all hear the one about Norman?" he continued.

"Norman who?"

"Stormin' Norman — the hostage."

I vaguely remembered hearing rumors that an oil worker had been taken hostage five months earlier by one of the tribes along the edge of the Empty Quarter. Billy tipped the brim of his hat to a three-hundred-pound woman in shorts who was eating a plateful of brownies.

"Norman was taken by the Bakil tribe, out in the desert somewhere around Marib. The oil pipeline cut right through their country. Hadn't received the promised benefits from the pipeline contractor or the government. Heard they wanted a school real bad. The Bakil treated Norman good, but shit! I know Norm — he's not the kinda guy to sit around and wait for a situation to clarify itself, if ya know what I mean. He lost his temper — blew up! He swore, jumped up and down. The Bakil were spooked, couldn't decide whether he was funny or crazy. They tried to quiet him down with whiskey, but Norm wouldn't take a drop. The Bakil had never heard of an oil man that didn't drink whiskey. Something wasn't right. They kept him until he started running around in front of their women without his shirt on. Dressed in cut-off blue jeans. Real short, like underpants. That was the turning point. Yemen Hunt sent out a negotiating team real quick, but by the time they arrived it was all over. Hell! The Bakil, fiercest tribe in the Jauf — they just let Norman go. I think they musta decided they didn't need the school that bad. Too much disruption. They'd messed with the wrong man." Billy took a final sip of beer, draining the can.

I left the festivities early, but kept Norman's story in mind, hoping to get the details from a more reliable source later. Returning to my hotel room that afternoon, I collected my bags and thanked the manager for his generosity. Out of a sense of decency, I couldn't justify accepting a complimentary room any longer. I also wanted to live in humbler surroundings. A cab took me to an older section of town outside the old city walls, where I could stay at the American Institute of Yemeni Studies, which I assumed to be a community of Yemeni and American scholars. The institute rented rooms at a reasonable rate, and a phone and kitchen were available.

Stepping out of the battered cab with my suitcase, I noticed plastic bags of human shit splattered against the metal front gate of the institute. I attributed the mess to neighborhood kids; it certainly didn't look like the work of a terrorist group. I pressed the intercom button, which had been missed by the barrage, and a buzzer sounded, so I could pass through the security gate.

At the front door I was confronted by a bespectacled, shuffling man of about forty who introduced himself as the resident director. He wore a checked flannel shirt rolled up to the elbows and khaki field pants aged to perfection. He had not received my letters of introduction and questioned me closely as to whether I had paid my $25 annual membership fee to the institute's business office in Portland, Oregon. Slightly amused, I suggested that he phone head office to check out my story. As he gave me a brief tour of the building, I found his clipped syllables difficult to string together into words. His eyes bulged at unexpected moments, and he had the irritating habit of walking off in midsentence. When the resident director wasn't talking to me directly, he made funny high-pitched "Hmmm?" sounds to himself, obviously enjoying a private joke. Within minutes of my arrival I realized I had made a mistake, but not wanting to spend the afternoon in search of a more suitable place, I took a room.

The institute was run along the lines of a freshman college dormitory. Notices taped to most of the interior wall surfaces outlined rules governing the use of the telephone, light switches, door locks, and private and public areas, as well as dust control, mail delivery, and number of guests permitted. A separate and more restrictive set of rules applied to those individuals wishing to entertain Yemeni guests. One could not sit on the toilet without being confronted with written instructions covering such intricate tasks as flushing and showering. "Report all leaks to the resident director; all who occupy this house will appreciate your cooperation" read a sign in the kitchen.

I grew to like the notices and later photographed many of them. On the walls of the common living room, lined with science fiction paperbacks and James Michener novels, I read the following:

> Use of washing machine: Members of the Institute — no charge. Nonmembers — ten riyals per load.

> Letters of introduction will be provided for members at no charge.

> Photocopies: Two riyals per page.

> Typewriter rentals: Members — no charge. Nonmembers — ten riyals per hour or fraction thereof.

The kitchen smelled of cockroaches, dust, and stale popcorn. Meals were not shared, and the residents hoarded their supplies of peanut butter, Ritz crackers, tins of beef stew, and other supermarket food in separate cupboards.

The resident director lived in mortal fear of being misquoted by visiting journalists or writers, and for this reason I was rated slightly higher than the substance smeared on the front gate. During our first and last conversation, he made it abundantly clear that despite his fluency in Arabic and four years in the country studying the social structure of the northern tribes, he didn't know anything, could make no introductions to anyone who did, and was unable to rent me one of the institute's four-wheel-drive vehicles, which had been purchased for that purpose. I had trouble even persuading the man to let me into the library. Judging by his hesitation, I anticipated a veritable storehouse of signed first editions by the great travelers of the Arabian peninsula: Carsten Niebuhr, Wilfrid Thesiger, Harry S. Philby, Charles Doughty, and Bertram Thomas. But once inside, I discovered a jumble of dusty books with no apparent filing system, dead plants, obscure research papers, three broken typewriters (one in Arabic script), and a photocopy machine that no longer worked. Material could not be taken from the library to be photocopied elsewhere.

The director watched over his domain with a zeal that left me totally mystified. On two occasions I witnessed European researchers leaving the grounds — one in tears, the other in a rage — because they had been turned away from the library, which was supposed to be open to the public. The man guarded the place like a mother hen, checking to make sure no one was using his laundry soap or stealing Lipton tea bags from his cupboard. After my second day at the institute, I remembered the plastic bags of excrement and could no longer be certain they had been thrown by Yemenis.

Two paleontologists and a geologist from the Museum of Natural History in New York were staying at the institute, and the director followed them around like a puppy wagging his little tail. At night the four of them drank Ballantine Scotch and, in hushed tones, discussed their search for early hominid fossils in Yemen. They chortled over sightings of alluvial fans, secondary graben floors, and globular stomatopoda in the way some men discuss women's breasts. I asked one of the scientists to identify a fossilized clamshell I had found in Wadi Zabid with Mohammed. The man held the shell fragment in the palm of his hand and regarded it in much the same way a butcher looks knowingly at a lamb chop.

"Jurassic," came his reply. "Not very old."

"How old?"

"About two hundred million years."

As a nonspecialist, I felt the shell was sufficiently old to keep as a souvenir.

Frank, the geologist, was older and less secretive about his work. I asked him what he had done before coming to Yemen to dig for fossils. His answer took me by surprise. He told me that he had worked on the moon.

"On the moon?"

"Yes, I helped map the surface of the moon, using satellite imagery."

According to Frank, the detail of the terrain on the moon as seen by U.S. satellites was so accurate that he could distinguish boulders less than ten meters in diameter. This comment gave me an idea. *Clea*'s hull was longer than ten meters. It occurred to me that satellite imagery might be a way of checking to see whether the sailboat was still on the beach of Uqban Island. I asked Frank if there were similar satellite images or aerial photos of Yemen.

"But of course," he replied. "LANDSAT has covered every square inch of the earth. There is also Spot Image USA — they have an office in Reston, Virginia. The standard aerial photos are also available, but we don't use them much anymore."

I asked him whether there were copies of these photos in Yemen. He told me that he knew of two sets, one at the Mapping and Survey Office and the other at the Ministry of Natural Resources and Oil. I asked what it would take to get a look at the photos.

"Permission from the Ministry of Information or National Security. Unfortunately, for you it is impossible to obtain clearance as an individual. If you had a very good friend in either of the two offices, you might have a chance."

I explained the story of the shipwreck and the journals buried on the beach, then asked whether he knew anyone I could talk to. He thought for a moment before writing a name on a piece of notepaper.

It came as a great relief to have finally met a genuine expert.

10

She Is Very Tired

"CAN YOU SEE ANYTHING?" I asked.

"No, the beach is completely empty — nothing in the water, either. If there was anything left of the sailboat, we would at least be able to see the shadow of the hull."

Nigel Dawson, who worked at the Ministry of Natural Resources and Oil, was showing me aerial photographs of Uqban taken on February 9, 1979, one year after the shipwreck. With a pair of stereoscopic viewing lenses, we scanned the entire nine-mile length of the island. The eight-by-eight-inch black-and-white photographs had been taken from 17,000 feet, but the detail was remarkably clear. By overlapping two adjacent photos and looking through the lenses, we could see the island in three dimensions. A forty-two-foot sailboat would have been visible on the clean sand beach. After looking at the island with great care, I wondered where the boat had gone. Someone must have taken the yacht off the beach, because not enough time had passed for the hull to have disintegrated. I thanked Nigel for his assistance and left the office.

Later that morning I opened a nautical chart of the area surrounding Uqban Island to determine where the looters might have come from. Khawbah and Al-Luhayyah, the two major fishing communities nearby, seemed the best bet, and I decided to make another attempt to reach these villages in hope of finding a way out to the island.

I found Gazem, a local guide, dozing on a teashop bench just off Saif Bin dhi Yazen Street, near the Department of Antiquities. I told him my plan. "You will never get a permit to visit Al-Luhayyah," he told me. "Visitors are never granted permission to visit the coast north of Hodeida."

Initially, comments such as these spurred me on. The more resistance I encountered, the harder I tried, and it took some time to realize that in a country like Yemen, this frontal approach to problem solving can only add to the futility of effort. I was beginning to lose my bearings.

Gazem went back to his nap, and I found my way to the travel permit office to fill out the standard form. I included Al-Luhayyah with ten innocuous destinations in the same general area. The man with the rubber stamp took the completed form but did not question me. The afternoon heat must have muddled his thinking, because thirty minutes later I was back at the teashop with my permit for the coast. Gazem was incredulous. We decided to leave that night.

Gazem had been born in the Ethiopian port town of Massawa in 1951. His mother was an Italian Catholic, but Gazem was raised as a Moslem by his Kashmiri father, who ran a fabric business near the harbor. Before working as a translator in San'a, Gazem had been a guerrilla fighter in Eritrea. Prior to the war he had been trained as a civil engineer, specializing in the construction and maintenance of public roads. He later put his education to good use: he excelled at blowing up roads, especially roads carrying government army vehicles full of soldiers or weapons. Following two years of fighting, he escaped on foot to the Sudan, then traveled to Saudi Arabia, where he surveyed roads for three years. There he met an Italian nurse, whom he married. They settled in Yemen and had two children, and Gazem now carried an Italian passport. He had not heard from his family for seven years.

Gazem spoke Italian, English, Afar, and Arabic fluently. He

was my idea of the perfect traveling companion: inconspicuous, fearless, and quick-witted. He could find humor in nearly any situation. Few details escaped his attention, and I would not have enjoyed driving down a road that he had mined with explosives. He was very thorough.

It was well after dark as Hussein, our driver, followed the northern road out of San'a. From the market town of Amran we took a road heading west, arriving in Hajjah just before midnight. After sleeping for a few hours, we started driving again. Before sunrise we had passed through the last army checkpost beyond Hajjah and were driving down a back road to Wadi Mawr and the coast. In six hours the heat would climb near 110° Farenheit, and we wanted to reach Al-Luhayyah before then. In low gear we moved down a rocky track that led to the valleys lost in darkness far below. Our headlights illuminated short sections of a two-lane road cut into the cliff face, but I could see little else at that early hour. Hajjah had been a royalist stronghold during the civil war twenty years earlier, which explained why the roadside was littered with the hulks of demolished armored personnel carriers. The rusted war vehicles had long since been stripped of their valuable parts.

At one point our bouncing headlights came upon a flat-roofed hut built two feet from the road against the cliff face. Alongside the hut there was just enough room to park a car. When I glanced into the structure as we crept by, I saw a human shape, wrapped in a blanket, lying on a rough wooden cot made of tree branches. A floor jack, air compressor, and hose were visible beside the bed. There was a pile of shiny mechanics' tools, and I could make out a blackened cooking area where a teakettle sat on a metal stand against one wall. An assortment of discarded tires lay about the ground in disorderly piles. The car's headlights moved on, leaving the building in darkness.

Farther down the road I concluded that the hut was a one-man tire repair shop. It was certainly in a perfect location for such a business. There were no villages for many miles, no competition, and on the rough road flat tires were common. People with tire problems would find themselves in a poor position to negotiate the price for repairs.

Morning light filled the sky as we reached the foot of the mountain. The road leveled out, and we passed through a village that looked like an open-air dormitory. Dozens of high, wood-framed cots strung with rope lay scattered across the road, so that we had to slow down in order to wend our way safely through the sleeping men. None of the blankets stirred as we passed. Sunrise was an hour away, but already I could feel the debilitating coastal heat in my lungs.

In the dry riverbeds, donkey caravans appeared, the animals loaded with stone cooking pots and hand-forged iron plows. The men who led the animals were taking their merchandise to Suq At Tur, the local weekly market. Turnip-domed reed huts and black-skinned people came into view. Traditionally, the olive-complexioned landowners lived on the mountaintops in fortified stone castles for defense, while the darker-complexioned tenant farmers, mostly of African descent, worked the flatlands and lived in communities of simple but elegant reed houses. This pattern of settlement continues in the Tihama.

The reed houses, which are typically fifteen to twenty feet tall, are built on circular mud foundations fifteen feet in diameter and are distinctly bullet-shaped. They have no internal supports, which lends a sense of spaciousness to the interior. The plastered ceilings and walls are nearly a foot thick, for strength and insulation. On the insides, the upper sections of the domes are often painted with colorful geometric and floral designs similar to simple embroidery. On the lower portions of the wall, dozens, if not hundreds, of brightly painted plates of varying sizes are displayed, sometimes covering every bit of wall surface. Considering the humid climate of the Tihama, the interiors of these buildings are remarkably cool and very pleasant to sit in. The roof is usually bound on the outside with patterned ropework, but I saw one house in Wadi Mawr where the classic design had been modified by setting an old car tire on the pointed roof, presumably to reinforce the tip of the dome. That morning I also noticed several reed houses crowned with homemade television aerials.

Women and young girls, dressed in ankle-length smocks, led their donkeys to the wells as the landscape became bathed in a warm orange glow. The sun had just risen. Other women were already drawing water from the stone-lined wells. Switching off the motor, we coasted to a halt to watch from a distance.

Above the ticking sounds of the cooling engine I could hear squeaking rope pulleys and the indistinct voices of the women. A black rubber bucket constructed from riveted sections of an old car tire rose into view, and a woman emptied its contents into a large funnel protruding from the top of one of the amphora-shaped terra-cotta jars hanging on the sides of a donkey. The women had wrapped lengths of black and red gauzy fabric around their heads, and many had stained their hands and feet dark red with henna. As they walked I could catch glimpses of their yellow and orange pantaloons beneath the long black smocks.

Before we drove on, Gazem collected a branch from a thorny shrub that grew at the side of the road. "*Solanum incanum,*" he said. "The toothache bush. There are many plants that these people use for medicine." He showed me how to make an efficient and disposable toothbrush by chewing the end of a freshly cut acacia twig. In the villages, charcoal is sometimes used as a dentifrice.

The car door slammed shut and we set off again along the rough track. I noticed a flowering desert rose and a variety of aloe plants, including *Aloe vera,* which is used for sunburn. Other succulents grew out of the rocky terrain. Off to our right, firewood collectors and their camels meandered through a landscape of huge purple boulders set on brown sandstone terraces. The camels were heavily laden with five-foot lengths of dry twisted wood, which the men had somehow split with their puny-looking axes. The wood collectors, dressed in typical Tihama fashion, wore white gathered skirts with matching jackets cut like sport coats. On their heads were tall, wide-brimmed straw hats similar to a witch's cap with a flattened peak. The camels carried hand-chiseled grinding stones and metal cooking pots.

These men and their camels were also on their way to Suq At Tur. I wanted to visit the market, but we didn't have time. The heat was upon us; it radiated from the ground and burned us from overhead, and the humidity soared. As we hurried down the road that followed the dry riverbed, conversation lapsed. There was only the sound of the bouncing car springs and the engine. At each bend in the road gravel spat from beneath the tires.

Flowering acacia trees with clusters of bright yellow blooms grew near the road, and we stopped to buy acacia honey at a lone stall constructed of flattened oil drums. Considering the lack of traffic on the road, the shop seemed a monument to optimism. In the darkened interior of the stall I could see shelves of old plastic bottles containing the thick amber liquid. Stacks of horizontal beehives, looking like logs, sat on low platforms in the nearby fields. Ten to fifteen hives were piled on each platform, to allow ventilation and to protect the honey from invading ants. Plastic sheets, looking very much like discarded shower curtains, covered the hives to keep the sun and rain out.

The beekeeper approached our car. He wanted twenty dollars for the liter bottle in his hand. The price didn't sound correct: Yemeni honey is arguably the best in the world, and a liter can cost sixty dollars or more in San'a. I wondered whether I was getting a bargain or honey diluted with sugar syrup, but Gazem assured me that in such a remote area there was little risk of adulteration.

He climbed out of the car to show me the two usual ways to check for purity. Removing the beeswax stopper from the bottle, he placed a single drop of honey in the dust. "If it remains in a ball, it is good. If the dust absorbs the drop, that means the honey has been mixed with water or sugar syrup." Our drop of honey sat perched on top of the dust. For the second test Gazem held a lit match next to the drop. Honey that contains sugar will burn. The drop didn't burn.

I paid the beekeeper and then passed the bottle around for

Hussein and Gazem to sample. We dipped our fingers into the bottle. I soon lost count of the flavors as they slowly melted into my mouth and tongue before drifting to my nose; the taste was sublime. I felt as if I had never enjoyed real honey before. By Yemeni standards, I hadn't.

The beekeeper smiled when he saw the expression of pleasure on my face. "For Madam!" he suddenly exclaimed in a rough manner. To emphasize his point, he made an upward thrusting motion with his fist and forearm. *Very Italian,* I thought to myself. I knew that Saudi men consider Yemeni honey to be an aphrodisiac, and therefore concluded that this was the message the beekeeper was trying to convey. The honey would make us virile. The recommended dosage was one tablespoonful per day. We drove to the coast with the flavor of honey in our mouths and the strength of ten men in our loins.

By the time we arrived in Al-Luhayyah, at 9 A.M., the heat was ferocious. The fishermen had not yet returned from the previous night's work, so we waited in a tumbledown café overlooking the waterfront. The building sat on a corner, and to aid ventilation two of the exterior brick walls had been knocked out. The work appeared to have been performed with a sledgehammer. Sweat rolled down my face and dripped from my chin, and my forearms left long wet patches on the wooden tabletop. Perched on stiltlike roots, mangrove trees grew thickly along a mudbank that ran parallel to the shoreline. The tide was well out, and the stink of hot mud and rotten fish entrails engulfed the town.

Seated at an adjoining table, three men shared a plate of what looked like a stack of eighteen-inch-wide whole-wheat griddlecakes soaked in yogurt. I couldn't imagine eating pancakes in such heat. The yogurt, I later found out, was curdled camel's milk. Gazem ordered two items for us. The first, known as hanid, was a blackened fish that I recognized as cold smoked mullet — a regional specialty, according to Hussein. A single lukewarm, oily morsel sat on my tongue for some time as my two companions reduced the mullet to a jumble of fine bones and a skull. I didn't bother asking for the recipe. "Good . . ." I managed to say, swallowing with difficulty. I wondered where I could wash the heavy smell of smoked fish from my hands and mouth. What I longed for was a simple glass of cold, freshly squeezed orange juice.

The fish carcass was removed from the table as a bowl full of what appeared to be premasticated Wonder Bread mixed in a light motor oil was set before us. Following Gazem's example, I took a small bit of the mixture in my fingers and placed it in my mouth. It was delicious, and as I chewed, my nose was filled with the thick perfume of well-ripened bananas, freshly baked bread, and honey. Fatut, as the dish is known, is made from leftover flatbread from the tandoor oven, bananas, warm clarified butter, and honey. Dates are sometimes added to the bowl before the ingredients are chopped with an inverted water glass.

From where we sat I could look down the streets of the ravaged town. During the days of the coffee trade, wealthy merchants had built elegant houses in Al-Luhayyah. Ornately carved wooden balconies shaded by delicate latticework now hung precariously from the plastered facades. Sea gulls perched atop coral-block walls that leaned in all directions. Carved door- and windowframes that deserved to be in the National Museum in San'a lay discarded in piles of salty rubble that had once been walls. Revenue from subsistence fishing would never enable the inhabitants to rebuild the town, and the central government had more urgent concerns than restoring Al-Luhayyah as a historical landmark for sentimental reasons. The city contains unique examples of Turkish Red Sea architecture, but most buildings are beyond saving. The people have built newer and plainer houses to the north and east of the old city center.

After our meal, Gazem asked the pancake eaters if they knew anything about a shipwreck on Uqban Island ten years earlier. The men were from Al-Luhayyah but claimed to know nothing of the incident. I didn't believe them, because the glow of the lighthouse is visible from town. People would have noticed immediately if the nightly sweep of the searchlight had stopped, and I was determined to find someone who remembered or was willing to talk. Our plan was to wait until the fishing boats came in so that we could ask someone to take us to the island.

A dust storm blew through town. As window shutters banged in the distance, I pulled up the bottom of my T-shirt to cover my mouth and nose. Through squinting eyes I saw a phantom shape advancing down the street. Dressed in a swimming suit, the figure seemed to float above the ground, his feet and lower legs obscured by the billowing clouds of dust. The man was balancing an object that looked like a barbell across his shoulders, but as he drew near, my vision of a Yemeni weightlifter faded and I could see that he was carrying a long stick with hundreds of silvery, dust-laden fish clustered at either end. The man wore a skin-diving mask over his eyes and nose, which allowed him to move through the storm in relative comfort. Minutes later, when the storm abated, the apparition had vanished.

Gazem, Hussein, and I waited an hour before the small fishing boats known as *huri* appeared on the horizon. The noise of their outboard engines drifted across the glassy surface of the water. We met them at the beach, and in a characteristic display of quick thinking, Gazem at once asked a fisherman to take us to Uqban. There was ample time to go and return before sunset; it was only 10:30 A.M. As I stood in the ankle-deep water, worrying about permits from the police and whether the man's boat could make the twenty-mile journey across the open sea, Gazem busily finalized the rental of the boat. The negotiations took no more than five minutes. For $70 the man would take us. I accepted the fee without question, even though I knew that $70 would have bought the boat. This sum represented an entire month's profit for the fisherman, but the price didn't strike me as exorbitant. He was taking a risk. We were strangers, and I knew that what we wanted to do was prohibited. After waiting ten years for this opportunity, I wasn't about to jeopardize our departure by arguing over a few dollars. It was more important to leave before questions were asked. I bought several bottles of drinking water while Hussein located a shovel. Seating myself in the thirty-foot-long open boat, I realized it was identical to the boat that had taken the major, his soldiers, and me to Uqban Island ten years earlier.

Waiting for our departure, I was dumbfounded at the ease with which Gazem had arranged transport. No one had tried to stop us. My excitement began to grow as I imagined myself on the familiar shores of Uqban Island. How would it feel to return? In less than two hours we could be digging in the sand. Surely I would find something buried on the beach. I carried an old photograph of the camp to help locate the spot. Details from ten years earlier came to mind: walking on the beach at dawn, the scalloped seashell that Suzanne had found to hold our soap, black manta rays leaping out of a turquoise lagoon, and diving sea birds with green webbed feet. I saw myself sitting in the shade of a low coral cliff watching a blue-and-white sail approaching the island.

As the fisherman began to push the boat away from the shore, my reverie was interrupted by a sudden silence that fell over the waterfront of Al-Luhayyah. The fishermen and customers who had been haranging each other over the morning's catch had stopped talking. I looked up and noticed a man who was clearly neither a fisherman nor a shopper. Unshouldering his Kalashnikov, he waved us back to shore. There was nothing to do but return. The man asked Gazem where we were going.

"Oh, just out to have a look at the mudflats and mangrove trees," he said with remarkable coolness.

The plainclothes policeman was unconvinced by this explanation. We waded ashore and soon found ourselves at the home of the chief of police, who received us shirtless and barefoot, dressed in a pair of striped pajama bottoms. His fingers bore fresh inkstains from an antiquated black fountain pen he held in his hand. By coincidence, this man was a distant relative of Hussein, our driver. These two spoke amicably for five minutes, but there was nothing the chief of police could do to assist us without written permission from the National Security Office in San'a or Hodeida. My permit was valid for Al-Luhayyah and the nearby coast, but not the island. He politely asked us to leave town before sunset.

During the conversation in Arabic, I heard the name Arafat mentioned several times. It didn't take long to make the connection between Yasir Arafat, the leader of the PLO, and the Red Sea islands, and it finally dawned on me why the islands lay within a military security area. I could appreciate why the coast was so carefully guarded if a PLO camp existed on one of the islands. But for whatever reason, it was abundantly clear that no one could visit the islands except the fishermen, and even they were watched closely.

It was maddening to realize that if it had not been for the untimely arrival of the policeman on the beach, I would be halfway to Uqban. The debilitating climate merely added to my sense of failure, but I tried to conceal my feelings of frustration. I decided that while we were in Al-Luhayyah, it would be prudent to contact the sheik of the fishermen. When I asked for him, however, I was told he was sleeping, so we returned to the café to wait.

Soon a man walked into the café and sat in a nearby chair. Given the heat and humidity, he looked unusually cool. We nodded politely to one another.

"Why are you come here?" he asked in an engaging manner.

"Tourist," I replied, assuming that the man wanted to practice his English. I wasn't in the mood for a language lesson.

"No, why are you come here?" he repeated.

"I want to visit the islands."

"No, let me tell you — you are come to ask about the boat."

Hearing this, Gazem moved closer. I asked the man what boat he was referring to.

"I am Mr. Mansur Hassan. I know everything."

"Everything? All right, where is this boat?"

"On Al-Murk Island."

"Wrong island," I replied. "The boat I'm looking for was wrecked on Uqban Island."

"Yes, but she not stay on Uqban." He laughed.

According to Mr. Mansur Hassan, a large storm had lifted the boat off the beach of Uqban a year after the shipwreck. The wind and waves had carried it eastward to the southwest reef of Al-Murk Island. This explained why Nigel and I hadn't been able to locate the boat in the aerial photos: we had been looking at the wrong island.

"Al-Murk, this is where she lies. I see the boat last year. She is on her side on the coral."

People gathered in the café to listen to our conversation. I pulled a nautical chart out of my shoulder bag, spread it on the table, and located Al-Murk. It was exactly five miles from where we sat. Judging by the currents and the position of the numerous reefs and islands, it seemed unlikely that the boat could have drifted eastward; the prevailing winds from the north would have pushed it to the south. I wasn't altogether certain that Mr. Hassan and I were talking about the same boat, so I asked him to describe in detail the vessel he had seen. Borrowing my pen, he began to draw a rough sketch. More people crowded into the café, blocking the stinking breeze from the mudflats. I felt suffocated in the still air, yet a sense of keen anticipation filled the room. Mr. Hassan drew with an unsteady hand, but there could be no mistaking the features. The cabin layout, mast, and placement of the steering wheel convinced me that he had seen *Clea*. He correctly described the maroon sails, the shape of the anchors, the location of the engine, compass, batteries, and other valuable fittings.

". . . clothes, books, colored pictures . . . a toilet here, radios, ropes — so many beautiful things!"

"You know the boat well," I remarked.

"Yes, I know everything, and I tell you why I know everything. I took these things myself. I was the customs officer." We both started laughing. I was amused that a government employee would so proudly announce his part in the looting of a foreign ship.

Encouraged by his admission and my friendly response, the other men spoke up. Gazem translated.

"I took the flare gun!" one cried out jubilantly.

"I took the gas bottles!" exclaimed another. "And he, my friend there, took the cooking pots. We took everything!"

The café was soon in an uproar as more people came forward with their stories of plunder. I remembered the scene of pillage as men swarmed over the boat in 1978. They had been driven off with gunfire. Spontaneous laughter broke out. United by this distant episode, we somehow found the frank admissions of thievery amusing.

No one in the café knew how I had arrived on Uqban Island or what the sailboat was doing on the beach. One man thought we had been repairing the hull. The small crowd was equally mystified as to our reasons for leaving the boat unguarded. Why hadn't we put her back in the water? The beach dropped off into deep water, they told me. It would have been no problem to refloat the yacht.

I explained the shipwreck, but I didn't feel like trying to explain the nature of insurance claims. Instead, I asked for an artifact from the boat. I wanted a souvenir. I offered to pay. A scrap of sailcloth, a book — anything would do.

The men laughed at my ignorance. "The things we took are gone now," one of them told Gazem. Ten years is a long time on this coast. Nothing lasts in the salt air.

I was referred to as "the man who was lost at sea." Coming from people who knew what a storm could do to a small boat in these waters, I took this title as a sign of respect. Many of these men had friends who never returned after a bad storm. A young boy of about twelve described *Clea* as he had seen her ten months earlier: "She has been in the sea for so long, and now she is very tired."

Another boy soon arrived to tell us that the sheik of the fishermen was awake and would see us now. I said goodbye to the men in the café, whose excited discussions continued as Gazem, Hussein, and I walked to the north of town. Keeping to the patches of shade as much as possible, we soon entered a courtyard, where we found Sheik Ali Abbas and two other men reclining on tall cots in the shade of his house. In the center of the yard an arbor covered with leafless grapevines provided little protection from the sun. The sheik offered tea, then came right to the point. Once again Gazem translated.

"You have come to ask about the boat. I will tell you what happened. The men in town have told you a storm brought your boat to Al-Murk Island. Ha! That is not the truth. Along with men from Khawbah, they dug the boat out of the beach during the first high tide and towed it to Al-Murk. It was hard work, but on Al-Murk we could visit it daily to take the things we needed. These men here, they know the story." He gestured to his companions.

One of the men confirmed the claim that the boat was on Al-Murk. "It is on its side in this much water," he said, indicating a level just above his knees. "Everything has been taken. Water fills the inside. It is difficult to approach. We don't go near it anymore. The boat is finished."

As he continued, I caught the sound of a commotion on the nearby beach. We couldn't see a thing from within the courtyard, but I judged the angry voices to be coming from the smoking ovens, where people had been preparing fish as we arrived. Sheik Ali Abbas allowed the furious argument to escalate for twenty minutes before he excused himself. A big man of about sixty, he had a stomach that protruded over his belt, and he walked with a peculiar penguin-like gait.

Half an hour later he returned to his cot, wearing a tired expression that suggested that life in Al-Luhayyah no longer held any surprises. As the leader of this obscure fishing community, he had seen it all before. Two men had been arguing over the joint ownership of a fishing boat. There had been a knife fight — nothing unusual. They had slashed each other with their blades, but no one had been killed.

The sheik drew himself up on the cot once again and yawned. I could see that he was bored with my questions. To speed the conversation to a conclusion, he mentioned that the two men who were sitting beside him had recently returned from fishing all night. They were tired. In such heat, was it not better to sleep? The sailboat was wrecked, I did not have permission to visit the islands, and nothing of value was left on the boat. What more was there to discuss?

But I continued, sensing that this might be the closest I would ever get to recovering my journals. I asked how the fishermen had discovered *Clea*. As I suspected, many people had noticed that the lighthouse was not working. Cautious by nature, the fishermen had waited to see what would happen next. One night the two men now sitting with the sheik were fishing near Al-Bodi, one of the outer islands near Uqban. They were perplexed when they saw colored flares in the sky, but they continued fishing. The men had no explanation for these lights, and not until several evenings later did they decide to investigate. They approached the southeast corner of Uqban sometime after midnight. I realized this must have been the night Georgik and Suzanne heard voices and saw sparkling lights on the water. A third man went ashore before dawn to have a look. Georgik and Suzanne had not imagined the voices. We had been watched.

"The man saw five people, two women and three men," Gazem explained with renewed interest. "He knew about your journeys to the lighthouse and the location of your camp, but he couldn't understand why your boat was on the beach. Soon other fishermen in the area came to know of the white people on the island. The fishermen waited and watched. When you left the island with the black men and their goats, they brought a large motorized dhow to the island and began removing things from the sailboat. They believed this boat was a gift from Allah. They worked through the night, loosening bolts on the engine, removing tools, and filling bags with the most valuable items. By dawn they were busy at the camp. They worked quickly, knowing the white people would soon return."

I asked if either of the two men had been at the sailboat when Georgik, Robert, and I had arrived with the soldiers later that morning.

"*Aywa!*" (Yes!) exclaimed one man. "The soldiers, they shot at us. The bullets passed overhead like this." He made a ducking motion. "We grabbed everything we could carry, but too much was left behind. We knew it was the end, so we ran. When the soldiers left we returned, but they had taken the best things."

Gazem told the men that I had been with the soldiers that

morning and had pleaded with them not to shoot anyone. On hearing this, one of the fishermen came over to where I was seated and shook my hand vigorously. I was equally delighted to meet him. Ten years earlier we had stood at the opposite ends of a desolate beach on Uqban Island. At that time he had been nothing more than one of many little black dots swarming over the yacht. We spoke for another half-hour about our different versions of what happened on the beach that morning, but the sun was already on the horizon. Unless we left soon, we wouldn't arrive in San'a before midnight.

In an unexpected flush of blind optimism, I envisioned myself returning to Al-Luhayyah within a week, two weeks at the most. I asked Sheik Ali Abbas if he could write a short letter to the National Security Police to confirm that *Clea* was now on Al-Murk Island. He refused to write the note and became irritated when pressed for an explanation. My persistence seemed to make him uncomfortable. Maybe he thought I was trying to seek compensation for the loss of the sailboat; that would have been the Yemeni way.

Gazem asked if we would be able to hire one of the fishing boats when we returned.

"*Inshallah*" (God willing), the sheik replied vaguely. He turned to engage the two fishermen in conversation, and we ceased to exist. We drove out of Al-Luhayyah just before sunset.

11

Dessert in the Desert

I AWOKE AT five the next morning after the long drive back to San'a. My eyes were closed, but through my bedroom window at the institute I heard the crunching sound of heavy-soled boots. The sound grew louder. Soldiers were running in step for morning exercise. They counted cadence in Arabic. One man sang out short plaintive cries, a pause followed, then a moving refrain thundered back from the ranks of young men. The voices were proud as well as powerfully evocative. From beneath my blanket I imagined a line of turbaned warriors with arms interlocked, at the edge of a dying fire, performing a dance at dawn before going into battle. The essence of Yemeni manliness, pride, and self-esteem was clearly conveyed as the soldiers passed by. The tramping sounds and voices gradually grew indistinct as they moved down the roadway. I fell back into my dreams and awoke two hours later.

The telephone was ringing. A man from Hodeida wanted to talk to me. I didn't know anyone in Hodeida. The caller introduced himself as Abdallah Kareem. Roughly translated, the man's name meant "the slave of God will provide." He announced that he could help me get clearance from the National Security Police to return to Uqban. When I asked how he knew my phone number, he ignored my question. It made me feel uneasy that a stranger knew of my plans. I asked who he worked for.

"I work for no one . . . and I work for everyone," he replied simply.

I understood his position immediately. He was a fixer, one of those shadowy figures who are indispensable in places like Yemen. Their sole mission in life is to facilitate unusual or nearly impossible projects. Ideally, they collect from all parties involved. I was pleased the Slave of God had called.

Abdallah Kareem questioned me closely regarding the events of 1978. He wanted to know the name of the sailboat, the dates, and particularly the names of any Yemeni soldiers I had met on Kamaran Island. I had the information with me. He asked if I would be at the same number later in the day. He would make some phone calls. When he called back at 5 P.M., he told me enough about the chronology of the shipwreck and details of my stay on Kamaran Island to convince me he was well connected with either the army or National Security.

"The boat is well known. We may have no computers here, but we remember these incidents very well," he said with a laugh. I wondered who he meant when he referred to "we." I asked about permission to return to the island.

"There is no problem, but it will take time," Abdallah cautioned me. I took this opportunity to let him know that I was agreeable to compensating him for his services, if that would help speed up the process.

"But of course!" he replied. He told me that he would call again when he had news. I waited for several days. During that time nothing happened, or, more precisely, none of the expected happened. We spoke on the phone frequently. First Abdallah's contact in the National Security Office was out of town, for unknown reasons. Then he was unavailable, owing to a student demonstration that had turned nasty in Ta'izz. As a result of a young woman's being insulted while collecting water, eight soldiers were to be executed. "It is a bother," Abdallah said, in a moment of supreme understatement. Then the Iraqi prime minister visited San'a. Security had to be arranged; an armed convoy of fifty vehicles was needed to escort him to and from the airport. My relatively trivial request was set aside.

I understood the unimportance of my plans, but my visa was valid for only thirty days. I was near the end of my fourth week in Yemen, and I wasn't confident I could get an extension. I soon grew anxious, then suspicious. How long could it take to get clearance? Another month? A year? A lifetime? I felt I was wasting my time. All I had to go on was Abdallah's voice over the phone, continuing to remind me that there were no problems. Lack of time is not considered a problem in Yemen.

One day I would be told "Everything is fine," the next day "It is not possible." Then it was merely a question of getting a letter. From the tone of his voice, I could tell the Slave of God was relishing the uncertainty. *Mumkin* (maybe) and *bukra* (tomorrow) were two expressions I got to know well. More days passed, but the letter did not materialize. I pressed Abdallah, but his standard reply was always "There is no problem . . . we have approval. You must be patient. Everything is being arranged."

I considered trying a different approach, but nothing came to mind. I soon had a new name for the voice on the telephone: Mr. Mafeesh Mushkilah, Arabic for "no problem." I wondered if he was simply incompetent, or perhaps an employee of National Security with instructions to block my plans with a variety of delays. By calling me frequently, he could keep me in one place. Although I had come to realize that Uqban Island was situated in a military security area, if the secret police wanted me out of the country, they would have simply picked me up and taken me to the airport. Perhaps I was being watched. One thing had become abundantly clear — the Slave of God was not providing me with anything tangible.

I decided to leave town for a day in order to relax and rethink my plans. Gazem would arrange a car and driver. I was interested in visiting two important archeological sites to the east of San'a, where the mountains meet the desert. Both destinations, Barakesh and Marib, are at the edge of the Rub'al-Khali desert,

the Empty Quarter. I also wanted to visit the ruins of two Sabaean temples in the same area. One, Mahram Bilqis, was dedi-
cated to the moon god Ilmuqah. The other, smaller ruin, consisting of five and a half closely spaced limestone pillars, is primarily
noted for the daring village boys who climb the thirty-foot pillars
and then slide down between them at great speed, using their
bare feet and backs to brake themselves.

These and other sites to the north and south were built along
the ancient trade route once linking Dhofar, in Oman, with Petra
and Alexandria. Camel caravans loaded with frankincense,
myrrh, spices, exotic animals, gold, silk fabric, and precious
stones had plodded this trail until a sea route joining the Medi-
terranean with the Far East was discovered in the first century
A.D. At that time the inland trade route began its long decline, as
the coastal cities grew in importance.

Gazem and I jostled each other as we dozed on the front seat
of the Land Cruiser next to Ali Mohammed, our driver. To avoid
the heat, we had left San'a before daylight, driving east toward
the Rub'al-Khali. I woke up during the long winding descent
to the desert floor. Searching for a notebook in my shoulder bag,
I came across a packet of astronaut ice cream. The blue-black-
and-silver label displayed a spaceman floating above the surface
of the moon. I knew I was carrying this freeze-dried version of
Neopolitan ice cream to the edge of the great desert in the middle
of the summer for a reason.

Unexpected gifts often accompany imminent departures to
far-off places. Minutes before I stepped onto my first plane flight,
from San Francisco to New York in 1968, a bystander in the departure lounge handed me a large watermelon. I took it on board
and carried it with me for two days before dropping it down a
light well from my room on the fifteenth floor of the Roosevelt
Hotel on East 45th Street. I still remember the forbidden thrill of
watching the green shape growing smaller and smaller until there
was nothing. Nothing, that is, apart from the surprisingly loud
report of a watermelon exploding at the bottom of a concrete
airshaft.

I have since found myself in possession of similar gifts, but undoubtedly the most unusual of these keepsakes was a gopher on a leash that was handed to me as I was setting off on a donkey journey near Band-i-Amir lakes in central Afghanistan in 1971. It was my prize for winning a two-hundred-yard, barefoot race against an Uzbeki potato farmer. I had told him that his donkey wasn't strong enough to carry me and that my legs were stronger than his donkey's.

"We'll see who has the strong legs," the farmer challenged me, hiking up his pant legs.

We ran two lengths of his freshly plowed field for the prize. Following the race, a great deal of money changed hands in the local teashop. But beyond the intrinsic value of the gopher, I appreciated the rodent on a deeper level. It was presented by the farmer as a gesture of friendship, a genuine souvenir to connect me with a person and a place in time.

In a similar spirit, the astronaut ice cream was given to me as a going-away present by a friend in California. It was an appropriate gift, lightweight as well as practical. Freeze-dried ice cream in the desert? I intended to enjoy it under adverse conditions. I would wait until I was overwhelmed by heat and the frustrations of travel. At that moment I would tear open the foil packet, eat the ice cream, and think of home.

Light was just coming into the eastern sky as the road straightened out, and I put the packet of ice cream back into my bag. Gazem was awake. Looking out the windshield, toward the north, he remembered a recent episode. Lighting a cigarette, he told me the story of the American oil worker who found a suitcase bomb in Wadi Jauf. "A pair of smoldering ankles protruding from his boot tops . . ." Gazem reminisced. "I hear that is all they found of the poor man. A terrible mistake. He had just arrived in the country. It happened to the north, not far from here."

Apparently the oil worker and his Yemeni driver had stopped on a remote road to investigate a suitcase sitting on top of a mattress. A suitcase at the side of the road? What could it mean? The two men discovered the secret minutes later. The resulting explosion was so powerful that investigators first thought the car had run over a land mine. Others suggested that a rocket-propelled grenade had hit it. But the explosion was too big for a grenade. When they examined the bodies, the car, the road, and the blast fragments more closely, the investigators finally decided that a bomb concealed in a suitcase had exploded inside the vehicle. Reconstructing the sequence of events, the American embassy officials came to the conclusion that the men had picked up the suitcase, brought it back to the car, and placed it on the passenger seat. The oil man had then clicked open the latches and lifted the lid. The driver must have been standing behind the oil worker, because most of his body was found.

According to Gazem, the suitcase had been left by one tribal group for another. There had been a dispute over water rights. Who could have guessed that two innocent strangers would come upon the trap in such an unlikely place?

As I listened to the story, I realized that I would have responded in exactly the same way. Curiosity would have compelled me to look in the suitcase.

Gazem finished his tale as we arrived in Barakesh. For nearly an hour we had followed an indistinct desert track. Stepping from the cab, I noticed that Gazem's eyelashes, hair, and shoulders were laden with fine dust.

Barakesh is considered to be the best-preserved ancient city in Yemen. Although it lies in ruins, visits are sometimes difficult, because two nearby villages claim jurisdiction over the site. To avoid violent conflict, the villages take turns extorting what they can from visitors on alternate days. It was still early, and we found ourselves completely alone. The ruined city is enclosed by a bastioned wall laid out in an ovoid shape, roughly three hundred yards long by two hundred yards wide. Constructed of smooth blocks of a beautiful calcite stone with chiseled margins, the wall reached a height of twenty-five feet. I poked around the slope of rubble at its foot; the site had never been excavated, and the temptation to pick through the debris was great. This fortified city had been inhabited for more than 1500 years.

I examined dozens of pottery shards decorated with a border of reddish brown ibex horns. Segments of brightly colored glass bangles were plainly visible on the surface of the ground where rainwater had cut shallow courses into the rubble. Climbing through a breach in the perimeter, I gazed across a city that looked like a complex sandcastle melted by gentle waves. Running my hand over one of the remaining walls, I decided that the mortar between the bricks might be a good place to look for older fragments. I reasoned that the mortar would have been prepared from nearby soil that considerably predated the walls. It was also more prone to erosion than the bricks, so that hard, imbedded objects would be easier to see. I was correct in my assumptions. Within twenty minutes I had eased the edge of a carved stone cup from between two bricks. Judging from the curve of the rim and the interior profile, I estimated the cup to be three and a half inches in diameter and two inches deep. The exterior surface was lined with a finely worked, fluted pattern. I put the fragment in my pocket.

I didn't have much time to enjoy my find or the beauty of Barakesh. As I walked back to the Land Cruiser for water, I heard a distant sound similar to popcorn striking the inside of a glass pot lid. Thirty yards from where I stood, the sand danced in little puffs. I failed to make the connection between the distant sound and the plumes of dust on the ground. There were also strange little *futt . . . futt . . . futt* noises, which corresponded with the puffs of sand. Each puff seemed to have an accompanying *futt*. I remembered old war movies on television, especially the parts where machine-gun fire strafed the beach. Suddenly I understood the relationship between the popcorn and the little flicks of sand. I was being shot at.

"Get down!" Gazem called out. Both he and Ali Mohammed had instinctively fallen to the ground the moment they heard the sound. Performing a crude imitation of Superman losing altitude rapidly, I knocked the wind out of myself. The popping sound subsided. We waited. When I looked up, a lone figure was striding briskly toward us. There wasn't much we could do, so we

stood up without dusting ourselves off and watched as the tribesman closed in on us.

"Just relax," Gazem told me quietly.

The tribesman turned out to be the ticket collector for the day.
It was Friday, the Moslem holy day. The man was irritated that
we had arrived so early. He wanted to know why Gazem and Ali
Mohammed were not at the mosque. Was it not a time to worship? And who had given us permission to visit? Where were the
permits? What, no permits? All right then, how about the
money? The man's interest shifted smoothly from religious to
commercial matters.

"He thinks we were planning to leave without paying," Gazem
told me. The tribesman was perfectly correct in this assumption,
but Gazem expressed surprise at the suggestion. A few uncertain
minutes passed, and then a cloud of dust miraculously appeared
on the horizon. The cloud grew into a vehicle, a long-wheelbase
Toyota Land Cruiser. More tribesmen? I wondered. What if this
man was collecting fees out of turn? The resulting confrontation
could be bloody. I fingered the cup fragment in my pocket and
directed my thoughts to distant places.

The vehicle came to a halt, and five corpulent German-speak-
ing men disgorged themselves onto the hot earth. Draped with
telephoto lenses and videocameras, they were completely oblivious to the situation. They began taking pictures — pictures of
the desert, the walls of Barakesh, each other, and finally, the
tribesman. I wondered what it would be like to see a man cut in
half by machine-gun fire. Gazem fell quiet as the tribesman, momentarily confused by the newcomers' fearless behavior, was
confronted by a portly man dressed in shorts, T-shirt, and a silly
light blue terry-cloth hat. I don't know what he was trying to say,
and I wasn't interested in finding out. Gazem caught my eye and
motioned toward our car, and we moved away from the group.
The tribesman had taken hold of one of the cameras, and there
were shouts of protest. As we climbed into the front seat and
eased the door shut, I heard one of the men shouting, *Das ist
meine kamera, du schweinhund!* We didn't wait for the reply.

Ali Mohammed started the engine and we moved off slowly. The scene was lost in our dust trail. I was relieved not to hear the sound of gunfire.

"Well, now!" Gazem exclaimed with a short laugh. "Let's go see the ruins at Marib."

Gazem and I made the standard tour of the Marib area. After he showed me the sluice gates of the great dam that had been built across Wadi Adhanah in the eighth century B.C., we examined a field of stones bearing Sabaean and Himyaritic inscriptions, nudged pottery shards with our feet, and then lost all interest in walking around in the midday heat. We drove on in search of the temple ruins at the edge of the Empty Quarter.

Sweat and dust were smeared over our faces and necks as we bounded across the desert. The stone pillars of Mahram Bilqis, our destination, soon appeared in the distance. The place is also known as the Temple of Refuge, a title that fit in perfectly with our plans. It was much too hot to go in search of the elliptical foundations in the surrounding sand dunes, so Gazem and I flopped down in the shade of eight magnificent limestone pillars to take refuge from the sun.

Shifting desert sands had long since reclaimed the ruins. The temple had been built for the worship of Ilmuqah, the moon god, a male diety regarded as the divine lover, affectionate and merciful. To the Bedouin, the moon is the giver of life and refreshes and guides men on their night journeys. Looking at the ruins protruding from the dunes, I remembered the moon depicted on the label of the astronaut ice cream. I felt for the packet in my bag; it was there. Ali Mohammed had fallen into a stupor in the front seat of the car. My shirt was saturated with perspiration, and a dusty paste clung to every exposed bit of damp skin. The moment had arrived. I ripped open the foil packet, snapped off two bits of freeze-dried ice cream, and handed one to Gazem. We ate in silence, absorbed by our own thoughts.

A thin line of men and their camels moved on the horizon. Their dark shapes quivered in the heat.

"Those people are as hard as rocks," Gazem muttered.

The Styrofoam-textured dessert crunched between our teeth, and the flavors of chocolate, vanilla, and strawberry mingled in my mouth. The ice cream was pretty good. I handed another piece to Gazem. A bead of sweat rolled down my face as I read the list of ingredients. The corn sweeteners, mono- and diglycerides, polysorbate 80, and artificial colors and flavors reminded me of home.

12

The School Project

WAITING FOR the Slave of God to look into travel possibilities with the National Security Police, I spent hours in the San'a teahouses with Gazem, following local gossip. It seemed perfectly reasonable that while I waited to collect my old stories, I should keep pace with the current ones. I became absorbed with the time-honored Yemeni tradition of taking hostages in order to bring attention to important grievances.

One morning, while taking tea with Gazem just outside the gates of Bab al-Yemen, I heard about the ordeal of the people of Al-Harum, an isolated village in Wadi Dahab near the Rub'al-Khali. In exchange for allowing the Hunt Oil pipeline to be constructed through their land, the government had offered to build a school. The pipeline contractor, Consolidated Contractors Corporation (CCC), promised to install an irrigation pump. Neither of these promises had been kept. During the construction of the pipeline, three young men from the village had been killed accidentally when their car collided with a truck owned by a Korean construction company. The company agreed to pay 180,000 riyals to each of the three families, bringing the total compensation paid to nearly $54,000. It paid the money to the Islamic Court, but because of unforeseen delays the funds had not yet reached the families of the dead men. There was no school, and now the people were being run down by construction vehicles. The villagers lost their patience.

In November 1987 the men of Al-Harum took their first hostage, a Lebanese employed by CCC. The hostage, as it turned out, was quite happy to sit around. He continued to earn his salary although he wasn't working, and he found the village relaxing compared to his neighborhood in West Beirut. During his two-week stay in Al-Harum he ate well, slept for most of the day, and spent the afternoons leering at the young women. What made the situation intolerable to the villagers was the fact that no one came to negotiate for the release of this freeloader. He proved useless as a hostage. The government would never build a school in exchange for this man, so they let him go.

In a second ransom attempt two months later, the same group of tribesmen captured the oil man Norman Whittle. I had not forgotten Billy's account of Stormin' Norman, and by good luck I later met Norman's girlfriend, Donna, who lived in the old city of San'a. At breakfast one morning she told me what had happened. It had all started with a phone call six months earlier. Donna had been expecting Norman after work when the phone rang. It was Hunt Oil. Norman would not be home for dinner. "He's been taken hostage," the voice said flatly.

Donna explained that she hadn't been surprised. She hung up the phone and returned to the kitchen to turn off the burner under the curried chicken. Taking a bottle of beer from the fridge, she sat down to think. She considered the possibilities, then let her mind go blank. Anything could happen, but she had been in Yemen long enough to know the value of patience. There was little point in either worrying or hoping.

As Donna was opening another bottle of beer, Norman was running through the night. He loped across broken ground, completely lost. In his spare time he ran for exercise, but this was his first opportunity to run for his life. Somewhere behind him in the darkness, armed tribesmen were looking for him. His captors should have taken his running shoes along with his car keys, because Norman wasted no time escaping. He simply ran over the nearest hill and disappeared from sight. A Yemeni tribesman carrying a twelve-pound Kalashnikov and wearing leather boots without laces cannot run nearly as fast as a frightened Welshman dressed in a T-shirt and cut-off blue jeans. Norman quickly outpaced his pursuers. By the time the moon was up, he had covered nearly twenty kilometers through totally unfamiliar territory.

When lights appeared in the far distance, Norman followed them until he came to a cluster of stone buildings. Dogs barked in the crisp night air as dark figures took him to a small room, where he explained his escape. He spoke little Arabic, but the villagers understood his story well enough. Congratulating him on his heroic run, they apologized for not being able to take him to the main road until the next day. Meanwhile, they offered their hospitality, and the simple dinner soon lulled Norman into a pleasant night's sleep. Before drifting off, he heard the men laughing quietly. Not until the following morning did he understand the joke.

As he slept, one of the men drove the rounds of the neighboring villages to see if anyone was missing a hostage. Norman had run to a different settlement, but unfortunately, the people in the area were all from the same tribe. When he awoke, his original captors were ready to take him back.

Returning to Al-Harum, Norman fell sullen and became uncooperative. Instead of taking tea with the people, he practiced his Arabic curses. Later in the day, on an impulse, he threw his walkie-talkie through the window of his Land Cruiser. Then he ate an orange and a can of jalapeño peppers from the ice chest in his truck, continuing to sulk. By early afternoon he had begun to bellow and scream. When this produced no response, he took off his shirt and ran around bare-chested. The villagers were bewildered by this totally uncharacteristic behavior. Never before had the tribesman taken a hostage who ran around half naked in front of their women. What sort of man had they brought into their village?

On the third morning of the villagers' ordeal, a Land Cruiser full of tribesmen arrived from nearby Wadi Jauf. Word had reached them that "their man Norman" had been taken. Norman worked in their territory and was therefore under their jurisdiction. The new arrivals argued that if anyone was going to take him hostage, they would. The men of Al-Harum began to regret their choice of hostage. Before settling matters with the government, they would have to negotiate with their neighbors over the right to hold Norman. A settlement was reached, and the men from Wadi Jauf withdrew.

Norman added to his captors' discomfort by refusing to accept their hospitality. The refusal to take food in Yemen, as in other Arabic and Asian countries, can mean one of only three things: that the guest feels the host cannot afford to provide food, which shames him; that the food is unclean or not well prepared; or that the guest has such a hatred for the host that he does not wish to diminish that hatred by sharing food. To refuse hospitality can be a serious matter.

The men tried to explain that they had nothing personal against Norman but were merely using him to open a dialogue with the government. They wanted a school for their children, and they knew of no other effective way to stimulate a serious discussion. However, their explanations fell on deaf ears; Norman continued to refuse to eat their food.

The man who had been assigned as Norman's host finally could take it no longer. Making the ultimate gesture of trust and friendship, he sent his lovely unmarried fourteen-year-old daughter to serve the strange white man his breakfast. The girl was unveiled and alone when she laid out the tray of food. She poured coffee and allowed Norman to look at her face, in order to show him that he was considered one of the family. She tried her best, but Norman remained unmoved. The family was distraught.

Norman continued to scream and make a nuisance of himself. I suspect that a Yemeni man behaving in this way would have been bound and gagged or simply knocked unconscious with a rifle butt. The villagers locked Norman in a stone tower, but he made such a commotion that they were soon forced to let him out again. He walked around freely, with confused men with rifles following him everywhere. The sight of a yelling, half-naked white man was too much for their sense of decency, however, and that night the men talked. They decided that Norman had to go. He was a nuisance they could well do without. He had violated every known rule of hostage etiquette. They decided to throw him out of the village the following day. The school project could wait.

Sensing that the end was near, Norman softened. He couldn't have been proud of his behavior, and perhaps to show the tribesmen he bore them no ill feelings, he sang English rugby songs, including "The Hole in the Elephant's Bottom," for their entertainment. Norman sang loudly and off key, and one can only imagine the effect his singing had on such people. It was just as well the assembled tribesmen and their families could not understand the raunchy lyrics. If they had, the songs might have cost the Welshman his life.

On the morning of the fourth day Norman found himself standing alone on the main road between Marib and San'a. The kidnappers, driving his Land Cruiser, retreated to the safety of their hills, and a passing truck brought Norman back to San'a, where Donna was still waiting.

The villagers had not had much luck, but according to Gazem that was not quite the end of their story. After their run-in with Norman, months passed before the men of Al-Harum felt confident enough to make a third attempt to get the school built. On the morning of April 20, 1988, Gazem was traveling the back road to Marib with Hussein, a tribesman from the north. Neither of them was armed. In the back, seated on either side of an ice chest filled with soft drinks and bottled water, were two BBC filmmakers on their first visit to the country. They were conducting a survey of the ancient cities along the frankincense route in preparation for a documentary film, and they spoke no Arabic. Rounding a corner on a mountain track, the four men encountered a row of oil drums and two parked trucks blocking the road. Armed men surrounded the car, and Gazem, Hussein, and the two filmmakers were taken hostage.

It was the second day of Ramadan, the month of fasting. During Ramadan it is not permitted to eat or drink or have sex during the daylight hours. People usually remain quiet throughout the day in order to conserve energy. By staying up late at night, they can sleep longer during the day. For this reason, at two o'clock the following morning the tribesmen were busy making tea and food. Hussein took this opportunity to escape by walking into the darkness and disappearing. There was a brief search, but the villagers returned without him.

Nothing much happened that afternoon. The captors didn't seem particularly unstable or murderous, a fact much appreciated by the two Englishmen, and an uneasy calm settled over the village. People moved about as little as possible, waiting for nightfall and the breaking of the fast. The following morning Gazem awoke to the sounds of birds at dawn. In the still air he also heard the far-off sound of helicopter blades beating the air. The *thump, thump, thump* of the big rotor carried across the barren hills. Something would happen that day. Hussein had found help.

The night of his escape, Hussein had walked for two hours until he arrived at a road. Not long after that a car approached. He explained to the driver that his own vehicle had broken down and he needed to go to Marib to buy new parts. The driver had not yet learned of the hostages, so when Hussein handed him 50 riyals, he took him to the main road. After arriving in Marib at dawn, Hussein contacted the army commandant, who was not only from his own tribe but a distant relative as well. Late in the afternoon two tanks, three Toyotas with fifty-caliber machine guns mounted in the back, and forty soldiers took up battle positions five hundred yards from the village. While the soldiers waited for the helicopter to arrive, the villagers prepared themselves for an attack.

At the sound of the helicopter, the guards turned to Gazem and told him quite simply that if the army fired on the village, they would kill him and the two white men. Gazem didn't bother translating these comments for the filmmakers. The helicopter landed some distance away. A man stepped out, and the helicopter left. The man walked into the village unarmed; he had been sent from San'a to negotiate with the tribesmen.

For the next five hours issues were discussed, and the outcome was fair to both sides. In return for the release of the hostages, the government would arrange payment of the 540,000 riyals for the deaths of the three young men. As for the school, the government promised to reconsider. It had gone back on its original offer because there weren't enough school-age children to justify the expense. The students had been directed to a regional school in a distant village, but this arrangement was not acceptable to the parents, who wanted to be with their children. The people of Al-Harum could keep the stolen vehicles, but on the condition they would not take any more hostages. The dispute over the irrigation pump would have to be addressed through the CCC representative in San'a. To assist, the government would pressure the company to make good its offer. Finally, the villagers would allow the BBC to return later in the year to film the archeological sights along the frankincense trail.

The government and the villagers stood by their promises. As Gazem and the two filmmakers prepared to leave Al-Harum, the tribesmen lined up along the road, apologized for any inconvenience, and then waved goodbye like a group of excited schoolchildren brandishing automatic weapons.

A political analyst at the U.S. Information Service in San'a found the settlement encouraging. The conflict had been resolved fairly, but more important, the tribal people had acknowledged the fact that the government might actually have something they wanted. It was possible that they were beginning to equate the central government with social services such as schools, medical clinics, and agricultural assistance. This represented a quantum leap in understanding for the fiercely independent tribes, whose combined private armies might still be capable of overwhelming the government forces. For generations the Yemeni and Saudi Arabian governments have endeavored to buy tribal loyalty. In a display of impartiality, the tribes, renowned for their ideological unreliability, have accepted payments from both governments and then done exactly as they have seen fit. The tribes along the border between Saudi Arabia and Yemen lack neither money nor weapons. The Saudis nurture unrest in the area, partly pending future oil discoveries, but primarily to maintain a weak government on their southern flank.

The political analyst cautioned that although a settlement had been reached, it was unlikely that the concept of taxes in exchange for government services would be embraced during this generation . . . or the next.

The people of Al-Harum were only partially satisfied, but they were willing to try the new style of negotiation. An armed delegation from the village would travel to San'a to encourage the government to build a school for their children. If this didn't work, they could always go back to taking hostages.

13

One Mind,
One Heart

GLANCING AWAY from the pandemonium that engulfed the official's desk, I noticed a dusty ivy vine suspended on a string. The vine had crept in one window, climbed the wall, crossed the entire length of the room on the overhead string, and then left the room through a different window. I was waiting my turn to apply for a visa extension. It was the end of my fourth week in Yemen.

White paint flaked from the ceiling, littering a beige carpet that bore the burn marks of thousands of cigarette butts toed out by anxious men. Chrome chairs upholstered in green velvet lined one wall, yet all of the thirty-odd visitors to the office were on their feet, with the exception of myself and whoever was seated behind the desk. I couldn't see the man because he was obscured by the pack of sweating applicants, who brandished dozens of passports in their fingers like fans of oversized playing cards. Each man specialized in a different nationality. One held only Egyptian passports, another Somali, and a third Pakistani. These men were practiced in the art of securing visa extensions to help foreign workers remain in the country. They also obtained exit visas that allowed Yemenis to find work overseas. The Korean, Chinese, Russian, British, French, American, German, Swiss,

Dutch, Italian, and Japanese passports waving about in the hot morning air revealed the complexity of foreign aid to Yemen.

One man opened his briefcase on the chair next to me. Inside I could see a jambia, a clip-on necktie, a bundle of qat, more passports, prayer beads, cigarettes, a Koran, a car license plate, a pair of rubber bathroom slippers, and a spray bottle of cologne. He seemed well prepared for a variety of situations.

The man behind the desk barked orders, and the tide of passport men surged forward and backward according to his commands. I could hear passports being slapped on the desktop. The official's voice ranged from a confidential murmur to terrific shouts of "Mahmoud!" at which point a stoop-shouldered assistant would shuffle into the room to carry out some thankless task. Desk telephones rang simultaneously, but the calls were left unanswered. I felt no need to push my way toward the official, as I had not yet prepared my reasons for a visa extension. I was officially allowed a one-month visit. It was my twenty-eighth day in the country, and I was feeling justifiably nervous about my status. I could fly across the Red Sea to Djibouti to renew my visa, but I preferred to avoid the extra expense of airfares and a hotel. More significant, if I left the country, there was no guarantee of being allowed re-entry.

Two young men entered the office. Their white skin was sunburned, and a two-day growth of whiskers darkened their cheeks. They wore rumpled cotton pants fastened at the waist with drawstrings, and the sleeves of their faded T-shirts were cut away, revealing tufts of underarm hair. Assuming Western privilege, they approached the crowd of men surrounding the desk. As the men parted, I caught my first glimpse of the seated official. He was a heavyset man. One side of his collar was turned up, and his necktie had been fastened in obvious haste. His huge stomach kept him some distance from the desk, and I noticed that one of his shirt buttons was undone. But despite these signs of slovenliness, I became aware of his clear and watchful eyes. In a gesture of exaggerated helpfulness, he held out his arms to the young men, with palms upturned, and cocked his head slightly to one side.

"And how may I help you?" he asked in English.

The men, who held Austrian passports, asked for an exit and re-entry visa that would allow them to bicycle to Aden, then the capital of South Yemen. Even I knew their request was as absurd as trying to obtain a re-entry visa to Israel for a round-trip journey between Tel Aviv and Amman. In 1988, the most common way for foreigners to go to Aden from North Yemen was via Djibouti.

Until quite recently relations between North and South Yemen were cordial but complicated because of their dependency on aid from countries with opposing interests. North Yemen, backed by the United States and Saudi Arabia, practiced free enterprise, while the economics and politics of South Yemen were influenced by the Soviet Union. The Yemens shared an acute need for money, but until the USSR left South Yemen or the recently discovered oil reserves near the Yemens' common border allowed for economic independence, national reconciliation seemed a remote possibility.

On May 22, 1990, North and South Yemen reunited to become the Yemen Republic. But this was of little help to the Austrian cyclists in the summer of 1988, and I wondered whether it was arrogance or stupidity that provoked them to announce their plan.

"You will not go to Aden," the official told them coolly.

"But we know that it is possible to go," they said, trying to convince him. "We must get the permits here."

"I will assure you, it is not possible," the official said in a louder voice.

"You don't understand —" one of the cyclists began. He was immediately cut off by the man behind the desk.

"No, my friend, it is you that does not understand. This is my office, and I am telling you that you cannot go to Aden."

"But we must go to Aden. We have bicycled all the way from Austria. It has taken us eight months to get this far. We have made our plans," they explained, using their best Western logic.

"You can go to hell, but you will not go to Aden!" the official bellowed at them. He pronounced *hell* like *hail,* and the Austri-

ans misunderstood his comment. They thought he was referring to an alternate destination in South Yemen.

"Where can we go?" one of them asked hopefully. His friend looked for the town on a map.

"To *hell* — you can go to hell! Do you understand *hell? Mahmoud! Mahmoud!*" The man was in a rage. The ignorance of these two white barbarians infuriated him. Specks of saliva flew from his mouth.

The Austrians were befuddled by the display of anger. They had cycled so far, and now this — a crazy man in the visa office. Their expressions of helplessness as they were ushered from the room were unforgettable. I never saw them again or learned of their fate. When I looked back at the desk, the official was staring at me.

"And you! Where do you want to go?" he demanded.

"Not to Aden," I replied.

The man sat back and smiled, obviously pleased with my answer. He broke out laughing. No one else in the room uttered a word. He invited me to sit in a chair near his desk. "Mahmoud! Mahmoud!" he yelled, and two cups of tea were soon brought. Abdullah Saleh el-Jeradi introduced himself and then asked why I had come to Yemen. I told him about the journals.

"Ah, so you are pursuing your dreams," he said. "And where do we find the answers to our dreams? We find them where the earth touches the sky — on the horizon. It is always so. You are chasing a mirage, but never mind, you will come to eat lunch with me."

He concluded the morning's work by dismissing everyone in the room with a wave of his arm. No one protested. Turning to me, he muttered, "One mind, one heart, one feeling . . . how can there be two?" I wasn't sure I followed his thoughts, but I nodded as if I did, hoping the meaning would come clear later. It seemed prudent to give the impression that we had established some sort of understanding. As we left the office for lunch, he added my passport to the dozens of others already bulging from his coat pockets.

Saleh el-Jeradi seemed to relish my company and acted as if we had met through mutual friends. He told me that he had once visited Washington, D.C., as part of a training program to study immigration surveillance procedures. His brother had lived in the United States for more than twenty years. One day during his training Saleh decided to type his brother's name into one of the terminals to see what he could find. The amount of information that appeared on the screen astonished him. Everything was there — especially the personal details of his brother's life, obscure facts that Saleh was unaware of. The report impressed him greatly, and the computerized information system provided him with his most lasting impressions of the United States (memories of public liquor stores and the Grand Canyon had faded with time). "Seeing is believing," he told me, using one of his most frequent expressions.

As the days passed, I wondered what had happened to my passport and visa application. Saleh seemed to be too busy entertaining me to take my concerns seriously. The afternoon after we met, he took me to a Yemeni wedding. At the lunch I found myself seated with five hundred men from the Hashid tribe, who had gathered in the dining room of an old summer residence of Imam Yahya. Yemenis eat quickly, and soon the long tabletops were ravaged as a result of the feasting. There were the usual joints of stewed mutton and a fatty soup of bone marrow and goat vertebrae. Terra-cotta pots bubbled with saltah, and my favorite Yemeni sweet, bint al-sahn — literally, the "daughter of the dish" — was served. Bint al-sahn is a round, strudel-like, layered egg bread topped with a sprinkling of blackened seeds and drenched in a mixture of honey and clarified butter. Shafout, a dish that I had heard of but never tried, turned out to be eighteen-inch whole-wheat crepes soaked in a tasty green sauce of yogurt and milk blended with garlic and chilis. Freshly minced coriander leaves gave the dish its greenish hue.

Seated across the table from me was a country cousin of the bridegroom who gnashed his teeth and belched loudly, obviously enjoying his meal a great deal. There was little conversation, as hundreds of arms crisscrossed the tabletops in search of food. We ate with our fingers. No women were present; they had gathered elsewhere. The actual wedding ceremony was to take place on the following day.

Automatic pistols appeared in nearly every waistband, and guards wandered between the tables with assault rifles slung over their shoulders, scanning the room carefully. When we had arrived, I had seen armed men roaming the gardens and the surrounding streets. Noticing my puzzlement, Saleh said, "One never knows what might happen at these gatherings." He patted his coat pocket.

Soon it was time for the platters of stewed sheep's heads. I continued eating, wondering about the proper way to eat a sheep's head. I didn't have to wait long to find out. There is a trick to cracking open the skulls. You place the thumb of one hand in an eye socket (with the eyeball still intact), and span the skull and grip the roof of the mouth with the fingers. The other hand grasps the lower jaw. A sharp twisting motion is accompanied by a sickening snap and a popping sound. When done properly, the slippery skull and jawbone come away in two pieces. Then you prise open the cranium.

Not every man could manage the trick, but the growling tribesman across from me was an expert. People handed him their sheep's heads, and for several minutes I watched as he skillfully wrenched the jaws away from a dozen skulls. It was not an appetizing sight.

"One mind, one heart!" exclaimed Saleh from across the table. Everyone's mouth and hands were covered in sheep fat and honey. By the time we rose from our chairs to wash our hands, the tabletops and carpeted floor of the dining room were littered with glistening jawbones and broken skulls.

The next two days passed in similar fashion, with much eating but no news of my visa application. I ate with Saleh's family one afternoon. The following day I was taken to an open-air restaurant that specialized in dishes from Wadi Hadramawt, in South Yemen. Sitting on straw mats in the shade of a whitewashed brick wall, we watched as young men prepared our meal a few feet away. They tossed what looked like wire coat hangers strung with meat into three-foot-wide fire pits dug into the earth. A large garbage-can lid was placed over the pit to help smoke the meat. When the meat was cooked, we were each handed a coat-hanger portion. The shared plate of rice mixed with cardamom pods, tomatoes, and raisins went nicely with the greasy morsels of charcoal-flavored goat.

The day my visa was to expire, I again mentioned my passport; I had not seen it in two days. Saleh worked a toothpick between his teeth as he asked how much time I needed.

"Two weeks?" I asked hopefully.

"Here," he said, producing my passport from his pocket.

"Seeing is believing," I replied. Saleh had given me six additional weeks. I was beginning to understand the Yemeni mind.

14

The Cafeteria of Hope

MY TOES ACHED with cold as I hurried to Bab al-Yemen, the southern gate through the old city walls. Stonemasons, carpenters, and general laborers hoping to be picked up for a day's work squatted in the morning sun, displaying the tools of their trade in buckets or on burlap bags. I was an hour late meeting Martin Plimsole, because my watch had stopped during the night. By coincidence, Martin had overslept as well, so that we arrived in front of Bab al-Yemen at the same time. He had brought a friend along — Kevin, who also taught English at the Bristol Language Institute. It was the beginning of the school break for them, the day we had settled on for our departure from San'a. With no particular destination in mind, we planned to go walking in the mountains for a few days.

None of us had eaten that morning, so we found a teahouse full of rough-looking men and hurried through a meal of fried beans, bread, and nutmeg-scented tea. The fresh green onions served with the meal tainted our breath for hours. Finishing breakfast, we set off on foot for the nearby taxi stand. When we arrived, the long-distance Peugeot 504 station wagons were queued up and slowly filling with morning travelers. We selected a sturdy-looking car and sat down in the middle seat to wait for more passengers.

Martin pointed through the front windshield to a veiled woman making her way across the large asphalted parking area. By local standards of dress there was nothing particularly remarkable about her clothing. She was dressed in a *sharshaf,* a black garment that covered her from head to ankle in veils and long pleats. The delicate fabric caught the breeze in such a way that every movement of the woman's body was accentuated with a billowy grace. The clues to her age, social status, and shape were too subtle for my untrained eye, but a Yemeni man would have read these signs at a glance. Her posture, hands, feet, and the quality of fabric told the story.

What made the woman's appearance unusual was the charcoal brazier perched on her head. Made of sheet metal, it was about eighteen inches in diameter and was supported on a two-foot-tall, slightly conical stand that flared at the bottom, so that it fit her head like a hat. She presented an odd sight, dressed in her black veils with a smoldering hat atop her head. The brazier left a line of dense white smoke high in the air, conspicuously marking the woman's course through the predominantly male crowd. The smoke trail reminded me of a steamship at sea.

Everyone was in motion. Men crossed the taxi area pushing identical green wheelbarrows filled with assorted merchandise. A three-foot mound of freshly scrubbed carrots was wheeled into view, dramatically backlit by the low morning sun so that they gave off a translucent orange glow. One man trundled by with a barrowful of shiny green melons stacked like cannonballs. The next man's wheelbarrow held a pile of freshly decapitated calf's heads. Vendors flowed along either side of our taxi, and my vision was soon confined to the view out the front windshield. There were wheelbarrow loads of long purple eggplants, freshly polished red apples from the Tihama, dusty mounds of toasted locusts, and what appeared to be daikon radishes. The radishes, known locally as *qushmi,* reminded me of a passage I had read by Ibn al-Mujawir, who visited Yemen in the thirteenth century. He had written about "The Edict of the White Radish":

The Daulah Gauhar told me that the radishes are sold split in four parts. Why? I asked him. Because it was told that a long time ago there was a woman that used one in her vagina. The sheik of the village, having heard about this, gave orders that radishes could only be sold if they had been split, and they have since made it a law.

The law had evidently been changed, because the radishes in the wheelbarrow were still intact — and of impressive proportions.

Another of the green wheelbarrows contained a human body. It was shaded by a large black umbrella and wheeled slowly through the crowds by a teenage boy, who walked between the long wooden handles. As they drew near, I could see the emaciated figure of a neatly kept man arranged on a blanket, his head lolling back with unblinking eyes. His disfigured limbs were folded in all directions, but he did not strike me as being grotesque. In one of his clawlike hands he clutched a microphone. A car battery, a loudspeaker, and a small amplifier were nestled in the blanket next to his body. He was broadcasting his request for alms. Yemenis give generously to the poor, and I saw many people put money into the wheelbarrow. The attendant made a well-practiced circuit of the taxi area before moving to the next stop. The wheelbarrow disappeared, and soon the amplified voice became indistinct in the commotion of the morning crowd.

A garland of sweet-scented jasmine flowers was thrust through the window at my side. I instinctively motioned the young girl away, but the thick perfume lingered for several minutes, and I soon regretted not buying the string of delicate white flowers.

When the taxi was filled, the driver collected 100 riyals from each of the eight passengers. In the back of the cab lay two spare tires (both flat), an engine block, a crankshaft, but no tools. As we started off, I noticed that the floor was covered with a floral-print linoleum. Magazine cutouts of unveiled, overweight women with bare arms were pasted to the door panels. The steering wheel, gearshift lever, and rearview mirror were carpeted, adding a whimsical counterpoint to the sober religious themes: three-dimensional postcards taped to the dashboard depicted scenes from the life of Mohammed, and the top border of the windshield was lined with glittering, multicolored decals bearing prayers from the Koran for a safe journey (possibly the owner's idea of collision insurance). The vehicle was more than a taxicab; we were passengers in a portable shrine, which paid homage to the Prophet while keeping us mindful of the pleasures of the flesh.

Kevin told us of an orientation speech reportedly given by the U.S. embassy hospital staff to single men working for Hunt Oil in San'a, in which the men had been instructed to swab themselves down with Clorox bleach before and after sex with Yemeni women. The possibility of an oil worker talking to a Yemeni woman, let alone touching her, was so remote that the precaution seemed ludicrous. It is much more common for Yemeni and foreign men to go to Djibouti for sex. Our laughter caused the driver to complain to the other passengers that Nasranis (followers of Jesus of Nazareth) never bothered to learn Arabic. He felt that we were excluding them from our joke. Martin replied in perfect Yemeni Arabic that this was entirely untrue. He told the Clorox story, and soon the conversation turned to women and sheep. Martin translated the comments for me.

"Are the English girls as good as sheep?" the driver wanted to know.

"I wouldn't have any idea. I have never had an English girl," replied Martin, without missing a beat.

"Do you get to see the faces of your Yemeni girl students?" another man wanted to know. He was scrunched in the back seat with a loaf of bread stuffed behind his jambia. Martin told him that several of the young women in his class lifted their veils during English lessons but lowered them before leaving the classroom. This response elicited an excited discussion that I couldn't follow but that reminded me of locker-room banter back home.

Martin asked if we were going to stop at the Girls, a popular restaurant on the San'a–Hodeida road that is run by two unveiled women. Nearly all the long-distance truckers and taxi drivers stop there to eat and to look at these hard-working women, about whom there are many lurid and highly unlikely stories.

"Will we eat with the girls?" Martin wanted to know.

"No, we will do other things with the girls," said the driver, chuckling.

"God willing," Martin replied. I laughed, but the other passengers fell silent. Smiling dreamily, they seemed lost in unlikely possibilities.

The man with the bread in his belt broke the reverie by recounting a sexual adventure in Hodeida many years earlier. "We were pillows for one another," he began (this is a Yemeni expression for lovemaking). "That woman from the Turkish quarter in Hodeida — she was the very best. I remember her. She was creamy chocolate brown and smelled of ambergris."

Other men described the intoxicating musky scent of women's clothes after being perfumed with *bakhour,* a light brown granular mixture imported from Aden and India. It is burned over charcoal in a small ceramic brazier that is placed beneath a four-foot conical frame of rattan. Clothing is draped over the frame, and clouds of perfumed smoke permeate the fabric. Alternatively, a woman can lift her skirts and stand over the brazier, allowing the smoke to waft into her underclothing. The scent, similar to that of frankincense or myrrh, lingers in the clothing and on the skin for hours.

I knew the smell of *bakhour* from my walks through the twisting lanes of San'a. One afternoon I had met a group of young women in one of those narrow passageways. Fully veiled in black, they walked toward me without a word or a glance to acknowledge my existence. I stepped aside, allowing them to pass by closely. Then they were gone. Continuing on my way, I was soon bathed in a delicate trail of perfume. For a moment I wondered where it had come from, but then I knew. The fragrance filled the laneway, lingering as a tantalizing reminder of the women with the perfumed skirts. The encounter made me appreciate fully the delicate pleasures of grace and modesty.

"Ah, happy talk!" exclaimed our driver as he accelerated down the road. So engrossed had we become in our discussions of sheep, women, and perfume that we had forgotten to stop at the Girls.

"We're almost to Bajil!" Kevin noted.

"Time flies when you're talking about sheep," I replied.

The mountain road straightened out, and I could feel the lowland heat. Following a wide graveled riverbed that held a ribbon of clear running water, we drove by garden plots of banana, corn, and sugar cane. Then we left the foothills and entered the Tihama. The section we crossed was utterly desolate. Scrubby acacia trees clung to life in the dry, sandy soil, and a hot wind from the north buffeted the car, making me feel drowsy as we approached Bajil.

The taxi dropped us off in a wind-whipped flurry of plastic bags and hot grit, so we took shelter in a restaurant to wait out the dust storm. We had our choice of chicken or goat. Kevin and I had the chicken, which was dry and stringy. Martin claimed that the goat was delicately flavored and succulent, but judging from the number of toothpicks he carried away after the meal, I doubted this. Outside, an ice cart emerged from a cloud of dust. It was pulled by a donkey, but no one appeared to be leading the animal. Nine rectangular ice blocks, each eighteen inches wide and nearly five feet long, were roped to the swaying wooden cart. Wet burlap sacking protected the ice from the sun but not from the dirt. The cart disappeared into the dust again, and we left the restaurant after the storm had subsided.

Bajil is an ugly town and is likely to remain so, because its buildings are made of reinforced concrete. The hideous shopfronts were put up soon after the completion of the nearby Bajil Cement Plant, in the days before concrete formwork techniques had been mastered by the local builders. The town is best known for its extensive collection of dented oil drums, tire repair shops, cement dust, embroidered women's dresses, and high-quality qat.

There is also a spiritual aspect to Bajil. Nearby a yearly festival known as the *ziyarah* of Wali al-Shamsi is held in honor of a local saint. The celebration has its origins in a Sufi/animist tale about a man by the name of Shamsi, who freed a nearby village from an ogre a thousand years ago. The monster demanded a yearly tribute of one virgin. It was not clear whether consumption or consummation was the goal of his desire, but Shamsi put an end to the ogre's appetites by cutting him up with a sword. Ever since that time people have come to Bajil to obtain *barakah* (blessings) from the saint's tomb. Wali al-Shamsi is also associated with childbearing, and barren women make pilgrimages to the tomb, hoping to become fertile.

Looking at the filth and the shoddy architecture of Bajil, I was intrigued at how a spiritual life could exist in such a place. A friend who witnessed the festival a couple of years earlier told me that it started out well, but sometime before dawn frenzied male dancers bared to the waist began to plunge jambias into their bellies as musicians played furiously on goatskin drums. The veneration of saints, self-mutilation, and fertility rites seemed wholly incongruous with the modern industry and squalor of the town. This juxtaposition of past and present is one of the most striking features of Yemeni society. In San'a I had seen men in hand-forged leg irons shuffling past storefronts selling computer software, and veiled women walking the streets with new color television sets balanced on their heads. In Bajil, a roadside town littered with derelict vehicles and reeking of sump oil, it was possible to observe a spectrum of human behavior that spanned more than a thousand years. But as far as I was concerned, the place was hot and ugly. I couldn't wait to get out of town.

Before leaving Bajil, we went shopping on behalf of Sheik Ibrahim Dabri, whom Martin had met on a visit to the mountains two years earlier. We located a perfume shop that was open at midday. The selection of scents was unremarkable, but we lingered over the variety of labels. There were Passion de Golf, Boom-Boom, Jigolo, No Man's Land, and others. Martin was looking for Sexational, but the shopkeeper had sold out and we had to settle for two bottles of Casino de Paris.

We hitched a ride out of Bajil in the back of a truck and two hours later arrived in a small village at the base of the mountains, where we took refuge from the sun in a *funduk,* an open-air boarding house — literally, "a place to obtain relief." The twelve-foot-high roof of corrugated metal was supported by unmilled rafters laid on tree-trunk posts set into the pounded earth floor. In the shade of this structure approximately eighty cots were arranged in groups of five or six. The exterior walls were clad with flattened oil drums.

No vehicles would leave for the mountains until late afternoon, and so to pass the next few hours we went to the marketplace to buy qat. There we met Mustafa, a handsome Somali man who taught English in the village school. There were no classes in the afternoon, so he joined us in the *funduk*. Mustafa told us that he had taught in the village for five years, but each year he returned to Somalia to visit his wife and children for two months.

Little interest was generated by our arrival in the *funduk*. I couldn't determine who was in charge, but our needs were taken care of without our asking. One boy brought bottled icewater to each of us, while another set up a tall water pipe. We separated our bundle of qat into three equal portions and began to chew, sipping water to quench the thirst that accompanies qat chewing. There was little conversation. I enjoyed the peaceful ambience. The other men showed a polite interest in us, but we were by no means the center of curiosity. This suited me, because I was nervous about the local officials. We had no permits to visit the mountains, and the longer we remained in the village, the greater, it seemed, our chances of being questioned were. Chewing qat did not strike me as the best method of finding a ride, but I had little desire to stand in the sun. At least in the *funduk* we were out of sight. Mustafa sent small boys to inquire about transport. Meanwhile there was little to do but relax, chew, and puff on the *mada'a* (pipe). A group of men wanted to know if we were Turkish or Iranian. Listening to Martin's Arabic, it didn't occur to them that English was our first language.

The qat began to make me feel very relaxed. As sundown approached, a television set mounted high on the wall of oil drums flickered to life. To coincide with the end of the nationwide afternoon qat session, an *oud* player performed on the screen for an hour. His voice and the sounds from the nine-stringed instrument were predictably soothing.

Absorbed as I was by the music, I hadn't noticed that most of the locals had quietly wandered off and the *funduk* was nearly empty. The sun had set. My serenity was interrupted half an hour later by the arrival of a stranger, who announced that a truck had been found. With our cheeks bulging with qat, we followed Mustafa quietly through a series of darkened laneways to an open area where two small roads intersected. I felt as if I had floated to this spot. I don't remember what became of Mustafa. There was no truck, but that didn't matter. I would happily have passed the night in that pleasant place, staring at the road and waiting for the sunrise.

Some time later I noticed two yellow headlights approaching. The familiar sight of Yemeni men hanging off the back of a Toyota Land Cruiser came into view. This reassured me that we would be in the mountains that night. I sat next to the driver. Cool mountain air blew through the cab as we bounced and lurched our way up an immense alluvial fan. The twelve-inch potholes that started on the outskirts of the village continued as far as the first set of single-lane switchbacks blasted into the mountainside. Beneath the star-filled sky, huge succulents (*Euphorbia ammak*) and large rocks loomed up in the headlights. The air was fragrant with the scent of mountain shrubs, but my enjoyment of the journey was hampered by the terrific jolts and bumps. Certain sections of the road were so precipitous that I got out to walk, and at these points the driver put on a special tape of Egyptian popular music. He turned up the volume of the female vocalist, engaged the gears, and somehow scrambled his way up the frightful inclines. The seemingly indestructible Land Cruiser was an even match for the skill and raw courage of our driver, and I was heartened to see that he had fortified himself with a tremendous wad of qat prior to our departure. A man in his right mind might have lost his nerve on that track.

Scattered lights appeared on the mountain, and a half-moon shone clearly above dark, jutting peaks. The road ended at the village of Al-Makrab. Arriving just before midnight, we were taken in at the village school by four Egyptian schoolteachers. The superintendent of the school, a Yemeni, was also still awake. He received us in the conference room, where we sat around the floor on cushions. He didn't strike me as being very pleasant, but then I couldn't understand a word of what he said. He kept a loaded pistol in his lap and exuded an air of indifference and self-importance. I was glad when he left the room. The four Egyptians, who stayed behind, were from a city in the middle of the Nile Delta called Tanta. From their descriptions the place sounded dreadful, but this didn't prevent them from talking incessantly about home and how much they longed to get away from the damp mountain air.

All I wanted was to go to sleep. The teachers were Scout-masterish and energetic, possessing a wholesomeness and sense of purpose that I had not witnessed since driving through Salt Lake City, Utah, in 1969. They commanded a group of admiring students, who vied with one another for the privilege of performing menial tasks: bringing us tea; cleaning up the conference room, which was strewn with teacups, qat leaves, and school papers; laying out rough-looking mattresses and wool blankets. Martin was handed the only set of keys to the outdoor water tank and toilet. At the edge of a precipice, we unlocked the padlock of the water faucet, washed our faces, and brushed our teeth, and then we returned to settle down beneath blankets that smelled like a sackful of two-week-old gym socks. We shared the room with three Yemeni men and four foul-smelling water pipes. The close atmosphere was made more unpleasant by the odor of stale tobacco, but I slept well.

The next morning, just before sunrise, I wandered up the hillside to the village square and asked the owner of a small teashop for warm water. He handed me an eight-ounce tin full of scalding water, which I let cool before rinsing my face and hands. The square was paved with damp flagstones and surrounded on three sides by handsome four-story buildings constructed of meticulously chipped blue-gray stone blocks. The arches, lintels, and round windows were finely proportioned. At one time the windows and doorways had been shaded with delicate wood overhangs, but in recent years most of the wood had deteriorated, and in its place were crudely worked sheets of rusted metal. The fourth side of the square opened onto a view of distant mountains graced with stone terraces that disappeared into the bank of clouds just below the village.

I sat on a cold metal folding chair in front of the teashop as the first direct rays of sun reached the village. There were no other customers at that hour, but I caught glimpses of bundled human shapes moving between the nearby buildings as I warmed my hands with several glasses of weak coffee. It was a fine morning, brisk and clear. The sun began to heat my face and clothing.

A man herded four sheep into the empty square. He didn't bother tying them up while he erected a metal tripod at the end of the square that overlooked the cloud-filled valley. The sheep were fifty feet from where I sat, and the smell of damp wool hung in the air. Pushing up the sleeves of his sport coat, the man laid one of the animals on its side. He immobilized the body with his legs and bent the head back until the throat was taut. A ten-inch knife appeared in his right hand. Facing north, toward Mecca, he put the blade to the right side of the animal's throat and muttered "Bismillah," cutting into the neck with a quick sawing motion that severed the windpipe and jugular vein. As the blade cut more deeply into the neck muscles, the animal seemed to be very much alive and struggling. The man adjusted his grip on its muzzle and with a wrenching motion cracked the head backward. The distinctive wet popping sound of snapping cartilage was audible where I sat. The head came away from the body. The man clung to the carcass as it tried to run away. But it was too late to run, and as the blood drained the convulsions subsided.

After hanging the animal from the tripod by a heel tendon, the man cut a slit along the inside of each leg and peeled the skin back, using his bare elbow for leverage between the skin and the still-quivering muscles. The skin came away in one piece. Then he opened the stomach cavity, pulled the small intestine out, and coiled it up like a limp garden hose. In the space of ten minutes the animal had been reduced to a pile of steaming, jointed meat. The man sharpened his knife on one of the flagstones before reaching for the next quaking animal. I had butchered farm animals myself, but there was something about the cool efficiency of this fellow's technique that unnerved me. I could too easily envision myself hanging from the tripod.

When Martin joined me for coffee, he pointed to a signboard written in Arabic above the doorway to the teashop. "How nice!" he exclaimed. "We are sitting in the Cafeteria of Hope. Unfortunately, there seems to be little hope for the sheep this morning."

"No hope at all," I replied, glancing at the second animal writhing in its own blood.

Sitting in the Cafeteria of Hope, I thought about fate — not only the fate of the four sheep, but also what had made me return to Yemen. If I had come to revisit the islands of the Red Sea and search for the traces of my past, what was I doing in a mountain village 150 miles from the coast?

Over the years, my notebooks had taken on a new significance. I didn't question that. Like writing on old parchment, the remembered pages had grown more delicate and precious with time. They represented a lost segment of my life, and for that reason I found it disconcerting that the longer I stayed in Yemen, the less I worried about finding them. The country was proving to be far more seductive and tantalizing than I had thought possible. That morning, for the first time, I was willing to admit that the search was not going well, and that maybe it wasn't important anymore. Accepting this fact, I caught a glimpse of my own fate. Regardless of what the notebooks contained, it was clearly my need to wander to remote places and lose myself in strange situations that had drawn me back to Yemen, and to the Cafeteria of Hope. At another time in my life, this same need had taken me on a journey of seven years.

The Egyptian schoolteachers appeared and explained that the governor of the province would be arriving at noon to lead a two-day meeting with the local sheiks at their school. Not wanting to be questioned by any officials, we thought it prudent to leave as soon as possible. We passed the last house on the main ridge behind the village before we stopped to look down on the cluster of stone buildings. Surrounded by mist, Al-Makrab appeared to be floating in the clouds. In the distance triangular black peaks pierced the sea of clouds, and in the foreground we could see several hundred schoolchildren assembled in the yard where the meeting would take place. Red and blue banners bearing words of welcome in Arabic script were jostled by the changing winds. A long row of more than twenty chairs had been set out, suggesting a large gathering.

Hours later, Martin discovered the keys to the toilet and water tank in his pocket. I tried to convince him that there would certainly be a second set of keys, but we all knew this was unlikely. I am sure the villagers still remember us as the stupid Nasranis who walked off with the keys to the toilet the day the governor came to visit. Martin intended to send them back with the first person going in the opposite direction, but at each opportunity we were so engrossed in conversation that he forgot. Soon it was too late. There were no more people on the trail, and we passed into the next valley.

Climbing steadily into a further set of mountains, we continued to gain altitude. The trails were good, and we had no difficulty finding our way. The views into the valleys and up the hillsides revealed little scenes of mountain life. A team of men worked on new terraces while women collected water from the stepped inner walls of a cistern and children led goats and sheep into the high pastures. Many of the fields lay bare, and dried stalks of sorghum, to be used as livestock fodder, lay bundled near the trail.

Calls echoed from one mountain slope to the next. "*Oooh* . . . *Ali!*" a voice drifted across a half-mile of open space separating two ridges. "*Oooh* . . . *Mohammed!*" came the reply. Shouts of one or two words conveyed messages and saved a walk of an hour or more. Later in the morning I saw men carrying Sony walkie-talkies with long antennas. These, I assumed, were for more private conversations.

I stumbled up the mountainside, following a rocky trail that meandered between the freshly plowed terraces. My legs and lungs were not up to the terrain nor to the exuberance of my two companions, and I soon fell behind as they strode out of sight. But I enjoyed the sensation of walking by myself. No people were visible as I moved across the mountain toward a slight dip in the ridge, where I joined the others at about 9000 feet. We sat on a pile of stones and ate a package of Burton's fig-roll cakes from Saudi Arabia. Scattered far below us, tiny stone villages clung to patches of land too steep or rocky for cultivation.

We would pass the night in one of these villages. As we descended the far side of the mountain, I could detect a subtle change of mood. The women's clothing was different: they wore knee-length black smocks embroidered with brightly colored thread, and those in the fields had hiked up their smocks to reveal baggy orange-and-black-striped pants that fit tightly at the cuff. Even from a distance I could see that the women had lightly colored their faces with ground turmeric, to protect their skin from the sun and wind but also to enhance their beauty. Their yellow-toned complexions flattered their clear wide eyes, which were lined with kohl. No one called out to us as we wandered across the high slopes of the valley, and I could sense that we had passed an imaginary border and stepped back in time.

After a while we stopped to ask directions from an old man who was training a young bull to pull the plow.

"This bull is still learning," he explained. "And as you can see, he is not enjoying his lesson today. Where are you going?"

"Mahall al-Dabri."

"Good, that is my village. There it is, over there — not too far." The cluster of stone buildings looked promising. There wasn't a television aerial in sight.

We said goodbye and headed toward Mahall al-Dabri, but long before we arrived the village sounds reached us. Hammers pounded sheet metal, and there was the distinctive *thump, thump, thump* of a diesel motor pumping water. Donkeys brayed, axes thudded into dry wood, and a multitude of hammers chipped at stone blocks for a new road. The excited voices of children laughing and playing mingled with the sounds of work. The confusion of random sounds suggested a community at ease with life.

Flanked by tall houses, the narrow pathway through the village included stone steps worn smooth, and there was the faint scent of donkey and goat droppings. Women with elaborately plaited hair appeared briefly at doorways and windows but showed little interest in our arrival. The smell of wood ash seemed to emanate from the cold stonework, and wisps of smoke drifted out of windows and short chimneys set on the flat roofs, where coffee beans were spread according to their color and state of dryness. The beans started out bright red, then progressed through several shades of purple until they attained a dark brown color. The familiar greenish beans were inside the dried husks. The rooftops were lined with large rusty tins from which sprouted fresh stalks of basil; women wore the long flowering sprigs behind their ears.

Walking through the village, I imagined that this must have been what life was like in seventeenth-century rural England. Everything in sight was crafted by hand: the stone walls, the clothing, the buckets, shovels, short-handled picks, and twig brooms. I took in these details quickly, because within minutes of arriving we were ushered into the sheik's house, where we would pass the night.

The *mafraj* (reception room) was illuminated by a bank of tall windows, above each of which were fanlights of colored glass set into delicate gypsum tracery. Knotted rugs covered the floor, and the walls were hung with cheap-looking carpets depicting various scenes: Mohammed's ascent to heaven, the Dome of the Rock in Jerusalem, and a caravan of camels crossing the desert at night. A gilded plaster clock in the shape of a clipper ship was mounted next to a flyspecked photo of President Ali Abdullah Saleh, and an ornamental niche decorated with plaster reliefs held a colorful row of Chinese Thermos bottles. On a far shelf I could see a miniature diorama of the Kaaba in the courtyard of the Great Mosque at Mecca. The center of the room was dominated by a large brass tray holding five *mada'a* and two large thermal jugs full of drinking water. A few older men, unconcerned by our presence, filed into the *mafraj* with bundles of qat to begin the afternoon ritual.

Everyone in the room assumed the same posture: right knee up, with left leg tucked comfortably in front; left elbow resting on a firm rectangular cushion. A young woman entered the room carrying a large terra-cotta pipe bowl, which she held in both hands as if it were an offering. The woman, who was scarcely taller than the four-and-a-half-foot water pipes, stepped to the edge of the wide brass tray to fasten the bowl to the top of one of the pipes. She was beautiful, and I found it difficult not to look at her. She was unveiled, and the sleeves of her long smock were rolled to the elbow. She approached the *mada'a* in much the same way a dancer approaches the exercise bar, with a sense of purpose and grace. The angle of her chin, the motion of her hands and fingers, the set of her shoulders, and even the shape of her little ankles and feet as she stood balanced on her toes fascinated me. The economy of movement lent dignity to her simple task, and I was charmed by these subtle gestures. Beneath her black smock, she had the flat chest of a young girl. This feature was not in keeping with the curve to her hips, small waist, and firmly shaped bottom. I wondered if the women in these villages bound their breasts for beauty, or out of modesty. The overall effect of the plaited hair, black eyes, turmeric-colored cheeks, and strong, graceful figure was lovely and enticing.

Having fit the bowl to the pipe stem, the woman brought the turned wooden mouthpiece to her lips and began to pull steadily on the pipe while twisting the bowl onto the shaft to create an airtight seal. Soon the flow of smoke was to her liking. She uncoiled the thick hose covered in purple velvet and then walked toward me, offering the mouthpiece and allowing our eyes to meet for the briefest of moments. I rarely smoke, but I could hardly refuse her offer. I took the pipe with both hands and placed it to my lips. The entire ritual seemed rich in secret gestures. The pipe gurgled. The woman waited for a moment, until the aroma of sweet, mild tobacco had filled my lungs and nostrils, and then left the room. I realized that the sight of the woman preparing the pipe was probably about as tantalizing to a Yemeni man as the sight of a woman vacuuming a living room rug is to a Western man, but this knowledge did not detract from my enjoyment of it. As an outsider, I took full advantage of my right to romanticize an unfamiliar situation.

Yemeni men continued to gather in the small, warm room, and the murmur of conversation around me produced a sense of well-being and companionship. The growing wad of qat in my cheek also helped. I appreciated Martin's translations, which gave me a feeling for the substance of the conversation. When compared to male bonding rituals in Western societies, qat sessions seemed very civilized. Sitting comfortably with a water pipe and a mouth full of leaves struck me as a much more intelligent and productive way to spend an afternoon than guzzling beer out of cans in front of the television or stupefying oneself after work in a bar full of strangers.

These thoughts were interrupted by Martin's account of a recent dispute in the village. It wasn't clear what had caused the argument, but there had been a scuffle between two women at the well. Blows were exchanged, and one woman had ended the discussion by stoning her opponent. Having observed the strength of the village women at work in the fields, I could well imagine the violent scene. The victor marched home, leaving the second woman bloodied and screaming for revenge. Quick and just resolutions of disputes are desirable in order to maintain village harmony, so the husbands of both women were called to the sheik's house, and the men of the village gathered to listen to the story. It was important for them to witness the judgment. The men chewed qat and smoked as each husband spoke for his wife, describing her injuries. The sheik levied fines calculated on a per-bruise or per-cut basis: one bruise was worth 50 riyals, while a cut or abrasion was worth 75 riyals. The injuries were totaled, and an amount was agreed on. There was an additional stipulation: if the total amount was not paid promptly, the families would not be allowed to use the well.

As dusk came down, I heard a group of men in the distance. I wasn't sure whether they were chanting or singing, but as they drew near I could detect a purposeful tone to their voices. Downstairs, a door was thrown open as a crowd surged into the ground-floor hallway. The sounds of shuffling feet and voices were amplified by the narrow stairway. Within moments, fifty men and boys had filed into the room where we sat. Once they had settled on the cushions arranged around the perimeter, the tempo and volume of their chant increased. We became wedged into this mass of new arrivals, so that we all sat shoulder to shoulder. A woman brought two small braziers of *bakhour* through the doorway, and great clouds of sweet, fragrant smoke filled the room, perfuming our clothing and skin.

I soon learned that less than an hour earlier, a young woman had died in childbirth. The men had gathered to acknowledge the death publicly and to pay tribute to the dead woman. No women were present, but wherever they were — either preparing the body or in their homes — the men's voices would reach them.

The chant didn't seem to have a beginning or end. It sounded as if they were saying, *"Hang-a hang-ila! Hang-a hang-ila! Hang-a hang-ila!"* The windows and doors were closed, and three additional *mada'a* were lit. The perfumed clouds of *bakhour* dissipated, only to be replaced by a thick pall of fresh tobacco smoke. For five minutes the chanting continued nonstop, but then a sayyid began reciting verses from the Koran. (Sayyids are a small but highly regarded group of north Arabians who claim descent from the family of Mohammed, and they are looked upon as holy. In some areas their touch is believed to cure.) The voices immediately fell silent as he recited, frequently exclaiming, "Blessings on the Prophet and his good and pure family!" There were choral responses from the crowd, and when the verses stopped, the chanting began again.

During a momentary lull in the chanting, Martin told me what the men were saying. *"La illaha ila Allah"* translates as "There is no god but Allah" — a reminder that death must be accepted as the will of God.

Two pressure kerosene lamps were brought in, and the room began to warm up from all the people in the confined space. As the chanting continued, the sayyid kept count with his strand of ninety-nine prayer beads. After two complete rounds, one hundred and ninety-eight chants, he would signal a stop by again reciting from the Koran. Over the next four hours the chant was repeated 70,000 times to honor the dead woman.

With the heat generated by the lamps, our bodies, and the water pipes, the room was growing unbearably warm and humid. The shrill yelling of the younger boys cut through the deeper bass tones of the older men, and the smoke, the qat, the powerful voices, and the extreme discomfort of sitting in one position for so many hours made my pulse race. Beads of perspiration stood out on everyone's forehead. The emotional state induced by the chanting and the close atmosphere fell just short of a frenzy. When the mouthpiece of the *mada'a* was handed to me, I pulled the sweet smoke into my lungs until the syllables of the chant became thoroughly jumbled in my mind. I passed the mouthpiece on and concentrated on breathing in order to fight off unconsciousness and an acute sense of claustrophobia.

Time was compressed; voices vibrated through my body, humming, pulsating, soothing and intrusive at the same time. The air pressure in the room seemed to increase as the bodies all about me rocked in time to the rhythm of the words. I relaxed and let the vibrations of the voices pass through me without resisting. Kevin had slumped into a corner, speechless, unblinking, stunned. I was alarmed by his chalky complexion but realized that I couldn't look much better. The windows were fogged up with condensation, and rivulets of water ran down the insides of the small windowpanes. At one point during the chanting I lost control of my hearing: words and syllables expanded and contracted as if distorted by the Doppler effect. I cleared my ears repeatedly by holding my nose and blowing until my ears popped. As the sweat streamed down my chest, I tried to focus on the sayyid's fingers. One by one he squeezed the beads between his thumb and index finger, counting the verses and controlling the tempo and energy level in the room. I concentrated on my breathing.

During a break, Martin leaned forward and asked Kevin if he was feeling all right. Kevin slowly blinked his eyes in response. The floor between our crossed legs was five inches deep in discarded qat leaves and stems.

"We all must die. Blessings to our fathers and mothers who have died before us and will rise up for the day of judgment!" called out the old man, and immediately fifty voices thundered in response.

Two men entered the room with armloads of qat and threw small bundles at our feet. We expressed our gratitude by selecting a few leaves, but passed the bulk to older and more important men. For visitors, it was polite to acknowledge the hospitality, but it showed good manners to offer the qat to others.

The 70,000 chants came to an abrupt halt, followed by a profound silence. The outpouring of emotion had left everyone spent. I couldn't move, but a short while later the men began to file out of the room. Half-submerged in leaf litter, I was incapable of speech.

Across the room, Kevin was mumbling to himself and laughing. "Hide the donkey . . . hide the donkey . . . behind the donkey, behind the donkey! That's what they were saying — hide the donkey — in a Scottish brogue. Imagine that!"

"Are you all right, Kevin?" Martin asked again.

"What? Me? Ha-ha-ha-ha-ha-ha-ha! *Yes,* of course. Hide the donkey!"

Kevin was not well at all.

When the men were gone, two little boys began sweeping up the qat leaves with twig brooms. The windows were not opened after the men left, so I went up to the roof to breathe in tremendous lungfuls of cold mountain air. I could see pinpoints of distant electric lights on the mountainsides. A bright half-moon bathed the surrounding coffee and qat terraces in a ghostly half-light, and the individual rocks of the terrace walls appeared to give off a dull luminescence. I stayed on the roof until I was shivering. Re-entering the *mafraj* was like stepping into a sauna filled with cigarette butts. The smell of tobacco, *bakhour,* and fresh human sweat was intense. I opened a window to air the room, but the Yemeni man who shared the room with us immediately shut it. I opened a more distant window, but he closed that one as well, fastening the latch with such conviction that I wondered if he was trying to keep in the heat or conserve the highly charged atmosphere created by the four-hour gathering. I wasn't sure, but I didn't attempt to open a window again.

Before sunrise I followed a winding stone pathway to a rocky outcrop that overlooked the village. In the foreground below me, a man approached the white courtyard and dome of the mosque, which clung to the edge of a precipice. Holding a tin of water in his right hand, he entered a roofless enclosure that looked like five stone-walled stables. I didn't understand his mission until he hiked up his *zanna,* an ankle-length dress, and squatted in one of the stables. Feeling foolish to have selected such a commanding view of the public toilets, I moved to a new spot in order to allow the other early-morning risers their privacy.

Sunlight bathed the village in an orange glow and brought the stone buildings to life. Shadows formed, defining space as human figures began to appear. Smoke drifted from high windows and chimneys. As a light wind carried the valley mist up the mountainsides, I saw a group of men leave the village carrying long bars and short-handled picks. They walked to a terrace facing the village and began to tunnel into the rock wall. Because of the lack of soil in the mountains, the dead are buried beneath the fields. I could hear the chinking sound of the tools against the stone.

I returned to the sheik's house as breakfast was being brought into the *mafraj.* We drank steamy weak coffee spiced with ginger. A damp flatbread, similar to a crepe or the Ethiopian *injera,* was brought to us on a thin aluminum platter, and hot ghee mixed with fermented cow's milk was poured over it. Squatting around the communal platter, we ate with our fingers. The hot bread, which was moist and fragrant, smelled of sorghum and wheat flour. Its upper surface had a spongelike appearance, which prompted Kevin to call the dish a Yemeni crumpet.

The funeral procession took place as we prepared to leave Mahall al-Dabri. Male voices called out from the upper part of the village to announce that the body was coming, and sobbing women and girls lined the flat rooftops. Beyond the women, purple mountain peaks were disappearing into the cloud cover. When the chanting men came into view, emerging from a lane between the stone houses, they carried a stretcher above their heads. The dead woman's body was wrapped in a simple white muslin shroud. The chanting and crying grew louder as the procession reached the flat ground below the village and drew close to the sheik's house, passing within six feet of where I stood. I could see that the stretcher was made of unfinished wood, and two new handles suggested recent repairs. "There is no god but Allah — blessings upon him," the men called out, half singing. Their voices echoed across the terraced mountainsides.

It was impossible not to be moved by the scene of communal grief. I was suddenly overwhelmed by a sense of profound humanity. The scene conveyed a feeling of sadness, but also one of unity and fate. I realized how privileged I was to witness that moment. Linking life and death, this last tribute served to reassure those left behind that when the day of their death came, they would be honored in the same way. There was a structure to these peoples' lives. They understood the routines of a day and of a lifetime. They were not dulled by the repetitious nature of their existence or frustrated by expectations of a life beyond their grasp. They lived in a state of harmony that I found enviable. The villagers knew how to recognize the significant moments. For them, life was infused with meaning.

I watched as only a stranger can in such circumstances — involved superficially, yet separated by culture. But as an observer I was surprised to find myself suddenly overcome by a real sense of personal loss. My sorrow was not for the dead woman, or her child, or the villagers. The procession stirred up feelings that I had repressed months earlier, at the death of my grandmother. There had been no ceremony and certainly no chanting of

70,000 blessings to mark her passage. The procession was only a short way down the path when, in my mind, I placed her body on the stretcher. The chanting entourage walked into the rising mist, which streamed up the slopes. The men appeared and disappeared in the clouds, but their voices carried clearly. I was filled with relief and a feeling of completion. That morning I found myself attending a funeral for my grandmother. I laid her to rest in a remote, high mountain valley of North Yemen.

Like Ants We Wander

LEAVING MAHALL AL-DABRI, we walked north as dense clouds closed in around us. We increased our pace to keep warm, but within a mile of the village we became disoriented. Lost in a sea of mountain mist, we followed narrow, rock-piled switch-backs that seemed to lead us in circles. Large patches of prickly pear appeared in the mist, and *Aloe vera* drooped listlessly from fissures in the cliff faces. During one ascent we broke through the cloud cover; in the sunlight the air was warm, and mountain peaks were visible in all directions. The distant views made me feel as if I had regained my sight. When we plunged back into the clouds, our vision became limited, and sounds provided the few clues to our surroundings. Young voices drifted to us, conjuring scenes of children taking their sheep to the mountain pastures. The distinctive thud of an axe bit into wood. Later we could hear the sounds of a *mizmar,* a double-reed pipe, and much later the distant voice of a woman singing.

I felt we were lost, but how could we be lost? There was only one trail, and we had no destination. What Martin thought was north, I took for south. Kevin was sure the direction was east.

As we stopped to discuss our differing opinions, an old man appeared out of the mist. Because he had his skirt hitched up to his waist, I could admire his spindly brown legs protruding from a natty set of blue-and-white-striped boxer shorts. His legs had the characteristic high calf muscles of mountain people. We exchanged greetings.

"Where is north?" Martin asked.

"North? What is north?" he replied. The term meant nothing to someone oriented by villages and fields. We were without a map and didn't know the names of any of the villages apart from those we had already visited.

Martin tried a different approach. *"Ain al-gibla?"* (Which is the direction of prayer?)

Without a moment's hesitation, the man gestured into the clouds toward Mecca, which lay to the north.

For the rest of the morning we followed this fellow through mountain scenery that reminded me of eleventh- and twelfth-century Chinese landscape painting. The cloud cover created a heightened sense of distance, isolating scenes and forcing the eye to leap from the middle distance to the far distance and back to the foreground. Winding valleys were filled with mist, and vertical space was divided by wispy layers of clouds in motion, which revealed a variety of vanishing scenes that left me with a feeling of infinite space. The tiny figure of a man appeared plowing a terraced field at the edge of a great precipice. The clouds shifted and the man disappeared. Higher up, a mountain peak became visible, shrouded in shaggy forest. As we walked along the trail, the clouds opened to reveal tremendous drops or distant stone villages clinging to the mountainsides.

Our guide left us at the base of a towering rock formation upon which sat a village known as Fingers. It took its name from five huge stone spires that rise dramatically from the mountaintop and point toward the sky. As we rested before climbing to the village, the head of a wrinkled old man appeared on the far side of a loose stone wall. He had been busy picking coffee beans by hand. When he saw us, he came close to the wall to speak.

"Where are you going?"

"To the mountaintop," replied Martin.

"Ah, like ants we wander," the old man remarked. He then

instructed Martin to produce pen and paper. "Now, write this," he commanded.

Martin started writing down his words in a neat Arabic script. "He's composing a spontaneous poem for us," he remarked after the first few lines.

There is a long tradition of spontaneous poetry in Yemen. At weddings in the past, men from each family challenged and entertained one another with eloquent or witty verses. Words, both written and spoken, used to carry clout. Not long ago, tribal disputes could be settled by poetry competitions instead of with bullets.

Our poem read:

> I ask you, merciful Allah, creator of heaven and earth,
> You who keep the moon and stars traveling by night, and the
> sun by day,
> To protect Toyota Land Cruisers and foreign strangers who
> climb to the mountaintops.
> And I conclude my prayer with a blessing on Mohammed, who
> is honored in all the lands.

When the man finished his recitation, Martin handed the poem over the wall. The man refused the piece of paper, explaining that the poem was for us — a souvenir of our visit, a prayer for a safe journey. We thanked him, then Martin pocketed the poem and we began our climb to the village.

We became lost in the maze of alleyways, and the first man we stopped to ask for directions glared at us with an ill-disguised look of contempt. This was surprising, because the next fellow we approached broke out in a wide smile and dragged us off to a qat party. We tried to explain that it was important for us to reach the next village before nightfall, but he would have none of our excuses. We were led to a large doorway that opened onto a room packed with men sitting on the floor. "Your uncles love you!" one of them cried out, inviting us to join the party. They were celebrating the return of a friend who had just spent twelve years working in Saudi Arabia. Someone brought us two bowls of food, one containing yogurt, the other a generous helping of lamb stew. We ate in haste, but before we could manage a polite exit, bundles of qat appeared. This meant we would have to stay for at least another hour.

We asked a man seated nearby if he knew the trail to our destination, the village of Al-Durahimi.

"The path is small," he replied thoughtfully.

"How small?" Kevin wanted to know.

"The smallest."

A discussion ensued concerning our intended route. I couldn't follow the details, but it was obvious that the men didn't want us to go. They claimed that the trail wasn't safe, but I suspected they wanted to amuse themselves with our company. Someone mentioned iron nails.

"Iron nails?" I asked with interest.

"Oh, they're nothing really — just part of the trail where it gets a bit steep," Martin explained. He had come the same way two years earlier with a French musicologist, but he seemed exceptionally vague about the details of the path ahead.

"It is too late . . . you won't be able to find your way if it gets dark . . . stay here where it is warm and chew qat . . . it will rain soon." The men gave us many good reasons why we should not continue, but we were determined to stick to our original plan, so we left Fingers in the afternoon. The walk to the next village would take at least two hours. Three hours of daylight remained, so we started off feeling confident. A light rain began to fall. Beyond the village the trail disappeared over a sharp drop-off before continuing downhill in a series of tight switchbacks. We carefully picked our way through cactus and loose rock, two hundred feet down the slope. The rain continued.

Martin had difficulty remembering the route, and we made several wrong turns in the terraces, where garden paths crossed the main trail. Repeatedly we were forced to retrace our steps. There was little chance of becoming seriously lost, but our trial-and-error method was costing us valuable time. Our provisions consisted of a single packet of Petit Beurre finest tea-time biscuits (product of Kuwait), half a liter of water, an eight-ounce spray bottle of Casino de Paris cologne, and a pack of Yemeni ciga-

rettes. Without matches, food, blankets, or shelter, we were totally unprepared to pass a night on the mountain.

Walking into a deep ravine choked with banana plants, Martin attempted to reassure us that he could recognize the significant landmarks. "Just to let you know I'm not lost," he said, "do
you see that big rock over there? Well, I took a shit just to the left
of it two years ago."

We took him at his word, but five minutes later we were again
stumbling from one rocky terrace to the next, surrounded by
more banana plants. The huge green leaves obscured the view in
all directions. Martin and Kevin plunged on as I paused to inspect a strange plant that looked like a succulent red dandelion
with white tips. The flower was perched on a three-inch brown
stem. This was *Scadoxus multiflorus,* the snake plant. Yemenis
believe that snakes eat the flower and live in areas where the
plant grows. When villagers are troubled by venomous snakes,
they can summon a snake man, who chants verses from the Koran until the snakes come quietly and allow themselves to be captured.

I was about to continue walking when I noticed a movement
on the mountainside above us. A man was carefully picking his
way down a steep trail. His eyes were on the pathway, and he
had not yet seen us. But as Martin and Kevin moved into an open
area, he instinctively dropped behind a bush. I wondered why he
was hiding.

For a moment I remained concealed, then I stepped out from
the cover of large green fronds and waved at the man in such an
exaggerated fashion that he couldn't very well pretend that he
hadn't seen me. He stood up. I gestured with my arms to ask him
where the trail went, and he turned and motioned straight up the
mountain in the direction he had just come from. Although we
were seventy-five yards apart, I could sense that he was mortified
to have been spotted first, especially by a stranger. People in
these remote areas have to be cautious. There are no police, and
the frequent land and water disputes are often settled with bursts
of gunfire on lonely sections of trail.

Following the man's gestures, we found the main footpath.

Minutes later we met the lone traveler, who wore a cream-colored *zanna* beneath a gray sport coat. A three-inch-wide leather belt covered with purple velvet held his jambia, and on his head was a light blue plastic shower cap similar to the kind provided by expensive hotels. Behind his jambia was a pistol, a pair of rubber thongs, and a large assortment of ballpoint pens. He wanted to know where we were going. It was unusual for foreigners to be in the area, especially on such a remote trail. The mountain people are extremely wary of strangers, and there was no mistaking the man's suspicions.

When we told him our destination, he looked at our feet and said, "*Mush tammam!*" I knew the expression: it meant "no good."

"What does he mean by 'no good'?" I wanted to know.

"He says the trail is very bad — we will never make it in our shoes. He thinks we should go barefoot," Martin explained.

"Barefoot? What on earth for?" I said. I looked at my feet, which were nestled in thick wool socks and a pair of very expensive New Balance running shoes. The shoes featured high, padded ankle supports, an adjustable lacing system, and patterned soles for traction. The breathable Gortex uppers were reinforced with leather. This footwear was designed, manufactured, and marketed for just this sort of varied terrain. What was the fellow talking about? When I glanced at his feet, I understood. Leathery yellow calluses covered his soles and grew up the sides of his feet. He could grip the mountain slopes with his toes and judge the rock surfaces by feel. Wiggling my tender toes, I realized that the man with the shower cap and bare feet had the superior equipment.

He shrugged his shoulders and continued down the trail, leaving us to our plans. We walked to the base of the mountainside, where the trail began to climb steeply. Kevin went first and disappeared into the mist, climbing steadily on all fours. There were scrambling sounds; a few small stones came down; then silence. I went next. Along one section I was forced to climb on hands and knees. Rain-laden bushes released a chilling shower at a touch. Reaching out to steady myself, I grabbed a cactus pad by mistake. Farther on, thorny shrubs pierced my hands in a dozen places. It was miserable going.

Kevin called out from somewhere above me, "Martin . . . are you sure this is the way?"

Below me came the reply: "Yes, it goes up for a while, as I recall. It gets somewhat worse, then better."

This vague pronouncement was not very reassuring, but it was the broken thongs next to the trail that worried me. The sight of split rubber toe straps in the mountains of Yemen should be taken as a danger sign. Where Yemenis can't walk without breaking their thongs, the average visitor should not go without a rope. I have watched village children follow their goats up rocky cliffs that no beginning rock climber in his right mind would attempt without a belay.

We climbed to a narrow saddle surrounded by thick shrubbery. A patch of ground had been cleared as a resting place, but with so little time to spare, we immediately started down a steep, muddy chute flanked by more thorny shrubs and cactus. Large granite splinters protruding from the slick earth provided treacherous handholds and footholds. This section of trail looked like a gigantic cheese grater; if one of us fell, many pieces of flesh and clothing would be left behind.

At the bottom of the chute we walked through a small forest that terminated at the edge of a forty-five-degree granite face. When we moved onto the rock, we were immediately chilled by a mist flowing from somewhere far below. The white clouds that swirled about us made me feel weightless, as if I were floating next to the mountain. But where were we? Gauging from the steepness of the slopes on the other side of the mountain, I imagined we were on an exposed rock face three hundred feet above the valley. But with visibility limited to one hundred feet, there was no way of knowing for sure. I confined my attention to figuring out how to get across the rock.

We walked upright most of the time, following crack systems and wide ledges, but frequently we had to crawl along narrow, root-filled bits of soil that appeared to be fastened to the granite with damp moss. I didn't like the look of those sections. We continued on, and soon the slope became so steep that when I stood upright, I could reach out and touch the rock wall with my hand. Sometimes we wandered blindly, finding our own separate ways. This careless attitude was the perfect prelude to a climbing disaster.

"Watch yourselves along this bit," warned Martin, tapping his walking stick on a section of loose granite flakes. As if to illustrate his comment, a flat stone became dislodged and clattered down the rock face, then launched itself into space. I counted the seconds to measure the drop, but time passed and there was only the sound of the wind in my ears. We continued climbing without comment. I was thankful for the cloud cover, which obscured what must have been a spectacular and terrifying panorama. I began to think about the iron nails. What were they? And if the going was this difficult now, what would the route be like when we arrived at the nails? The rain came down in large cold droplets that pelted our backs and made the rock slippery. We lost our way, then Kevin found a fragment of broken thong and we followed his lead.

Martin called out the names of birds. "That's an African sunbird — note the flash of iridescence on its chest . . . Ah, and a hammerkop — hammerhead in English, you know. Surprised to see him up here in this weather." He mumbled something about a cinnamon-breasted rock bunting, but I was too busy looking for footholds to pay much attention. I assumed he was making these comments to break the tension. Unfortunately, this was not the case. His nonchalance was entirely due to impaired vision. Rain droplets had speckled his glasses for the previous half-hour, and he was not aware of our dangerous footing.

The rock now angled at sixty degrees. Kevin and I clutched the wet stone like a pair of migrating limpets. Another bird flashed by. I scarcely took note of it, but a moment later, without warning, Martin let go with his hands and performed the astonishing feat of standing upright on a nine-inch-wide ledge. Feeling secure behind his rain-spattered spectacles, he knew no fear.

"But I say, wasn't that Tristram's grackle?" he exclaimed.

"Martin . . ." I started to speak but could not complete my thought.

"No, I'm quite sure it was — that distinctive patch of red beneath its wing." Martin stood planted, as if his feet were encased in concrete. He hung his cane over his left forearm and then removed his glasses. Looking off into the middle distance, he proceeded to wipe down the lenses with his shirttail. The sight of him standing there in the wind was magnificent and horrifying. I tightened my grip as I waited to see what would come next. Thirty feet above us, Kevin was frozen to the rock with his head averted. He did not want to watch Martin's plummeting form disappear into the clouds below.

"You know, it's damned irritating not to be able to see properly with the rain on my spectacles. You two are lucky to have good sight." He squinted once again before replacing his glasses, then fell silent as he glanced downward. With his cane still hung on his elbow, an expression of surprise came over his face. He seemed to hesitate, suspended between the mountain and the clouds.

"Good Lord!" he muttered.

Turning to look over his left shoulder, he swayed briefly before reaching out with his free right hand and grabbing the mountain. We continued the climb in silence, and it wasn't until the following afternoon that Martin renewed his interest in bird life.

We moved up the rock face another three hundred feet before arriving at a dirt trail. The path wandered over a slight rise before leading onto a knife-edge ridge, where we stopped to rest for a few minutes. The rain had let up, but we were soaked, and it would soon be dark. We moved along the ridge in single file, uncertain of how far we had to go. During the two-thousand-foot descent that followed, the cartilage beneath my kneecaps was ground to a gritty paste of pure misery.

"The nails — I can see the nails!" Kevin called from ahead. I caught up with him, and we stood in silence, horrified at the sight of a row of two dozen iron rods projecting eighteen inches from the rock wall. Lengths of hand-hewn stone had been laid end to end on top of the rods to form a makeshift ledge, and smaller stones had been used to fill in the gaps. The drop wasn't quite vertical, but it was steep enough that if you lost your footing, you would careen down the mountainside and end up as an unrecognizable sack of splintered bones and battered pulp at the bottom.

Martin decided to find an easier route. He groped his way back to the ridge, but within minutes he had lost his cane over a far more frightening cliff. I watched it slide down the mountainside before disappearing from sight, spinning slowly end over end into the clouds. Martin rejoined us at the iron rods.

Fearless Kevin offered to go first. He started across the ledge upright, but within twenty feet he had assumed an unorthodox but more sensible position, moving on all fours in a crablike fashion, with feet first and stomach uppermost. As he worked his way across, I could hear the ledge of loose rocks shifting beneath his weight. I was mentally preparing myself for the crossing when the mist cleared. As cultivated terraces appeared five hundred feet below me, I felt ill. My cheeks flushed. I wanted to wait for the mist to obscure the view, but there was no time. It was getting dark, and we had to get off the mountain. I crawled on all fours, with the yellow stripe on my back facing downward. At the halfway point I decided to conquer my fear of heights by looking down. I looked, and immediately regretted doing so. I completed the crawl without taking another breath.

Martin moved toward the ledge. His glasses were again covered with raindrops, but somehow the sight of him blinking and groping his way along, half blinded by the rain, seemed incredibly funny. A rock tumbled down the cliff, and we all laughed.

"Oh God, I wish I was back in Tanta!" Martin joked as he reached the safety of solid rock.

"To Tanta!" we cried out in unison.

The trail improved, and soon we were off the mountain, sloshing our way into the village of Al-Durahimi. People were surprised to see us, especially at such a late hour. Where had the Nasranis come from? We hung around a couple of open doors looking miserable, but no one extended an invitation to enter, although one man stopped us to find out where we had come from.

"From Fingers," we told him.

"Impossible! There is no road from Fingers," he replied suspiciously.

"We took the footpath," Martin explained.

"The footpath . . . ? There is no god but Allah!" the man concluded, clearly astonished that three strangers would attempt that route unaccompanied.

We walked through the village with the squelching sound of our shoes echoing down the mud- and dung-splattered laneways. A young boy approached. Did we need a place to stay? He led us to the Scientific Institute, a vocational training center for village boys.

"Would you like to stay with the Egyptian teachers or the Somali teachers?" our guide asked as the rain drummed down on our bare heads.

"The Somali teachers," Martin replied, remembering our talkative Egyptian hosts from two nights earlier. As he spoke, a head popped up unexpectedly from behind the school wall.

"Where are you from?" the head asked in English.

"Britain, and the United States. Where are you from?"

"Tanta!" came the reply. I heard a muffled snort from Kevin as he struggled to contain his laughter.

Out of politeness, we entered the concrete-walled bedroom shared by five Egyptian teachers. Each man had a bed and a nightstand. There was space for little else in the room, which was only about fifteen by fifteen feet. Mosquito nets, brown and limp with age, hung above each bed.

While students swarmed into the room to practice English and speak Arabic with Martin, we were served cups of hot black tea, but for some reason our hosts were oblivious to our wet clothes and chattering teeth. After we had talked to the teachers for half an hour, we were summoned to the sheik's house. We walked for another twenty minutes in the rain to get there. I was drenched, and by the time we staggered up the spiral staircase leading to the upper floors of the sheik's house my knee and ankles were emitting disturbing popping noises similar to the sound of wooden pencils being snapped in half. Having arrived in the *mafraj*, we changed into dry sarongs, T-shirts, and warm sweaters. When I removed my wet socks, I noticed that my feet were waterlogged and three of my toenails had been blackened by our descent. We sipped cups of hot qishr, an effusion of ground coffee husks and ginger, and watched a program on Yemeni television: double-exposed over a scene of breaking waves, a man in a cheap suit was playing a flute. For dinner we were served bowls of rich, fatty goat soup.

Martin was drawn into a discussion with a young man who was intrigued to know how an intelligent, learned man could not be attracted by Islam. The sheik's brother, in the meantime, wanted to know if we were married. Kevin and I said that we had girlfriends at home but that Martin, at age twenty-nine, was still single. When asked why he had not married, Martin told the men he was saving himself for an elderly heiress. The men immediately advised against this, claiming that "all women live to be two hundred years old," a Yemeni expression that means no man outlives his wife. "Take a young woman who can give you children," they suggested kindly. Martin thanked them for their advice before continuing with his explanation of why he had not become a Moslem.

I fell into conversation with Kevin, who told me that cloves were sometimes offered with qat to counter the dry, unpleasant taste of the leaves. According to Kevin, cloves were only offered to married men. I wanted to know why.

"The Yemenis believe that chewing a clove will produce a stonker."

"A what?"

"A stonker — you know, on bonk," he repeated in a conspicuous North Midlands accent.

"On bonk?" I asked, confused by this expression as well.

"Christ! A stonker! A stiffie! The Yemeni men figure you'll get an erection if you eat cloves. That's why they don't offer them to unmarried men."

I finally understood. "Well, if they offer us qat and cloves, couldn't we tell them that Martin practices animal husbandry?"

Kevin didn't think our hosts would be amused. Probably not.

A small polite group had gathered around Martin, who was still searching for a convincing reason why he had not converted to Islam. He hadn't yet found one when I fell asleep forty-five minutes later.

At dawn I eased open the wooden shutters near my mattress, and a stream of brisk air blew over my face. I looked above the village and beheld a terrifying sight: the mountain. I could see where we had climbed the day before. The narrow ridge above the iron nails was touched with a thin line of yellow light. Higher up, I located the approximate spot where Martin had stood to clean his glasses. By rough estimate, I judged the fall to the rocks (not including bounces) to be at least one thousand feet. I felt grateful not to have had a view as we scrambled through the clouds the day before. From the warmth and safety of the bedroom, it was difficult to imagine a footpath traversing those towering rock walls.

I closed the shutters to keep out the light. The four Yemeni men who shared the room with us looked like corpses. They slept on their backs, completely covered by their woolen blankets.

Before anyone was awake, I went to the bathroom to wash my pants, rinsing out the mud in a plastic bucket half filled with cold water. Climbing into the wet pant legs was pure torture. I shivered until we were back on the road, and my legs gave off steam until the pants dried in the sun.

We walked for two hours on a graded road before being picked up by the first vehicle that came along. Leaf springs strained as the Land Cruiser lurched down the steep mountain track, which was littered with rock rubble and silt from the previous day's rain. As we moved ahead cautiously, villagers busily cleared debris from the road. A truckload of armed tribesmen came into view, climbing a steep section of the track, headed in our direction. As they drew near we pulled to one side, but they blocked us by stopping in the middle of the one-lane road, and a man came over to find out what we were doing. Martin mentioned that we had been visiting Sheik Ibrahim Dabri. This was the truth. The men didn't change their grim expressions, but they allowed us to leave the mountains.

The road flattened out as we entered the top of an inclined wadi system that drained to the west. Tamarind trees and umbrella-shaped acacias reappeared. Far off to our left, an abandoned saint's tomb came into view, set on a hill covered with cactus. Consisting of a set of cream-colored domes surrounded by a high stone wall, it looked like a monument to mother's milk.

Continuing toward the sea, we passed open-air classrooms shaded with vast corrugated metal roofs and filled with young boys. We bounced down the wide valley, swaying from side to side in a lazy motion. I could feel the coastal heat drying the skin on my face until it became taut. Proud, black-skinned Somali men strode along the roadside, looking magnificent in their turbans and ankle-length robes of pure white cotton. We left these dignified figures choking in yellow clouds of billowing dust. When the roadside garbage reappeared, I knew we were getting close to civilization. We bounded along the sand track for another hour before arriving at the paved coastal road that runs between Hodeida and the Saudi Arabian border. I could not see the coastline, but I knew it was only twenty miles away. We were less than forty miles from Uqban Island. My journals were so close, but there was nothing for me to do but wait, because no one would take me to the island without government permission.

We caught a ride south to Hodeida. It was 1 P.M. when we arrived at the qat market, where the consumer frenzy was intimidating. The Hodeida market specializes in *shami* qat, the *grand cru* of qat. Taxis, minibuses, trucks, motor scooters, bicycles, and private cars jammed the entrance to the parking area, and horns blared and men screamed as unarmed traffic police tried unsuccessfully to keep order with their silly whistles. While truckers unloaded burlap bags full of fresh leaves, thousands of men milled around the stalls, checking the merchandise. Sweat flowed over coffee-colored cheeks bulging with chewed leaves, and veins stood out on the necks and foreheads of both venders and buyers.

I entered the crowd of jostling customers, but immediately felt helpless in the tide of bodies. Leaves were shoved in front of my face with shouts of "*Tammam! Tammam!* Best quality! Look! Look!" I didn't have the strength to worm my way into the maelstrom of shoppers to search out a bargain; the heat and confusion within that heaving sea of green leaves and damp bodies was too much for me. We made our purchases at the edge of the market, then limped to a row of nearby restaurants.

Half stupefied by the excitement of the qat market, I could feel my legs beginning to stiffen from the previous day's walk. I was overwhelmed by the intensity and strangeness of what we had seen over the past seventy-two hours. I sat at our table trying to order my thoughts, but the strangeness continued. A man brought my order of fish and rice to the table. I waved the flies aside and stared at my lunch. My lunch stared back. A large fish head, with eyes intact, was looking directly at me from the center of a bed of steaming rice. There was little sense in sending it back. *Bismillah*, I ate. The cheeks were delicious.

Driving to San'a that night, we were stopped repeatedly at roadblocks, where soldiers armed with assault rifles thrust their flashlights and faces into the interior of the taxicab. We handed our identity papers to the soldiers through windows on one side of the vehicle as qat stems, empty water bottles, plastic bags, and crumpled cigarette packs were thrown out the windows on the opposite side.

We drove into the night. I stared out the window at the darkened countryside. I saw the Cafeteria of Hope and the bloody sheep carcasses; a funeral procession chanted in the mist, and a beautiful mountain woman in perfumed skirts smiled at me. Martin stood on a thousand-foot cliff cleaning his glasses with his shirttail. I felt dizzy. Sometime before midnight we arrived in San'a. When I woke up the next day at noon, I knew there were going to be problems. I couldn't move my legs.

16

The Bathhouse

I COULDN'T STAND. Surely an ice pick had been driven into each of my kneecaps. Every sprain from years of walking came back to torture me. A taxi driver helped me to the front door of Hammam Ali, a bathhouse at the edge of the old Jewish quarter. Out of modesty, I had never used a Yemeni public bathhouse before. The thought of sudsing myself up in some dank, fetid grotto filled with half-naked, sweating strangers did not appeal to my sense of hygiene or safety. Certainly a visit would be interesting, but I wasn't altogether sure I needed the experience. It was my kneecaps that finally convinced me to go — I needed to steam my legs back to health.

Tottering barefoot on a smooth reed mat, I changed into a sarong and left my clothes with the bath keeper. I rinsed my feet with a ladleful of cold water before painfully groping my way through a steam-filled labyrinth of underground stone passageways that connected a series of temperate and hot rooms. The floor was slippery, and I moved uncertainly in the dim light. At last I entered a room where I found a group of men dressed in damp *futahs* lying on the floor, their bodies glistening with sweat. Hot steam filled my lungs as the door thumped shut behind me. One fellow sat against a stone trough, ladling water over his head. Another sang quietly while three younger men danced in a row along one wall. An older, dignified-looking man spat an expertly aimed ball of phlegm into one of the two corner drains and then motioned me to take a place in the center of the room.

"*Tammam, sadiq?*" (Everything all right, my friend?) a young bath attendant asked me as I limped across the damp stone floor. Someone behind me poured a bucket of hot water over my head. The attendant washed down an area where I was to sit. I eased myself onto the floor but found it too hot, so I slid closer to the wall, where half a dozen bodies lay perspiring in silence. I wasn't sure what to do next. I wasn't ready to lie down on the slick, worn stones.

Out of the steam and darkness a voice spoke to me. "Medium, *sadiq* — it is only medium. Yesterday? The floor, it was like fire." The voice eased my anxiety without diminishing the mystery of this dark bathing place. Near the wall opposite the dancers, I lay on my back and looked up at the domed roof with its four small glazed skylights, one of which cast a beam of light across the room, illuminating a shaft of rising steam. Within minutes of entering the heated chamber, perspiration was pouring from my body. The room had an earthy, sensual smell that I found pleas- ant. I must have been several yards below street level, but after negotiating all the steps and odd passageways, I was completely disoriented.

Feeling comfortably lost in this underworld of hot stones and moist air, I recalled my tour of Hammam al-Maydan weeks ear- lier. I thought of the animal bones and stiffened hides the stoker had shoved into the furnaces. The realization that goat horns, car tires, rubber thongs, and cow patties were probably burning just a few feet beneath me did not detract from my enjoyment in the slightest. The steam and hot stones bathed my body in a va- por of soothing warmth, and I soon became lost in my thoughts and sensations.

Partially obscured by steam, the three young men continued their dance. A stranger invited me to follow him through a short vaulted passageway to an adjoining room. I could hardly see as he poured a bucket of tepid water over me. I did the same for him, and we returned to the hot room. I was beginning to enjoy myself. More men arrived, some of them with children. At random moments bodies would rise from the floor to engage in unusual calisthenics: pull-ups from stone ledges, knee bends, and bizarre twisting motions from the waist. They waved and flapped their arms before flopping back onto the hot stone slabs. The exaggerated sounds of dripping water, the heat, and the movement of bodies, in the darkness made me feel as if I were in a damp cavern near the center of the earth, where people never saw the light of day or breathed cool air. Lying among the other bodies, I relaxed as the sweat poured from my skin. At ten- to fifteen-minute intervals men left the hot room to cool off, but I was content to steam myself into oblivion.

"*Sadiq* — come, please."

One of the attendants was speaking to me. He opened a damp wooden door and led me into a room lined with stone benches, where other bathers were being scrubbed by slim young men. I handed my attendant a plastic bag containing a bottle of shampoo and a bar of sandalwood soap. With a gesture, I asked whether I should remove my sarong. The man shook his head, then poured hot water over me. Grabbing a bundle of palm fiber that looked and felt very much like a pot scourer, he began to scrub my limbs with long practiced strokes, and the dead skin and dirt were soon rolling off me. He went at me so vigorously with a pumice stone that I would not have been surprised to see blood, and I wondered if, in his enthusiasm, he was removing the body hair along with the skin. He frequently rinsed me with hot water poured from a section of old inner tube.

The man knew his job well, and the treatment continued without a word being exchanged between us. My hair was shampooed twice, then I had an elaborate head and neck massage that quickly reduced me to a spineless lump of jelly. The attendant sudsed my body until I was covered in a frothy coat of fragrant sandalwood-scented bubbles. He washed my feet and hands, cracked my knuckles and my neck, and could easily have dismembered me for all I cared. Seldom have I felt so clean or pampered.

The man motioned that I should wash my private parts, and after I did so he poured another cascade of hot water over my body. But this was not the end. Another complete sudsing ensued as his strong hands worked over my calves and thighs. The pain was spectacular, but I was incapable of uttering a word in protest. My feet tingled and then suddenly went cold, and my toes were numb by the time a cold sweat broke out across my brow. I must have stayed in the hot room too long. I became nauseated, then dizzy. I recognized the signs of an imminent blackout and leaned over to put my head between my legs, but it was much too late for such measures. I don't know how the bathing ritual ends under normal circumstances, because the room started to tilt at an angle; I had the distinct impression that someone was lifting the far end of the solid stone bench. But the bench remained perfectly stationary as I fell sideways onto the floor. That is all I remember.

I must have been washed down and helped to an adjoining cool room, because it was there I found myself sometime later. Stretched out on a stone slab, I had no idea where I was when I awoke. There was no recollection of time passing or movement from one room to the next. There was a voice.

"*Tammam, sadiq?*" One of the bath attendants was speaking to me. I perceived only darkness and coolness.

"Yes . . . *tammam,*" I replied without opening my eyes. A hand touched my shoulder reassuringly, then withdrew.

Sometime later, not trusting my balance, I moved cautiously to the edge of a wide stone pool to ladle water onto my legs. My eyelids and lips were covered with salty perspiration. Returning to the slab, I lay down and closed my eyes once again. The smell of the beach on Uqban Island came back to me. I could see the familiar curve of shoreline, and in the distance, sitting motionless on the horizon, was a lone blue-and-white sail. Lying there, I finally accepted that the point of my journey had shifted. When I first returned to Yemen, the country and people merely provided an exotic backdrop for my search, but as I was caught up in the maze of events and personalities, I found myself focusing more on the present. Perhaps there was more sense in embracing new experiences than in endlessly wandering about in search of the old ones. After all, it wasn't exactly the Holy Grail I was looking for. Without abandoning my hopes, I felt the burden of my original plans fall away, and I was left with a wonderful sense of relief.

I doused myself with another bucket of cold water to clear my thoughts, shivering as the water flowed down my sides and onto the stone platform. Steam rippled through two parallel shafts of sunlight that pierced the darkness. I heard far-off voices, muted and unintelligible. Safe within the subterranean warmth of the baths, I drifted back into the comfort of my thoughts.

The Yemeni men were much more modest than I had expected. They covered themselves completely from waist to ankle with their long *futahs*. Eye contact was discreetly avoided, and prolonged conversation between strangers was confined to the well-lit changing room. I had heard stories that the women often went naked in the *hammam*, but this seemed unlikely. According to Martin, the women are allowed to use the baths on an average of three days a week. They go to wash, but it is also still customary for Yemeni women to visit the baths to purify themselves after menstruation. The women from a household often bathe at the same time, and like the men, they enjoy dancing in the hot rooms. Their days vary according to the bathhouse, but as a rule, men always have the use of the baths on Friday, the holy day.

The *hammam* may also be rented before a wedding. A day or so before the wedding night, the bride visits the baths with her friends, the women of her family, and the women from the groom's family, who are thus given an opportunity to inspect the merchandise. The groom bathes with his friends and relatives just before "the night of entry," the night the bride's veil is lifted, the bride and groom see each other for the first time, and the marriage is consummated. In the older houses of San'a there is a special room just off the *mafraj* called the Flower Room, within which the unveiling and deflowering take place.

Lying on my back in the damp heat, I found myself trying to

imagine such a night. When I sat up later, I could see a row of young boys kneeling. Dressed in identical striped bath towels, they faced a *mihrab*, a niche set into the wall of the changing room that indicates north, the direction of prayer.

I felt foolish for not having come to the baths before. My fears of disease and low morals were completely unfounded. The sort of random sexual adventures associated with Western bathhouses were unthinkable. Hammam Ali was a model of cleanliness and piety. Most of the seventeen *hammams* in San'a are associated with a local mosque, and men often use them for their ablutions prior to prayer. Public bathhouses have existed in San'a since ancient times and are modeled after the Roman baths found in Egypt and other parts of North Africa. Hammam Yasir is said to be at least one thousand years old, and many of the other bathhouses are four hundred years old.

After ladling cold water over my feet one last time, I returned to the changing room, feeling refreshed. The bath keeper handed me a dry towel, then helped me out of my wet sarong, which he laid out to dry. I rested for another twenty minutes, then got dressed and paid the bath keeper 30 riyals, the equivalent of $3. This sum included a tip for the attendants who had taken care of me. People smiled and nodded kindly as I stood up to take my leave.

Stepping onto the street, I felt as if I had been underground for several days. My legs were weak, but there was no pain as I wobbled down a laneway crowded with dusty sheep.

It Was Not Written

17

Two French archeologists invited me to move out of the American Institute, where I had been staying, and into an old Yemeni house they had recently finished restoring. It was located in Al Qa, the Jewish quarter of San'a. Over the years they had put together a fine library full of books, maps, photographs, and other reference materials covering Yemen and the Middle East. At sunrise I could usually be found writing at one of the two library desks. A diffuse light filtered through alabaster windows, and beside me there was a pot of hot black tea flavored with Yemeni honey. I would continue working until late morning, when Miriam, the fifty-year-old Somali cleaning woman, would arrive. My brief conversation with her never varied.

"*Bonjour, monsieur,*" she would say, making eyes at me.

"*Ahhh . . . bonjour, Madame Miriam,*" I would reply.

Covering her mouth with both hands, she would then break out in a spasm of belly laughs. Miriam weighed about two hundred and fifty pounds and was the delight of my mornings. She was the first person I saw each day.

After her arrival I would take a walk. Afternoons were frequently spent chewing qat with Martin and his friends. Wednesday was a special day at the house: as many as a dozen people would congregate for lunch in the high-ceilinged dining room on the third floor. The windows of the room overlooked an old neighborhood of family compounds, vegetable gardens, and leafy trees. Minarets and television aerials pointed into the sky, where black birds circled overhead on the warm updrafts.

One of the regular lunch guests had a friend who worked for Air France, so there were bottles of Bordeaux on the table, as well as pâté de campagne, aged Brie, and individual rounds of goat cheese to spread on warm mulouj, the chewy Yemeni equivalent of a baguette. There were bowls of mixed green salad sprinkled with freshly picked miniature tomatoes, and crisp baby cucumbers tossed in a mustard-and-tarragon vinaigrette. Large terra-cotta pots of cassoulet (minus the pork) were brought to the table, and there was chilled fruit for dessert. One day a crème brûlée was served, followed by French roast espresso. After two months of drinking qishr, I enjoyed the coffee immensely.

The company was made up of a diverse group of Koranic scholars, art historians, architects, photographers, employees of the French embassy, and a curator from the National Museum. At one of these lunches the conversation came around to a Frenchman by the name of Erich Frager, who had been kept in Hajjah prison for nearly two years without standing trial. A woman from the embassy provided sketchy details of his arrest, but little else was known about his situation. His extreme isolation intrigued me, and I decided to visit the man.

The morning I arrived by taxi in Hajjah, I went directly to the marketplace to buy bags of almonds, raisins, oranges, apples, cigarettes, and other items I imagined Frager might like, or might use to trade with the guards or other prisoners. Leaving the market, I realized I didn't know the Arabic word for prison. I walked to the police station to get directions, but unfortunately, the guards at the front door spoke no English and would not let me enter the building. Moving back a step, I put down my bags and said, "*Nasrani.*" I held my wrists together as if handcuffed.

"*Fra-zhay! Fra-zhay!*" the guards cried out excitedly. They immediately understood that I wanted to take food to the only Christian in Hajjah prison. One of them took me by the hand

and led me to the nearest intersection, where he motioned me to stand out of the way, on the footpath. Stepping onto the busy roadway, he leveled his AK-47 at the oncoming traffic. The motorists reacted by honking and swerving around him as if he were nothing more than a stray dog in the road. I began to fear for his safety as he tried to commandeer a vehicle to take me to the prison.

Not wanting to run down an armed policeman, a taxi skidded to a halt. The policeman banged his weapon on the hood of the car and engaged the driver and his passenger in a horrible argument. I thought there might be bloodshed until I realized that the men were merely discussing price and destination. I was shoved into the back seat, and as the cab thundered down the road I could hear the policeman gleefully calling out, "Fra-zhay! Fra-zhay!" The Frenchman obviously enjoyed a large following in the town.

At the front gates of Hajjah prison, I was not searched. The bags of fruit explained all.

"Fra-zhay?" inquired the gatekeeper.

"Fra-zhay!" I nodded in reply.

I was led to a quiet building set in a corner of the walled compound. In a concrete room on the second floor I found the Frenchman taking a late morning nap. Frager shared the cell with two dozen other prisoners, and I found him sleeping on a mattress on the floor. He climbed from beneath his blanket fully dressed and greeted me warmly. Smoothing down his hair, he sat across from me at a small writing desk neatly arranged with books, pens, an ashtray, and a small wooden box containing an expensive brand of miniature cigars from Cuba. Set to one side was a stack of notebooks. These turned out to be his prison diaries. They reminded me of my own diaries, and I was quick to realize that those pages were his most treasured possessions.

Frager was given one small loaf of bread each day and, like the four hundred other prisoners, was totally dependent on his friends and fellow inmates to provide him with food and whatever else he needed. No sooner had I handed him the two plastic bags full of fruit than he was distributing the contents to men whose families lived too far away to visit regularly. Members of the French community in San'a sometimes made the six-hour round-trip journey to Hajjah to deliver food and keep him company for an afternoon. As a foreigner, he was allowed to drink wine, although he did so infrequently out of respect for his Moslem cellmates.

He did not seem surprised by my arrival. I introduced myself by telling him of my time in jail on Kamaran Island ten years earlier. The story established an immediate rapport between us, and he spoke openly about his situation.

During the construction of a new hospital in Hajjah, Frager, a thirty-two-year-old civil engineer from Paris, had been in charge of organizing the local builders. The project, which was funded by Saudi Arabia, had a duty-free license for the transport of building materials from Saudi Arabia to Yemen. From the beginning, Frager suspected that Yahya Selba, the Hajjah subcontractor in charge of transportation, was using the license to import more materials than were necessary for the construction of the hospital. The excess, which turned out to be truckloads of reinforcing rods, sacks of cement, and electrical and plumbing goods, was being off-loaded before reaching the hospital and then sold at a large profit.

Frager was not involved, but there was little he could do to control the use of the license. He had lived in the Middle East long enough to know that the contractors would make his work difficult if he interfered with the operation. It was impossible for him to inspect the trucks crossing the border, so he made an agreement with his transporters that he would pay only for materials delivered to the work site. He felt that as long as the hospital was built properly and on time, he could tolerate a moderate amount of corruption. What difference could it make to his work?

He soon found out, when the government auditing office in San'a ran a check on the hospital project. Frager was accused of smuggling and soon found himself in Hajjah prison, awaiting trial.

Following his arrest, three associates of Yahya Selba decided to take extended holidays in Aden and Saudi Arabia. The Hajjah prosecutor promptly put the remaining Yemeni transporters in prison, but only temporarily. These businessmen bought themselves out within hours, for amounts as high as 50,000 riyals each. Frager did not have the presence of mind to do likewise. While he sat in prison preparing the proof of his innocence, the Hajjah court began inquiries into his personal wealth and the assets of his company.

Frager was accused of smuggling everything from one thousand tons of toilet bowls and washbasins to $10 million worth of cement and electrical fixtures. One day the prosecutor from Hajjah wanted $500,000 in fines; the following week the amount was reduced to $100,000. The Frenchman viewed all this as the court's way of testing his patience and his ability to pay. His company was bankrupt following the cancellation of the hospital contract, and Frager had no money of his own.

"Then why are they bothering to keep you?" I asked.

"In Hajjah, the prosecutor and court are entitled to ten percent of the final settlement. Justice is not their primary concern."

Setting aside the conflicting accusations and legal discussions of Frager's guilt or innocence, the simple fact remained that Hajjah and the surrounding province have always been a major smuggling area. Hajjah is scarcely 250 kilometers by road from the Saudi border. Within half a day, a truck can deliver trailerloads of anything from pirated Michael Jackson tapes to cabbages to heavy weapons. The customs officials on the border are only too happy to facilitate the flow of goods, and one can safely say, without fear of contradiction, that smuggling was well established in the area before the arrival of this French civil engineer.

The reasons behind the easy movement of goods across the border are not difficult to understand. Hajjah province, a powerful royalist area, is allowed certain "trade concessions" by the San'a government in return for not stirring up old political issues. San'a stays out of local business matters, and Hajjah doesn't get involved in national politics. Anyone stepping forward to defend Erich Frager would have to point the finger at

Yahya Selba, the man in charge of transporting materials to the hospital. Such an accusation is unlikely, as Yahya Selba's uncle is the chief adviser to the National Security Police in Hajjah. To consolidate his position in the community, Yahya Selba had recently made a "donation" of half a million riyals to the poor people of Hajjah during Ramadan. Things were not looking good for the Frenchman, who naively held onto his belief that his innocence would ultimately lead to his release.

After the first few months, Frager told me, he had settled into prison life. He grew to enjoy the sense of fellowship, and his Arabic improved immensely. He shared his cell with murderers — not criminals in the Western sense of the word, but men of principle who had upheld their tribal obligations by killing other men. The strength of the tribal system is based on specific rights and responsibilities, and avenging a death can be an obligation.

In Yemen there is little stigma attached to being put in jail. Indeed, a prison sentence can often enhance a man's position in his community. It is an important rite of passage, especially for young men. Once a person is in prison, it is considered unmanly for him not to wear leg irons, because that would mean the guards did not consider him brave or clever enough to try to escape. During the Imam's time, a common punishment was to put a man's weapons in jail. Without his jambia and rifle a man would be ashamed to be seen in public, so he would stay in his home until his weapons had served their time.

Frager found it easy to maintain a sense of humor, as Hajjah prison was an excellent place to observe the human comedy on a daily basis. That afternoon I noticed one of the guards shuffling around the cell block wearing a set of leg irons. Frager told me that the guard was guilty of letting the wrong prisoner out of jail for the day. The man he had released was being kept for his own protection, because the family of the man he had killed refused blood money. When two of the family members spotted the murderer walking through the marketplace one morning, they lost no time in unshouldering their automatic rifles and riddling him with bullets. The guard wore leg irons as punishment for his mistake.

Respected and trusted prisoners enjoyed certain privileges. Occasionally they could spend the entire night with their wives, provided they returned to the prison early the following day. One man had been sentenced to sixty-five days, but he asked to leave after thirty-five days because of previous business commitments. His request was considered by the prison director, then granted, on the condition that a family member take his place. The man's father sat in prison for ten days, and then one of his nephews filled in. When the sixty-five days were completed, the nephew was released. Justice had been served, responsibility shared.

This criminal justice system tests the limits of conventional Western thinking. Not long after Erich Frager arrived to serve his unspecified jail term, he witnessed the following scene: A man wanted to put his wife in prison for throwing a stone through the screen of the family television set. The woman seemed to have temporarily lost her senses. The husband asked his father-in-law for advice, and the father-in-law suggested leaving her in prison for a few days to quiet her down. The husband, thinking this a good idea, led his veiled wife to the prison gates, where he discovered that they would have to wait several hours for the women's section of the prison to open. To pass the time, he wandered through the jail, inspecting the men's cells. In Frager's cell one of the prisoners asked him why he had come to the prison. When the story of the broken television and the angry wife came out, the convicted murderers were shocked. A large commotion ensued.

"Can't you settle the law at home?" one prisoner sneered.

"Have you nothing better to do with your time?" cried out another man.

Several prisoners ridiculed the husband; others gave advice. Despite his humiliation, the husband listened. He reconsidered his original plan, then changed his mind. Thanking the men, he returned home with his wife. The prisoners were justifiably satisfied with the fairness of their decision.

Frager explained to me that during his most recent day in court, the judge had "joked" that he should pay him 400,000 riyals in return for an easy sentence. The Hajjah prosecutor and Yahya Selba's uncle were also present.

"But I am innocent," Frager insisted.

"If you want to be innocent and not play the game with us, you can stay in jail," the prosecutor and the judge told him.

Frager said that he would appeal.

The men laughed. "You want to appeal?" they said. "All right — that will add six months to your stay in prison. After that we can again discuss our terms and your innocence."

Compared to these men, the prisoners in Frager's cell looked like a group of distinguished jurists.

Having spent time in jail in the Middle East under similar circumstances, I was familiar with the issues. I asked Frager whether he placed a dollar value on his freedom. Certainly he could afford to pay something.

"The point is, I am innocent," he insisted.

"Surely you must realize by now that your innocence is not the issue. It is a question of money."

"I refuse to admit guilt."

The idealist looked at the pragmatist; the pragmatist looked at the idealist. I wished him luck. We shook hands, and I passed through the prison gates just before nightfall. During the three-hour drive back to San'a that evening I had ample time to mull over the details of the Frenchman's story. As I saw it, Frager's biggest mistake was in not accepting kickbacks from Yahya Selba in the first place. At least then he would have had the money to buy his release from prison. As of late 1990, Erich Frager remained in his cell, patiently awaiting a miracle. Apart from the sympathy I felt for him, his problems helped me put my own into perspective. Compared to his situation, my difficulties in trying to return to Uqban Island seemed utterly trivial.

Back in San'a I continued to visit the baths at Hammam Ali, and slowly the pain in my knees disappeared. The weeks went by. I washed my clothes more often than was necessary, and when there was nothing left to wash and my legs felt better, I spent long hours walking through the old city. My sense of purposelessness was intermittently acute; I began to wonder with increasing frequency if it was time to leave.

I was contemplating this thought during one of my daily walks when I came upon a German man lost in an alleyway of the old city. He was short and bearded, and his shiny pate had been reddened by the summer sun. He was in a panic, claiming that the National Security Police were following him. Within five minutes I had heard his story. The lost man, who turned out to be a professor of art history, had been put through some fairly unpleasant moments, but I couldn't help finding them quite amusing. His fears of being pursued by police thugs were unjustified, but I understood his confusion.

The professor's original plan had been to visit an old girlfriend from his art school days in Berlin twenty-five years earlier. The two of them had written over the years, and finally, at her suggestion, his trip to Yemen had been arranged. Who knows what he anticipated before his arrival, but one thing became clear to me as he blurted out his story — the sojourn in San'a had gone badly.

Shortly after he arrived, the professor attempted to visit his friend at the home she shared with her Yemeni husband and their two children. The husband, who had earlier consented to the visit, changed his mind when the German man appeared. He forbade the professor to enter the house. The woman was caught between her loyalty to her husband, who in the Yemeni setting was acting entirely within his rights, and her desire to make contact with her friend and the memories of her past. The two managed to see each other in a neutral and public place, and nothing questionable went on between them, at least by European standards.

During his stay in San'a the professor mooned about the old city, wandering from one disaster to the next. He was constantly getting himself into difficulties while performing the most innocent acts imaginable. Within a very short time he had been arrested twice. The first time was for operating a tape recorder in the marketplace. He knew no Arabic, but was accused of recording private conversations. The local merchants quickly concluded that this was the work of a spy, and the police took the professor away in a van. In a later incident he was arrested for photographing a wall. He had been attracted to a fine example of Arabic script, which proved to be an obscene reference to the buttocks of a woman by the name of Afra, on a wall near the Great Mosque. Angry neighbors surrounded the man and claimed that he was mocking Islam by composing a photo of the obscenity with the Great Mosque in the background. The professor did not understand the people's outrage. Again the police were summoned, and again the German was taken away in their van.

It was shortly after his second encounter with the police that I met him. He wore a harried look and was sweating profusely, and he had convinced himself that he was being followed. Over the next few days I occasionally caught glimpses of him wandering through the old city with his camera and notebook. There was something about his posture and gait that aroused even my suspicions. The man seemed flighty and directionless. It was not until after I left Yemen that I learned what finally happened to him.

One day the Yemeni husband could no longer tolerate the professor's presence. How could it be that there was nothing going on between his wife and this strange man? Had the fellow not flown thousands of miles and spent tens of thousands of riyals to see her? And why did he linger in the country? The husband's family and neighbors thought about these questions as well.

Feeling that his honor was in question, the husband drove to the private house where the professor was staying and knocked loudly on the door. When the door opened, the husband slammed the bespectacled art historian up against the nearest wall with the butt of his Kalashnikov and indicated the quickest route to the airport. After that incident, the professor's activities took on a greater sense of purpose and direction. He was on the first available flight back to Germany.

Abdallah Kareem, the Slave of God, who had promised to arrange my permit to return to Uqban Island, continued to be entertaining as well as masterful in his presentation of good and bad news, but I realized that he was becoming increasingly vague. I was amused, but his behavior made it difficult to sustain serious interest in returning to the island.

It came as no great surprise when he finally stopped phoning me. When I called him, a new voice answered and claimed that Abdallah Kareem had left the country. "Business in Jidda," I was told.

"When will he return?" I wanted to know.

"Tomorrow. Or maybe next week . . ." the voice replied uncertainly.

The phone call marked the end of a frustrating scenario, and I never again heard from the Slave of God. I decided to try the frontal approach and went to visit the National Security Office alone. Because of the rumored persuasion techniques used there, the building is known as the Fingernail Factory. I was politely spared my fingernails, but my request to visit the island was neither granted nor denied.

One morning my situation was clarified by a sympathetic official who took me aside. "Don't wait for an answer that will never come," he said. "There may be no substantial reason why you cannot return to Uqban, but believe me, you have no hope. You are looking for ghosts. There is nothing for you here. Go back to your country."

Yemenis, like other devout Moslems, recognize five types of human behavior. According to the Koran, an act is obligatory, permitted, neutral, reprehensible, or prohibited. There are no other possibilities. I asked the official if he was familiar with the passage from the Koran that states "That which is not expressly forbidden is permissible."

"Yes," the man said with a laugh. "A wise thought, indeed, but regretfully, it does not apply to foreign strangers wishing to visit military security areas in the Yemen Arab Republic in 1988."

With this conversation I ran out of ideas. Returning to my room, I lay down on my bed. I needed a day to contemplate the true nature of things, especially the meaning of my stay in Yemen. I realized that it was unlikely I would have experiences to top my walk with Martin and Kevin or the journeys to the Rub'al-Khali and the Tihama with Mohammed and Gazem. Nothing was to be gained by prolonging my frustration about Uqban Island. I had lost my appetite for chasing vanished realities. It was time to leave the country, and surrender whatever obscure hopes I still entertained that the journals could ever be recovered.

The departure came quickly. I booked my flight and had one last dinner with Martin in the old city. He was late, as usual, and I waited for an hour outside the restaurant before he arrived on his bicycle, breathless. He had been playing the piano for a Yugoslavian-Irish opera singer by the name of Dagmar. "Wagnerian proportions," he exclaimed, summing up the woman's vast bosom and girth.

We reminisced about our walk through the mountains and talked about how fate and circumstance dictate so much of life in Yemen. Martin kindly pointed out that it was highly unlikely I could have located the notebooks even if National Security had allowed me to go back to Uqban. "Don't worry about the stories you lost," he said. "There are always more to come, and it only takes a few good ones to keep us going." I agreed. We said goodbye. I packed my bag and went to bed early.

Three hours before dawn I was sitting in the waiting room of the San'a airport. The place was filled with row upon row of Yemeni men wrapped in white cloth, wearing identical terrycloth shawls draped over their shoulders. These men were hajis, pilgrims on their way to Mecca. The room smelled of bath soap and their scrupulously shampooed hair. At the edge of this gentle throng of devout Moslems sat a rabbi dressed all in black, with ringlets of gray-black hair descending from beneath the brim of his beaver hat. Incongruous as he appeared, the rabbi seemed completely at ease with the pilgrims, who in turn took no unusual notice of this Orthodox Jew.

The rabbi and I were aboard the same flight to Paris. When the seat-belt sign blinked off, I walked down the aisle to where he was seated. I couldn't resist asking what he was doing in Yemen.

He turned out to be Yusef Becher, from Williamsburg, a predominantly Hasidic neighborhood in Brooklyn.

"I come to serve my people," he told me.

Following the exodus of 45,000 Yemeni Jews to Israel during Operation Magic Carpet in 1949, the remnants of the Jewish communities became more scattered. Religious traditions were further threatened by the removal of ancient texts, including Torahs and Talmudical books taken by the departing migrants. There had never been a burning of holy books in Yemen, and many of the volumes and scrolls were priceless. The Yemeni Jews needed replacements for these holy books, and Rabbi Becher responded to this need.

He described his work as social and religious. Since 1979 he has distributed Torah scrolls, prayerbooks, Bibles, and other religious texts to the Jewish communities in the remote mountainous north of Yemen. These items are sold for a small sum, which is immediately redistributed within the villages. The money is used to keep up Talmud-Torah classes, to subsidize the training of scribes, to support the old and sick, and to provide for poor, devout men who need assistance with the bride price.

I asked about the rumors of persecution of Jews in Yemen.

"To the contrary," he replied. "Yemeni society is tolerant. The situation here demonstrates how well Jews and Moslems can live together without the interference of Zionism and Israel. Yemeni Jews are very orthodox, but they also chew qat with their Moslem neighbors."

In addition to religious texts, Rabbi Becher sold shofars (ram's horns for blowing on Rosh Hashanah, the Jewish New Year), as well as kosher stainless steel knives for slaughtering animals. The cut must be as painless as possible, and a chip in the blade will make the meat unkosher. The rabbi took a delight in pointing out details. Local Yemeni knives, I learned, are good for only five or six chickens before they need resharpening. Using the American-made stainless steel blades, a village butcher can cut up to two hundred chicken throats without fear of the meat's being unkosher.

The photos were next.

"Here, look at this," he said, pointing to what looked like a shallow bathtub chiseled into a stone wall. The bathing area was for women to perform *peuilla,* the obligatory immersion and cleansing following menstruation. Sexual relations are not allowed before *peuilla.*

"They use rainwater whenever possible," Rabbi Becher explained. "It is yet another example of how Yemeni Jews are observant."

He then asked what I had been doing in Yemen. When I told him, he lifted one eyebrow.

"Do you know the difference between the intelligent man and the wise man?" he asked.

"Tell me."

"The intelligent man is capable of overcoming problems and difficulties the wise man would have avoided in the first place."

I returned to my seat with that illuminating thought. The next time I looked down the aisle Rabbi Becher had tied a small black box to his forehead. His eyes were closed, his lips moved. The box, known as a tefillin, contained handwritten bits of Scripture. A white shawl lay over his shoulders. The beaver hat rested beside him on an empty seat. Rabbi Becher had begun his morning prayers.

Outside, the aircraft engines roared steadily. All about the rabbi there was movement, as Yemeni women emerged from their black cocoons. Veils were removed; female faces appeared. A black pleated garment designed for modesty and concealment fell away to reveal a beautiful young Yemeni woman dressed in a checked Western-style shirt, Wrangler jeans, and cowgirl boots.

Watching Rabbi Becher, lost in prayer amid this metamorphosis, I realized that my journey had come to an end. I surrendered my last hope of retrieving my journals. It was a relief to let them go.

18

It Was Written

YEMEN CHANGED ME. The country may not have taught me how to give up, but at least I had discovered how to surrender temporarily with grace. The sheer adversity of the place had attracted and repelled me before finally overwhelming both my patience and my hope. But even after I consciously set aside my dream of digging up my notebooks, the momentum of my crazy quest continued. The most important lesson I learned from my visits to Yemen had to do with how infinite possibilities can present themselves when one gives fate a fair chance.

Back home, eight months after leaving Yemen, I received a letter from Nick telling me that his toilet project had been completed at a cost of $49,000. This worked out to $7000 per stall, as predicted. He also mentioned that the people of Al-Harum, the village that had taken Norman hostage, had succeeded in their efforts as well: the government had built them a school. Heartened by their accomplishments, I was again reminded of my failures. Following Nick's letter a series of incidents made it increasingly difficult for me to let things simply be, and it wasn't long before the lessons I had learned about fate and how to let go began to fade from my mind.

One day a postcard arrived, inviting me to an exhibit of photographs of Yemeni architecture to be held at the American Architectural Foundation in Washington, D.C. I decided to go. Standing in front of a concrete wall hung with a line of framed photos, I examined one of the images closely. The sixteen-by-twenty-inch Cibachrome print showed the exterior wall of a Yemeni tower house. The photographer had captured the architectural details and, inadvertently, the less savory features of two drop toilets that projected from the brickwork on the upper floors. The splattered catchment area was just visible at the bottom margin of the photograph.

I fell into conversation with a well-dressed Yemeni man standing next to me.

"What is it about the toilets," he asked, "that visitors to Yemen find so intriguing?"

"Their height?" I ventured. We both laughed.

"Have you ever visited Yemen?" the man asked politely.

"Yes, several times. During my first visit to your country, in 1978, I was thrown in jail for ten days."

"Really . . . and where was that?"

"On a small island northwest of Hodeida. You have probably never heard of it."

"Which island?" the man asked in a pleasant voice as he turned to face me.

"Kamaran."

"Which part of the island?"

"Near Kamaran harbor, on the east coast."

"Which building?"

"The old British residency on the hill."

"Which room?" he continued as his smile broadened.

"Climbing the front steps, it is the main room on the left. There is a picture of the last British resident on the wall."

"And one of his wife as well," the man added. "In 1952 I was imprisoned in that same room for two days. Imam Ahmed exiled me from the country for my political beliefs. I went to live in Cairo."

He offered his hand. I took it, and in this way I met His Excellency Mohsin Alaini, the Yemeni ambassador to the United States.

People moved about the exhibition space, sipping wine and commenting on the fine photographs, while the ambassador and I discussed the room on Kamaran Island. The lure of Yemen took hold of me once again. The evening coincided with the end of Ramadan, and I was invited to the ambassador's house, where a large group of people had gathered to celebrate Id al-Fitr, the Festival of the Breaking of the Fast. Headless carcasses of roast lamb set upon silver platters were cut up and served by uncomfortable-looking white men wearing starched chef's caps. Accustomed to presliced meat, the caterers were unsure of themselves when confronted with a whole cooked animal.

After dinner, the ambassador asked if I had ever considered writing about my experiences in Yemen. I told him I had five hundred pages of manuscript without an ending.

"I think I might be able to help you find that ending," he replied.

Five months later the mud of Al-Luhayyah oozed between my toes as I waded into the flat, warm sea. A few feet from shore I stepped into a fishing boat that smelled of rancid shark oil and puréed dates, a concoction that had been applied to the interior of the boat to preserve and season the wooden planks. The smelly oil also stuck to our skin and clothing. I was accompanied by Mr. al-Kibsi, an agent of the National Security Police in San'a, two local fishermen, a boatman, and a policeman from Hodeida. In the bottom of the boat lay a shovel I had bought that morning for 50 riyals. At the last minute I purchased six one-liter bottles of water. The other men had provisioned themselves for the forty-mile round trip with several packs of cigarettes. We had no food apart from a package of glucose biscuits.

During the drive from San'a the previous day, Mr. al-Kibsi had asked me repeatedly why I had come all the way from America to look for some notebooks buried on Uqban Island. He couldn't quite get his mind around the idea. But his confusion was nothing compared to the confusion of the men in Al-Luhayyah when we arrived in the middle of a qat party at the house of the *mudir,* or headman, that afternoon.

Fifteen months had passed since my previous visit to Al-Luhayyah. I remembered well the men's smirks, and their parting comments: "Of course we would like to help you . . . anything we can do . . . yes, yes, there is no problem, provided you come back with someone from National Security." Those men figured I had about one chance in ten thousand of ever returning to the village, let alone with the secret police. I had been forgotten until the moment Mr. al-Kibsi and I walked into the qat session. Scanning the room as I sat down, I thought several of the men might choke on their wads of qat. Their looks of cool detachment were quickly transformed into expressions of profound disbelief, and I found it difficult to conceal my great pleasure at the sight of their growing discomfort. It wasn't difficult to read their thoughts: how had I made arrangements with the National Security Police, and was I back to prosecute the looters?

Ali Abbas, the sheik of the fishermen, was summoned to confirm my story, but regrettably he could not attend due to a sudden illness. Other men whose names I remembered from my last visit were also unavailable. The people in the room could not leave without drawing attention to themselves, and a feeling of unease prevailed as I explained to the *mudir* my reasons for wanting to return to Uqban Island. Clearly everyone in the room thought I was either out of my mind or lying. In their view, I had to be looking for buried money or weapons.

The cool breeze and flat seas promised a pleasant two-hour journey to Uqban, which lay twenty miles to the west, just over the horizon. The fifty-five horsepower outboard motor rumbled to life, and the little boat moved smoothly past tumbledown buildings and half-submerged hulks of abandoned dhows. Dozens of sleek red-and-white fishing boats sat placidly at anchor as we followed a circuitous channel through the mangroves and out to sea. The crumbling Turkish citadel set on the hill behind the city grew indistinct in the low morning haze as we met the first ocean swells. It was a beautiful, calm morning, an auspicious beginning to the day. I was lulled into a half-sleep by the vibration of the motor and the motion of the boat as it cut its way through gentle waves.

I awoke with a start. Six miles out to sea the motor died. We cleaned the two spark plugs with a fishhook, which was our only tool apart from the rusted plug wrench. We pumped gas directly into the cylinder heads before replacing the plugs. Pulling on the rope starter, we couldn't manage to coax a single cough out of the motor. There was no spark. When I checked the wiring, I found such a rat's nest of loose connections and frayed wires that I didn't know where to begin my search.

The motor was hot, and without the slightest hesitation, the boatman opened a bottle of drinking water and emptied it over the engine to help cool it off. It occurred to me that this was an interesting way for the man to use "his" bottle of water. One has to be either deeply religious or a fool to waste water like that in such a situation. Sea water would have done the job just as well. There was no shade as the sun began to burn its way into the cool morning air, and with five liters of water for six people, I figured we were on our way to the promised land, or that other place. I took my turn pulling on the rope starter until my fingers bled. Before long, the rope snapped off at the engine housing. So much for preventive maintenance.

"Son of a bitch . . . *why me?*" I asked myself out loud. No one replied.

Consumed by frustration, I sat down to rest, taking a deep breath and then exhaling with a loud sigh. It was going to be a long day. To ease their tension, my fellow passengers began to smoke furiously. Pushed by the waves and the morning's offshore winds, we were drifting farther out to sea. The remaining water was quickly consumed, and there were no islands or other boats in sight. We didn't even have a set of oars. Two hours later, a low sand island appeared. We drifted toward it, hoping to be washed ashore or at least to pass close enough to try swimming to it. I couldn't believe I was going to be shipwrecked in the Red Sea a second time.

Just as it seemed likely we would miss the island, we sighted a small fishing boat on the horizon. Blinded by the low morning sun behind us, the men in the other boat were well past us before they noticed our waves for help. What followed was a typical Yemeni rescue operation. I was obliged to pay the equivalent of $15.36 to the fishermen in the other boat to compensate them for the time and fuel it took to tow us back to shore. This amount was more than a fair price. If they had not seen us, our chances of survival would have been small. From where they picked us up, there was nothing but open sea all the way to the east coast of Africa, 125 miles away. Without food, a sail, water, or oars, we might have lasted a few days. It is difficult to place a dollar value on human life, but that morning, by dividing $15.36 by the six of us in the boat, I calculated that I was worth exactly $2.56 to a Yemeni fisherman: the approximate price of two smoked mullet.

Instead of being swept out to sea, we returned to Al-Luhayyah after four hours on the water — badly sunburned, but otherwise intact. During our lunch of bread dipped in a purée of yogurt and tomatoes, Mr. al-Kibsi voiced a thought we all shared: "We were very lucky. Fishermen don't usually go out that far. We could have died." I was in complete agreement. Things could have turned nasty very quickly.

"What would you like to do now?" he asked me. He envisioned the drive back to San'a that afternoon.

"Find another boat," I said.

"What . . . ?" he replied in disbelief.

The other men looked up from their meal, and I could feel their eyes taking in the full measure of my madness. It felt good. We finished lunch and located another single-engine boat. On our second attempt, we succeeded in reaching Uqban Island.

During the two-and-a-half-hour journey, I occupied myself by observing the sad state of Mr. al-Kibsi's clothing. He had picked me up the previous day dressed in a regulation black wool suit, a white shirt open at the neck, and a pair of nicely polished black leather shoes with dark socks. He looked smart in the hotel lobby, but by the time we were on our way out to the island for the second time his shoes and socks were missing, his pant legs were rolled above his muddied feet, and the skin on his ankles was broken in several places. He sat in a sorry-looking cardboard box on the bottom of the boat, in an unsuccessful attempt to keep the seat of his pants dry. The armpits of his soiled white shirt were ripped out, and two buttons were missing from just above his belt. I don't know what had become of his jacket. He had wrapped a red-and-white scarf around his head to protect his sunburned face from the driving salt spray that lay crusted on our skin and clothing. I could not help but feel sorry for Mr. al-Kibsi. He had tried so hard to help me. Dirty, seasick, exhausted, and with little idea of what possessed me or what he was going to do about his suit, he never once complained.

At half past three in the afternoon of October 17, 1989, I once again waded through the shallows of Uqban Island. Buffeted by a hot afternoon breeze, I stood on the wet sand, less than twenty yards from where our camp had been in 1978. Returning to that beach was like stepping into a dream, and I was overwhelmed by the thrill of being back on that obscure piece of land that meant so much to me. As the memories closed in and the years fell away, I felt as if I had entered my dreams and was trespassing on sacred ground. I was afraid I had returned to a place where I had no right to be.

A garbage-strewn fishing camp was situated where our beach kitchen had once stood. Empty oil tins, plastic bottles, and other floating debris bobbed at the water's edge. I imagined Georgik and Suzanne sunbathing on the beach amid the litter. Instead, hundreds if not thousands of dried and stinking shark carcasses lay in piles above the high-tide mark. The stomachs had been gutted for the valuable shark oil, and the fins and tails had been cut away to be sent to Singapore, where they would be packaged and exported as shark-fin soup. Bits of frayed plastic rope protruded from the sand. There were discarded nets and thousands of rusted tin cans. Rubbish lay strewn along the beach as far as I could see. On a low sand hill, a four-poster Tihama cot with a canopy of cardboard and corrugated tin overlooked the lagoon where I had once spent a morning watching giant manta rays leaping through the surface of the blue-green water.

Struggling to set these memories and impressions aside, I focused my thoughts on one thing only: digging. We had to return to the coast before nightfall, and with the morning's delays, that left me with less than an hour to find the spot where I had buried the notebooks. Grabbing the shovel, I paced the approximate area and tested two places without success. I walked back and forth across the sand, trying to remember the site of our garbage trench. I was not in my right mind. Stupefied by the heat and the events of that morning, I stumbled about in confusion. I knew the direction of the trench from our camp, but I could not remember the precise distance. Once I found the filled-in trench, it would simply be a matter of following it to the end nearest the water. Beneath that spot I hoped to find my journals.

I dug at random and found nothing. The work was not easy. Of every three shovelfuls of dry sand, two shovelfuls seemed to fall back into the hole. The afternoon sun was intense, and after the first twenty minutes the other men lost interest in my search. They rested in the shade of the low coral cliffs, paying little attention to my efforts.

Continuing my search, I found our latrine, which was in a remarkable state of preservation. Long after human life vanishes, I suspect, plastic tampon applicators will inherit the earth. Further digging in the same area produced more blisters and increasing panic, but nothing else. Then I felt the tip of my shovel slide off a smooth object buried in the sand. It was a bottle. The label was still perfectly legible: lime cordial from Sri Lanka. I remembered the synthetic flavor of the bright green syrup. The next shovelful produced tin cans rusted beyond recognition. I unearthed a piece of fabric: yellow Ripstop nylon with zigzag lines of stitching in maroon thread. It was a test piece from the day Georgik adjusted the bobbin tension on the sewing machine and stitched the sails for the dinghy. After eleven and a half years buried in the dry sand, the fabric and thread were in perfect condition.

To establish the direction of the garbage trench, I walked a few paces toward the shoreline and began to dig in a line parallel to the beach. I soon located an empty marmalade jar. As I dug my way to the end of the trench, the boatman approached me, pointing to his wristwatch to let me know I had fifteen minutes before the boat would have to leave. Digging with a renewed sense of urgency, I soon littered the surrounding sand with old aluminum beer cans, empty Johnny Walker Scotch bottles, and mango chutney jars from Madras.

Digging deeper, I uncovered what appeared to be a scrap of white plastic. Pulling on it, I realized that it was the corner of a bag. I pulled again, but the bag would not come loose. I felt the skin on my forearms tingle. Setting down the shovel, I got on my knees and brushed the sand away with my fingers. I felt a flat surface and the edge of a solid object inside the bag. It was my notebooks. After waiting so many years, with all the setbacks, I had expected nothing. Stunned by my discovery, I became oblivious to the broken blisters on my hands and my sunburned skin.

The reclining figures in the shade began to stir. Making a quick decision, I shoved the parcel into my shoulder bag, afraid that National Security would confiscate my find; then I continued digging as if nothing had happened. I like to think I was motivated more by prudence than by dishonesty, but regardless of these fine points, I had little interest in having secret police agents thumb through my past.

It was time to go. I shouldered my bag, and Mr. al-Kibsi walked with me to the waiting boat. While I showed him the piece of yellow fabric that I had found buried in the sand, the fishermen took a good look at my excavations. They assumed I was looking for money or weapons and wanted to remember the exact spot. I am quite confident that since that afternoon they have spent many a fruitless hour digging up that beach in search of their own fantasies.

We rode the ocean swells back to Al-Luhayyah and arrived just at sunset. By the time we were ashore it was dark. I passed the night in the *mudir*'s house, surrounded by sleeping tribesmen cuddled up with their weapons. Haunted by a strange feeling of unreality, I couldn't sleep. It was difficult to believe that my search had come to an end. Light finally crept into the sky, but I remember little of the journey back to San'a that morning, apart from the additional, welcome weight in my shoulder bag.

In San'a I showed the notebooks to a friend who was familiar with the details of my search over the previous two years.

"*Mabrouk,*" he told me — you are blessed.

"*Allah kareem,*" I replied — Allah provides.

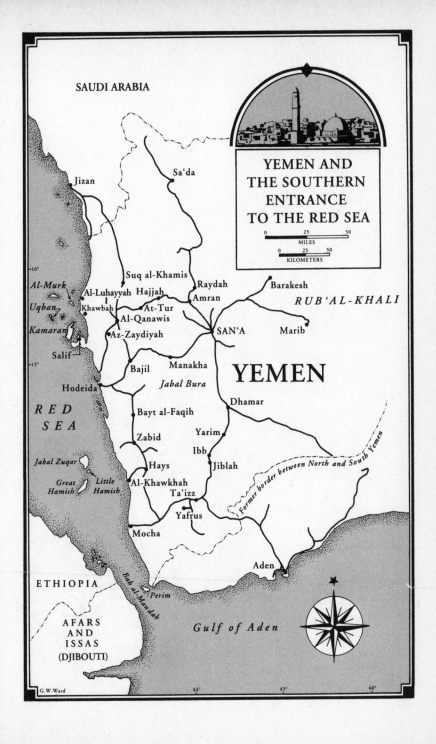

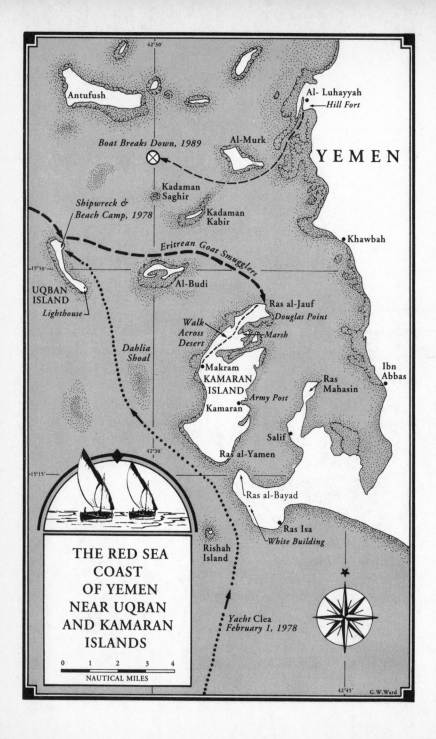

42°30'

Antufush

Al- Luhayyah
Hill Fort

Boat Breaks Down, 1989 ⊗

Al-Murk

Y E M E N

Kadaman
Saghir

*Shipwreck &
Beach Camp, 1978*

Kadaman
Kabir

Khawbah

Eritrean Goat Smugglers

15°30'

Al-Budi

UQBAN
ISLAND

Lighthouse

Ras al-Jauf
Douglas Point

*Walk
Across
Desert*

Marsh

*Dahlia
Shoal*

Makram
KAMARAN
ISLAND

Ras
Mahasin

Ibn
Abbas

Army Post

Kamaran

Salif

42°30'

Ras al-Yamen

15°15'

Ras al-Bayad

Ras Isa
White Building

THE RED SEA
COAST
OF YEMEN
NEAR UQBAN
AND KAMARAN
ISLANDS

Rishah
Island

*Yacht Clea
February 1, 1978*

0   1   2   3   4
NAUTICAL MILES

42°45'

G.W.Ward

Bibliography

Al-Hubaishi, Ahmed, and Muller-Hohenstein, Klaus. *An Intro-duction to the Vegetation of Yemen*. Eschborn, Federal Re-public of Germany: German Agency for Technical Cooper-ation (GTZ), 1984.

Costa, Pablo, and Vicario, Ennio. *Yemen, Land of Builders*. New York: Rizzoli, 1977.

Daum, Werner, ed. *Yemen: 3,000 Years of Art and Civilisation in Arabia Felix*. Innsbruck: Penguin, 1988.

Dorsky, Susan. *Women of Amran*. Salt Lake City: University of Utah Press, 1986.

Fayein, Claudie. *French Doctor in the Yemen*. London: Robert Hale, 1957.

Kennedy, John G. *The Flower of Paradise: The Institutionalized Use of the Drug Qat in North Yemen*. Dordrecht, the Neth-erlands: D. Reidel, 1987.

Lewcock, Ronald. *The Old Walled City of Sana'a*. Paris: UNESCO, 1986.

Lewis, I. M. *Ecstatic Religion: An Anthropological Study of Spirit Possession and Shamanism*. Harmondsworth, Eng-land: Penguin, 1971.

Marechaux, Pascal, and Marechaux, Maria. *Villages d'Arabie Heureuse*. Paris: Chene/ Hachette, 1979.

——. *Arabian Moons: Passages in Time Through Yemen*. Singapore: Concept Media, 1988.

Niebuhr, M. Carsten. *Travels Through Arabia and Other Countries in the East,* vol. 2. Trans. R. Heron. Edinburgh: R. Morrison and Son, 1792.

Serjeant, R. B., and Lewcock, R. *Sana'a: An Arabian Islamic City.* London: World of Islam Festival Trust, 1983.

Stevenson, Thomas. *Social Change in a Yemeni Highlands Town.* Salt Lake City: University of Utah Press, 1985.

Stone, Francine. *Studies on the Tihamah: The Report of the Tihamah Expedition 1982 and Related Papers.* Essex, England: Longman, 1985.

Varanda, Fernando. *Art of Building in Yemen.* Cambridge, Mass.: MIT Press, 1982.

ABOUT THE AUTHOR

ERIC HANSEN is the author of *Stranger in the Forest: On Foot Across Borneo*. He has traveled extensively through the Middle East and Asia over the past twenty years, and now lives in northern California.

VINTAGE DEPARTURES

A Wolverine Is Eating My Leg by Tim Cahill

Journeys through Himalayan rapids, the Grand Terror of Montana, and Dian Fossey's forbidden zone, all told with a special blend of sharp insight and crazed humor.

"Irreverence is a specialty of Tim Cahill's generation, and he ranks among its apostles."

—*Washington Post*

A Vintage Original/0-679-72026-X/$11.00

Coyotes: A Journey Through the Secret World of America's Illegal Aliens by Ted Conover

Disguised as one of many illegal aliens, Ted Conover makes a perilous nighttime journey across America's southern border, experiencing all the special terrors and surprising sense of camaraderie that inhabit the world of the *coyote.*

"Ted Conover lived the bizarre life of the Mexican illegals. . . . A devastating document, this one must be read."

—Leon Uris

A Vintage Original/0-394-75518-9/$11.00

The Good Rain: Across Time and Terrain in the Pacific Northwest by Timothy Egan

Traveling from rain forest to English garden, mountain top to river gorge, the Seattle correspondent for *The New York Times* reveals the Pacific Northwest as a land of both unparalleled beauty and frenzied exploitation.

"A celebration of natural bounty, a warning that too much has already been lost . . . Egan is a worthy spokesman for his homeland, a fluent and crafty writer."

—Richard Nelson, *Los Angeles Times*

0-679-73485-6/$10.00

Bad Trips, Edited and with an Introduction by Keath Fraser

From Martin Amis in the air to Peter Matthiessen on a mountain top, some of the best-known writers of our time recount sometimes harrowing and sometimes exhilarating tales of their most memorable misadventures in travel.

"The only aspect of our travels that is guaranteed to hold an audience is disaster. . . . Nothing is better for self-esteem than survival."

—Martha Gellhorn

A Vintage Original/0-679-72908-9/$12.00

Samba by Alma Guillermoprieto

An exuberant account of the rhythms and rituals of samba—that sensuous song and dance marked by a driving rapturous beat—and its key place in the lives of the poor people of the *favelas,* or villages, near Rio de Janeiro.

"The single best book ever written about the central place of music in the life of the Third World."

—*Washington Post Book World*

0-679-73256-X/$11.00

Motoring With Mohammed: Journeys to Yemen and the Red Sea
by Eric Hansen

A fascinating introduction to a land of haunting ancient customs and terrifying modern-day politics, as well as unparalleled desert beauty.

"Picaresque, beguiling, and great fun."

—Diane Ackerman, *The New York Times*

0-679-73855-X/$10.00

Video Night in Kathmandu: and Other Reports from the Not-So-Far East
by Pico Iyer

Images of the Far East—comical, poignant, and unsettling—that make up "a magical mystery tour through the brave new world of Asia" *(The New York Times).*

"Delightful . . . Pico Iyer's remarkable talent is enough justification for going anywhere in the world he fancies."

—*Washington Post Book World*

0-679-72216-5/$12.00

Running the Amazon by Joe Kane

"The story of the first expedition to run the entire length of the Earth's longest river . . . a terrific adventure . . . a torrent of stories from the first dusty road to the final champagne drunk at the Atlantic."

—*Los Angeles Times Book Review*

"Kane's eloquence lends his story a you-are-there quality."

—*Cleveland Plain Dealer*

0-679-72902-X/$9.95

Making Hay by Verlyn Klinkenborg

"A heartwarming yet unsentimental vision of the men and women who pour their lives into the land."

—*Seattle Times/Post Intelligencer*

"Takes one of the least common denominators in rural American life and gives it real glory . . . funny, learned, elegant and accurate."

—Thomas McGuane

0-394-75599-5/$5.95

In Bolivia by Eric Lawlor

In an odyssey that takes him from the bizarre decaying capital of La Paz to the suspected site of the Incan city of gold, Eric Lawlor's wit and keen eye sustain him through a series of peculiar misadventures as he travels in a land he sometimes feels time has forgotten.

"Eric Lawlor searches out the essence of the country. . . . *In Bolivia* is funny and terrible, sad and angry."

—Moritz Thomsen

0-394-75836-6/$8.95

Into the Heart of Borneo by Redmond O'Hanlon

An account of the 1983 journey into the heart of Borneo by a British naturalist with the knowledge of a trained scientist and the wit of a born comic writer.

"Within this intrepid travelogue lies the soul of Monty Python. . . . Every misstep of the way, O'Hanlon employs a dry, self-deprecating style that cannot disguise [his] gift for fresh and arresting description."
                                                                                          —*Time*

0-394-75540-5/$10.00

The Road Through Miyama by Leila Philip

A beautifully perceptive look at the cultural roots of Japan, as seen through the eyes of a young American woman who spends a year in a small southern village as an apprentice to a master potter of a centuries-old craft.

"As perceptive and evocative as Japanese *haiku* and a delight to read."
                                                                          —Edwin O. Reischauer

0-679-72501-6/$9.95

Iron & Silk by Mark Salzman

The critically acclaimed and bestselling adventures of a young American martial arts master in China.

"Dazzling . . . exhilarating . . . a joy to read from beginning to end."
                                                                                        —*People*

0-394-75511-1/$10.00

In the Shadow of the Sacred Grove by Carol Spindel

A moving memoir of an American woman's difficult and gradual acceptance into the daily life of a rural West African community.

"I was unprepared for the quietly gathering power of this respectfully inquisitive study of modern life in a small West African village. It poses, and answers, questions about the lives of a proud and shy people."
                                                                                  —Alice Walker

A Vintage Original/0-679-72214-9/$10.95

You Gotta Have Wa: When Two Cultures Collide on the Baseball Diamond by Robert Whiting

An American journalist gives us a witty close-up view at *besuboru*—Japanese baseball—as well as an incisive look into the culture of present-day Japan.

"[It] will please baseball fans and enlighten anyone interested in Japanese-American relations."
                                                                    —James Fallows, *Atlantic Monthly*

0-679-72947-X/$10.95

Available at your local bookstore or call toll-free to order: 1-800-733-3000.
Credit cards only. Prices subject to change.

VINTAGE DEPARTURES

Available at your bookstore or call toll-free to order: 1-800-733-3000.
Credit cards only. Prices subject to change.